A CHOICE OF DAYS

H.L. Mencken

A CHOICE OF DAYS

Essays from
HAPPY DAYS,
NEWSPAPER DAYS,
and **HEATHEN DAYS**
selected and with
an introduction by
EDWARD L. GALLIGAN

Vintage Books
A Division of Random House
New York

Library of Congress Cataloging in Publication Data
Mencken, H. L. (Henry Louis), 1880-1956.
A choice of days.
1. Mencken, H. L. (Henry Louis), 1880-1956—
Biography—Addresses, essays, lectures. 2. Authors,
American—20th century—Biography—Addresses, essays,
lectures. I. Title.
PS3525.E43Z517 1981   818'.5209   81-40084
ISBN 0-394-74760-7   AACR2

CONTENTS

Contents

INTRODUCTION

IN the mid-1930's, when he was writing the earliest of the pieces in this book, H. L. Mencken had plenty of excuses for self-pity. The decade had begun with Mencken riding as high as a man could. He was then the best-known and most influential man of letters in the country, cursed by his chosen enemies, admired by the intellectually ambitious, and ignored by no one who could read. In March of 1930 he published what he considered the best book he had ever written, *Treatise on the Gods*. And in August of that year, after years of gleefully proclaiming the virtues of bachelorhood, he married Sara Haardt and promptly became an intensely contented husband. Yet by 1934 his reputation and influence had shriveled.

He had resigned his editorship of *The American Mercury*, which had flourished mightily in his heyday in the late Twenties but was now losing circulation with practically every issue, and his *Treatise on Right and Wrong* was receiving reviews that were at best tepid and at worst derisive. Then, in May 1935, his wife died of tubercular meningitis.

A fifty-five-year-old man who has suffered such losses in both his private and public lives is a candidate for a case of the boo-hoos, but Mencken was made of tougher stuff. He turned to his type-writer, not to a crying-towel, and produced the Fourth Edition of *The American Language*. This was, for all practical purposes, a new book on the subject he had first explored in 1919, and it won a mostly new and astonishingly large audience. To recoup fame and fortune with a fat volume of philology is one of the gaudiest, most improbable feats on record.

That same year he commenced another enter-prise, less gaudy but ultimately more impressive: the writing of a series of essays in autobiography. He began tentatively; one essay appeared in 1936, another in 1937, none at all in 1938. Then in 1939 the gates of recollection opened wide, and easy, unpretentious, deeply humorous, lucid essays came flooding out during the next few years. Nearly all were first published in *The New Yorker* and were later gathered in the three books

—*Happy Days* (1940), *Newspaper Days* (1941), and *Heathen Days* (1943)—from which this volume has been put together. If there is a single foggy phrase or clumsy sentence in any of these works, I have failed to notice it, and I am positive that there isn't a whisper of self-pity in them. They are the recollections of a happy man; in fact, Mencken subsequently regretted that he hadn't simply labeled the last two books *Happy Days II* and *III*.

His explanation for his happiness varied from book to book. In *Happy Days* he credits it, appropriately enough, to having had a "placid, secure, uneventful" childhood. In *Newspaper Days* the credit goes to his good fortune in having been a reporter in a major American city at the turn of the century: "It was the maddest, gladdest, damndest existence ever enjoyed by mortal youth." But he gives his most sweeping explanation in the preface to *Heathen Days*, which ranges over his whole life:

> Like any other man I have had my disasters and my miseries, and like any other author I have suffered from recurrent depressions and despairs, but taking one year with another I have had a fine time of it in this vale of sorrow, and no call to envy any man. Indeed, I seem to have been born without any capacity for envy, and to the fact, no doubt, is due a large part of my habitual tranquility, not to say complacency.

Whatever the explanation, gaiety bubbles up on every page of these books, as it did on nearly every page Mencken ever wrote. He was rash enough to feel always that he was a free man and to comport himself accordingly. Where or how he acquired that powerfully gay conviction is impossible to tell. Perhaps the determinists are right and it was unreasonable and unrealistic for him to do so. Yet for Mencken freedom was as real as Baltimore crabcakes and good beer, and just as tasty. The marvelous thing about the *Days* books is that, like Mark Twain's "Old Times on the Mississippi," they re-create the experience of freedom so vividly that even a behavioral psychologist would have to feel liberated while reading them. And though they are blessedly free of any urge to instruct, an attentive reader can learn a great deal from them about what is necessary to keep the conviction of freedom flourishing.

Good luck is basic. Mencken argues that he was lucky all his life—lucky to be born into a family such as his, lucky to live in a city like Baltimore, lucky to get into the newspaper business at the turn of the century, lucky to find just the right openings in magazines at just the right times, lucky to live in a country that supplied him with things to laugh at in such abundance, lucky to have had such teachers, editors, publishers, acquaintances, and friends. Yet luck has a way of coming most often to a person with the courage to trust in it. Mencken had the courage, and with it the obstinacy to go his own way. For a charming illustration, see his account in "Allegro Con Brio" of the way he broke into the newspaper business by laying siege to Max Ways, editor of the Baltimore *Herald*. But note, too, the passing references in various essays to his refusal to move from Baltimore when he was making his way in the magazine business. Then as now, an ambitious young man *had* to live in New York, but Mencken nonetheless demonstrated, first with *The Smart Set* and then with *The American Mercury*, that it was possible to live in Baltimore and be the best editor in New York. To step outside the *Days* for a moment, one might also note that in both World Wars, when Mencken's views on Germany became unpalatable to the publishers of the *Sunpapers*, he gave up writing his columns rather than change or even mute his ideas.

Mencken expected other people to go their way as stubbornly as he went his. One sees in this volume his relish of the idiosyncrasies of the people he writes about, and the horror of reformers which led him to formulate (in "Drill for a Rookie") Mencken's Law: "whenever A annoys or injures B on the pretense of improving X, A is a scoundrel." And if other people's ways led them to denounce *him*, that was fine with Mencken. In fact, in 1928 he had his wife-to-be cull choice examples of denunciation from his clipping books, and published them under the title *Menckeniana: A Schimpflexikon*. His invariable rule was never to reply to or protest an attack on himself, no matter how scurrilous it might be. There was nothing saintly about this: usually he had goaded his attackers with satire, and there was nothing in the policy to keep him from sinking more barbs, skillfully, gleefully, in their tender hides. His restraint derived in part from a polemicist's understanding that by replying to an attack you only give more force to it, but fundamentally it was a product of his belief—perhaps the deepest one he held—that anyone should be free to say whatever he feels like saying about anything or anybody at any time.

Mencken came to be on remarkably good terms with a number of his adversaries, such as that well-known advocate of Prohibition, Bishop James Cannon, Jr., of the Methodist Church. There were exceptions, of course—he refused to soften his harsh judgment of William Jennings Bryan when Bryan died suddenly after the Scopes "Monkey" Trial, and he seethed with hatred of Franklin D. Roosevelt, especially after the President did a nicely malicious job of making a fool of him at the Gridiron Club Banquet in 1934. But on the whole, Mencken thought that he had been lucky (again) in having opponents who possessed qualities one could respect; throughout his life he enjoyed the company and the correspondence of people who stood on the other side of issues he engaged with unflagging zest. The last essay in this collection, "Vanishing Act," is a piece in evidence, for it recounts a visit this most notorious of heathens paid to the site of Carthage in the company of a Catholic bishop. Grief prevented any mention in the essay of his other companion on that trip, his wife; but we can note that the author of "The Sahara of the Bozarts" and hundreds of other gibes at Southern life and culture had married the loyal daughter of a prominent family of Montgomery, Alabama.

Competence, not ideology, was Mencken's test of any man or woman. As he put it in the Preface to *Heathen Days:*

> I simply can't imagine competence as anything save admirable, for it is very rare in this world, and especially in this great Republic, and those who have it in some measure, in any art or craft from adultery to zoology, are the only human beings I can think of who will be worth the oil it will take to fry them in Hell.

All three volumes of his *Days* reflect his admiration for competence, and they reach comic heights in celebrating it in unlikely places or forms: in champion beer drinkers (see "The Days of the Giants"), in all-night hack drivers (see "A Girl from Red Lion, P.A."), and in Democratic mayors (see "Romantic Intermezzo"). One suspects that he could have mustered some admiration even for the "papuliferous exegete" who drove him out of the Y.M.C.A. (see "Adventures of a Y.M.C.A. Lad") if the fellow hadn't chosen such unrelentingly platitudinous texts to expound. Certainly he respected his own competence. There was no false modesty about him; he knew how very good he was as a newspaperman, as a magazine editor, and as a prose writer.

It may seem a strange thing to say about a self-confident man who took particular delight in playing the part of the cockiest kid in town, but the truth is that Mencken wrote out of a superb self-negligence. Early and late, his images of himself are comic and derisive. "There is a photograph of me at eighteen months," he reports in "Introduction to the Universe," "which looks like the pictures the milk companies print in the rotogravure section of the Sunday papers, whooping up the zeal of their cows. If cannibalism hadn't been abolished in Maryland some years before my birth I'd have butchered beautifully." And at forty-four, according to "The Noble Experiment," he tried to talk his way past a suspicious doorman in a speakeasy by pointing out that no Prohibition agent ever looked "so innocent, so moony, so dumb." In this, as in many other respects, Mencken is at one with the great comic artists; from Cervantes on down, they savor their own ridiculousness, care nothing about how they look to others, and get on with whatever the moment has brought to them.

What all moments brought to Mencken was the chance to pursue further his love affair with the American language. He contemplated, studied, analyzed, categorized, exercised, chastised, embraced, adored, celebrated, and enlarged our language as faithfully and as playfully as any fond lover in history. One cannot put a date to the beginning of that love affair. Quite possibly it preceded the perception of the great burst of lights outside his father's cigar factory on September 13, 1883, which he cites (in "Introduction to the Universe") as the earliest of his earthly recollections; perhaps it was even simultaneous with it, for he seems to have perceived language as another, even more dazzling burst of lights. It would be pleasing if one could argue that it was engendered by his discovery in 1889 of *Huckleberry Finn*, which he describes (in "Larval Stage of a Bookworm") as probably the most stupendous event of his whole life. But the truth is that a love like that is as dateless as the poets and songwriters say it is.

It permeated every sentence he ever published. He quotes for us (in "Allegro Con Brio") his first piece of reporting, written when he was eighteen:

A horse, a buggy and several sets of harness, valued in all at about $250, were stolen last night from the stable of Howard Quinlan, near Kingsville. The

county police are at work on the case, but so far no
trace of either thieves or booty has been found.

Anyone who has ever tried to teach writing to
eighteen-year-olds will testify that the structure
of the first sentence (note the nicely unobtrusive
"valued—" phrase) and the diction of the second
(note "at work on" rather than "investigating,"
and "no trace of either thieves or booty") demon-
strate an unusual sensitivity to the nature of
American English. And the last piece that he
wrote for the Baltimore *Evening Sun*—a caustic
discussion of the efforts of the Baltimore Park
Board to enforce its rule against racially mixed
tennis games on the public courts, which was published two weeks before he had his incapacitating
stroke—shows the same finely tuned sensitivity:

> A free citizen in a free state, it seems to me, has an
> inalienable right to play with whomsoever he will,
> so long as he does not disturb the general peace. If
> any other citizen, offended by the spectacle, makes a
> pother, then that other citizen, and not the man
> exercising his inalienable right, should be put down
> by the police.

In between, he wrote and published a prodigious
number of sentences. Inevitably, some were silly
and some were trite, but all, I think, were written
so as to come smoothly off an American tongue or
fall comfortably on an American ear. His defini-
tion of Puritanism can serve as a single famous

example: "The haunting fear that someone, somewhere, may be happy."

His prose style is astonishing for its flexibility,
its clarity, and its force. It served equally well his
purposes as a newspaper reporter and columnist,
a literary critic, a polemicist, a philologian, an
editor, and an autobiographical essayist. It is so
personal as to be almost instantly identifiable,
yet so plainly useful that subsequent generations
of American essayists have gone to school on it.
It is easy to label its most important quality: it
can strike both high tones and low in a single
coherent, speakable sentence. Mencken had a huge
vocabulary, quite possibly the biggest in the history of American literature, and he used it both
freely and exactly. But he also had a horror of
pomposity and a delight in sardonic, deflating
turns of speech, which are the hallmarks of
American humor. Thus, he had the resources to
write about practically any subject accurately,
and the wit and drive to make himself clear to any
moderately educated reader. That is the combination that everyone writing nonfiction for a general
audience sweats to master.

In all of his work, but nowhere more gaily than
in the essays in this volume, Mencken offers his
reader the gift of delight in language. Like Mark
Twain, who extends the same gift to his readers,
Mencken denies any purpose in the essays save to
entertain. Well, maybe they had to make these de-

nials in order to get on with their work, but certainly we should not pay any attention to them. *Happy Days, Newspaper Days,* and *Heathen Days* possess, as I have suggested, the same general purpose as "Old Times on the Mississippi" and *The Adventures of Huckleberry Finn:* to celebrate and illuminate the experience of freedom. All agree that the greatest kind *and* source of freedom is the freedom to play with language.

That may be what Richard Wright took from Mencken when, as a poor, barely literate black boy in Memphis in the 1920's, he managed to get hold of some volumes of his *Prejudices.* That Wright started his remarkable journey in reading and writing with a book of Mencken's will astonish educators who preach that novice readers must be raised on a diet of simple words; that he later acknowledged his debt to Mencken will puzzle and perhaps even offend those who "know" that Mencken was a racist because he didn't refer to black people in a respectful, liberal way. A good response is to point out that Wright turned to Mencken because he read an editorial in a Memphis paper furiously condemning him for his latest irreverent comments on the Old South. Wright judged that anyone who could elicit that response from a Memphis newspaper must be worth reading. I imagine Wright did find racism in Mencken; after all, Wright was among the first

to show that in our culture no one is entirely free
of racism.

But whatever Mencken was, he was openly; so
it is Mencken who gives the best response to the
charge of racism. "I was," he states in the Preface
to *Happy Days*,

> a larva of the comfortable and complacent bour-
> geoisie, though I was quite unaware of the fact until
> I was along in my teens, and had begun to read in-
> dignant books. To belong to that great order of
> mankind is vaguely discreditable today, but I still
> maintain my dues-paying membership in it, and
> continue to believe that it was and is authentically
> human, and therefore worthy of the attention of
> philosophers, at least to the extent that the Mayans,
> Hittites, Kallikuks and so on are worthy of it.

That's Mencken. Loyal to his family, enjoying
his comfort, and always refusing to be a reformer,
he upholds the bourgeoisie, warts and all, but he
does so with a double-edged irony so as to nick
both its defenders and its critics. If the bourgeoisie
is racist in word as well as deed, far be it from him
to adopt genteel liberal language; rather, he will
most frequently refer to colored people (which
was the polite term of his day) as either "Afra-
mericans" or "blackamoors," relishing the preposterous quality of both terms.

A valid sample of Mencken's attitude on racial
matters may be found in "Gore in the Caribbees,"

where he describes the celebration in the presidential palace the night of Menocal's victory. Thousands of well-wishers rushed in, including scores of officers from his army. "Some of these officers were indubitably Caucasians, but a great many were of darker shades, including saddle-brown and coffee-black." Everyone, His Excellency included, fell to hugging and kissing everyone else. "It was an exhilarating show, but full of strangeness to a Nordic. I observed two things especially. The first was that, for all the uproar, no one was drunk. The other was that the cops beat up no one."

A few words of explanation are in order about the selection of the essays for this volume. The number—twenty—was set by Mencken: that is, he put precisely twenty essays in each volume of the *Days*, even though he had far more material on hand. ("My Life as Author and Editor," in four typescript volumes, and "Thirty-five Years of Newspaper Work," in three typescript volumes, are on deposit in libraries, with the restriction that they be closed to everyone until 1991.) The order was also set by Mencken. When I re-read *Happy Days*, *Newspaper Days*, and *Heathen Days* to make the selection, I discovered that each of these seemingly casual, almost off-the-cuff books is far more subtly integrated than I—or, I think, anyone else—had realized. The integration derives much more from the music of his prose than from conventional narrative techniques. Simple chronology determines the sequence of the essays, but they are linked to each other, and embedded in their books, by modulations of tone rather than by cross references or by lines of narrative development. (Thus, in editing this volume I found that I had only six cross references to deal with; in four instances, I could simply change the number of the "chapter" Mencken referred to to conform with the numeration in this volume, and in the other two, where he was referring to essays not in this volume, I could delete the references without any loss of clarity.) To cite only one example, "Adventures of a Y.M.C.A. Lad" belongs in time with the essays in *Happy Days*, for it deals with his childhood, but its sardonic attention to the god-awful platitudes of the pious ties it firmly to "Gore in the Caribbees," "The Noble Experiment," and the other essays in *Heathen Days*. I was thus led to conclude that I would do the least violence to Mencken's artistry by arranging the pieces I selected in his own order.

Accordingly, one will find here seven essays from *Happy Days*, then seven from *Newspaper Days*, and finally six from *Heathen Days*, all in the same order in which they appear in their respective books. That the twenty are so neatly spread over the three books is essentially an accident, at least as far as I am concerned. Certainly, I did not set out to do this; my aim was simply to pick out twenty of the best essays that would hold together reasonably well in a single volume. I suspect that any editor would arrive at substantially the same result, give or take a few selections; indeed, I suspect that in some corner of his mind Mencken arranged things so as to produce this result. If that is an exaggeration, it is certainly no exaggeration to say that Mencken was in full control of his books and brought them to a high pitch here and flattened them there for the same reason that any artist writing a longer work will vary its pace and effect. The "best" essays were spread over the three books—deliberately, skillfully, rightly.

Since I had so little to do with it, I can in all modesty argue that this is a genuine razzle-dazzle of a book, one that is in a class with the very best of American humor. But a wise reader will remember that it is only a selection. Essays remain in each of the *Days* that are every bit as good as the ones I have chosen, and no mere selection can do justice to the rhythm and unity of the original books. *Happy Days*, *Newspaper Days*, and *Heathen Days* are works of comic art.

Mencken was 62 when *Heathen Days* was published on March 1, 1943. During the next several years he worked mostly, though by no means exclusively, on the two Supplements to *The Ameri-*

can Language. In the summer of 1948 he became an active reporter again, covering the Republican, Democratic, and Progressive parties' national conventions with nearly all of his old clarity and zest. But on November 23 of that year, a little more than two months past his 68th birthday, he suffered a massive stroke which, with massive irony, centered on the part of his brain that controlled language. He recovered enough to live for seven more years, dying January 29, 1956, but he was never again able to read or to write, or even to speak other than haltingly. Although surely there wasn't a day during those seven pointless, hideously frustrating years on which he would not have died gladly, he endured without whining. H. L. Mencken was made of very tough stuff indeed.

Kalamazoo, Michigan   Edward L. Galligan
September 1979

FROM

HAPPY
DAYS

1880-1892

I

Introduction to
the Universe

AT the instant I first became aware of the cosmos
we all infest I was sitting in my mother's lap and
blinking at a great burst of lights, some of them
red and others green, but most of them only the
bright yellow of flaring gas. The time: the evening
of Thursday, September 13, 1883, which was the
day after my third birthday. The place: a ledge
outside the second-story front windows of my father's cigar factory at 368 Baltimore street, Baltimore, Maryland, U. S. A., fenced off from space
and disaster by a sign bearing the majestic legend:
AUG. MENCKEN & BRO. The occasion: the
third and last annual Summer Nights' Carnival of
the Order of Orioles, a society that adjourned *sine
die*, with a thumping deficit, the very next morning,

and has since been forgotten by the whole human race.

At that larval stage of my life, of course, I knew nothing whatever about the Order of Orioles, just as I knew nothing whatever about the United States, though I had been born to their liberties, and was entitled to the protection of their army and navy. All I was aware of, emerging from the unfathomable abyss of nonentity, was the fact that the world I had just burst into seemed to be very brilliant, and that peeping at it over my father's sign was somewhat hard on my still gelatinous bones. So I made signals of distress to my mother and was duly hauled into her lap, where I first dozed and then snored away until the lights went out, and the family buggy wafted me home, still asleep.

The latter details, you will understand, I learned subsequently from historians, but I remember the lights with great clarity, and entirely on my own. They constitute not only the earliest of all my earthly recollections, but also one of my most vivid, and I take no stock in the theories of psychologists who teach that events experienced so early in life are never really recalled, but only reconstructed from family gossip. To be sure, there is a dead line beyond which even the most grasping memory does not reach, but I am sure that in my own case it must have run with my third birthday. Ask me if I recall the occasion, probably before my sec-

ond, when I was initiated into the game of I-spy by
a neighbor boy, and went to hide behind a wire
screen, and was astonished when he detected me —
ask me about that, and I'll admit freely that I recall nothing of it whatever, but only the ensuing
anecdote, which my poor mother was so fond of telling that in the end I hid in the cellar every time she
started it. Nor do I remember anything on my own
about my baptism (at which ceremonial my father,
so I have heard, made efforts to get the rector
tight, and was hoist by his own petard), for I was
then but a few months old. But not all the psychologists on earth, working in shifts like coal-miners,
will ever convince me that I don't remember those
lights, and wholly under my own steam.

They made their flash and then went out, and the
fog again closed down. I don't recall moving to the
new house in Hollins street that was to be my home
for so many years, though we took possession of it
only a few weeks later. I don't recall going into
pants at about a quarter to four years, though it
must have been a colossal experience, full of pride
and glory. But gradually, as my consciousness
jelled, my days began to be speckled with other
events that, for one reason or another, stuck. I recall, though only somewhat vaguely, the deck of an
excursion-boat, *circa* 1885, its deafening siren, and
the wide, gray waters of Chesapeake Bay. I recall
very clearly being taken by my father to a clothing-
store bright with arc-lights, then a novelty in the

world, and seeing great piles of elegant Sunday suits, and coming home with one that was tight across the stern. I recall a straw hat with flowing ribbons, a cat named Pinkie, and my brother Charlie, then still a brat in long clothes, howling like a catamount one hot Summer night, while my mother dosed him with the whole pharmacopoeia of the house, and frisked him for outlaw pins. I recall, again, my introduction to the wonderland of science, with an earthworm (*Lumbricus terrestris*) as my first subject, and the experiment directed toward finding out how long it would take him, laid out in the sun on the backyard walk, to fry to death. And I recall my mother reading to me, on a dark Winter afternoon, out of a book describing the adventures of the Simple Simon who went to a fair, the while she sipped a cup of tea that smelled very cheerful, and I glued my nose to the frosty window pane, watching a lamplighter light the lamps in Union Square across the street and wondering what a fair might be. It was a charming, colorful, Kate Greenaway world that her reading took me into, and to this day I can shut my eyes and still see its little timbered houses, its boys and girls gamboling on village greens, and its unclouded skies of pale blue.

I was on the fattish side as an infant, with a scow-like beam and noticeable jowls. Dr. C. L. Buddenbohn, who fetched me into sentience at 9 p.m., precisely, of Sunday, September 12, 1880, apparently made a good (though, as I hear, somewhat rough) job of it, despite the fact that his surviving bill, dated October 2, shows that all he charged " to one confinement " was ten dollars. The science of infant feeding, in those days, was as rudimentary as bacteriology or social justice, but there can be no doubt that I got plenty of calories and vitamins, and probably even an overdose. There is a photograph of me at eighteen months which looks like the pictures the milk companies print in the rotogravure sections of the Sunday papers, whooping up the zeal of their cows. If cannibalism had not been abolished in Maryland some years before my birth I'd have butchered beautifully.

My mother used to tell me years afterward that my bulk often attracted public notice, especially when it was set off dramatically against her own lack of it, for she was of slight frame and less than average height, and looked, in her blue-eyed blondness, to be even younger than she actually was. Once, hauling me somewhere by horse-car, she was confronted by an old man who gaped at her and me for a while with senile impertinence, and then burst out: " Good God, girl, is that baby *yours?* " This adiposity passed off as I began to run about, and from the age of six onward I was rather skinny, but toward the end of my twenties my cross-section again became a circle, and at thirty I was taking one of the first of the anti-fat cures, and beating it by sly resorts to malt liquor.

My gradually accumulating and clarifying memories of infancy have to do chiefly with the backyard in Hollins street, which had the unusual length, for a yard in a city block, of a hundred feet. Along with my brother Charlie, who followed me into this vale when I was but twenty months old, I spent most of my pre-school leisure in it, and found it a strange, wild land of endless discoveries and enchantments. Even in the dead of Winter we were pastured in it almost daily, bundled up in the thick, scratchy coats, overcoats, mittens, leggings, caps, shirts, over-shirts and under-drawers that the young then wore. We wallowed in the snow whenever there was any to wallow in, and piled it up into crude houses, forts and snow-men, and inscribed it with wavering scrolls and devices by the method followed by infant males since the Würm Glaciation. In Spring we dug worms and watched for robins, in Summer we chased butterflies and stoned sparrows, and in Autumn we made bonfires of the falling leaves. At all times from March to October we made a Dust Bowl of my mother's garden.

The Hollins street neighborhood, in the eighties, was still almost rural, for there were plenty of vacant lots nearby, and the open country began only a few blocks away. Across the street from our house was the wide green of Union Square, with a

fishpond, a cast-iron Greek temple housing a drink-
ing-fountain, and a little brick office and tool-house
for the square-keeper, looking almost small enough
to have been designed by Chick Sale. A block to
the westward, and well within range of our upstairs
windows, was the vast, mysterious compound of the
House of the Good Shepherd, with nuns in flapping
habits flitting along its paths and alleys, and a high
stone wall shutting it in from the world. In our
backyard itself there were a peach tree, a cherry
tree, a plum tree, and a pear tree. The pear tree
survives to this day, and is still as lush and vigor-
ous as it was in 1883, beside being thirty feet higher
and so large around the waist that its branches
bulge into the neighboring yards. My brother and
I used to begin on the cherries when they were still
only pellets of hard green, and had got through
three or four powerful bellyaches before the earliest
of them was ripe. The peaches, pears and plums
came later in the year, but while we were waiting
for them we chewed the gum that oozed from the
peach-tree trunk, and practised spitting the imbed-
ded flies and June bugs at Pinkie the cat.

There was also a grape-arbor arching the brick
walk, with six vines that flourished amazingly, and
produced in the Autumn a huge crop of sweet Concord grapes. My brother and I applied ourselves
to them diligently from the moment the first blush
of color showed on them, and all the sparrows of
West Baltimore helped, but there was always

enough in the end to fill a couple of large dishpans, and my mother and the hired girl spent a hot afternoon boiling them down, and storing them away in glass tumblers with tin tops. My brother and I, for some reason or other, had no fancy for the grape jelly thus produced with so much travail, but we had to eat it all Winter, for it was supposed, like camomile tea, to be good for us. I don't recall any like embalming of the peaches, plums and pears; in all probability we got them all down before there were any ripe enough to preserve. The grapes escaped simply because some of them hung high, as in the fable of the fox. In later years we collared these high ones by steeple-jacking, and so paid for escape from the jelly with a few additional belly-aches.

But the show-piece of the yard was not the grape-arbor, nor even the fruit-trees; it was the Summer-house, a rococo structure ten feet by ten in area, with a high, pointed roof covered with tin, a wooden floor, an ornate railing, and jig-saw spirals wherever two of its members came together. This Summer-house had been designed and executed by my mother's father, our Grandfather Abhau, who was a very skillful cabinet-maker, and had also made some of the furniture of the house. Everything of his construction was built to last, and when, far on in the Twentieth Century, I hired a gang of house-wreckers to demolish the Summer-house, they sweated half a day with their crowbars

and pickaxes. In the eighties it was the throne-
room and justice-seat of the household, at least in
Summer. There, on fair Sunday mornings, my father and his brother Henry, who lived next door,
met to drink beer, try out new combinations of tobacco for their cigar factory, and discuss the credit
of customers and the infamies of labor agitators.
And there, on his periodical visitations as head of
the family, my Grandfather Mencken sat to deter-
mine all the delicate questions within his jurisdiction.

My mother was an active gardener, and during
her forty-two years in Hollins street must have
pulled at least a million weeds. For this business,
as I first recall her, she had a uniform consisting
of a long gingham apron and an old-time slat-
bonnet — a head-dress that went out with the Nineteenth Century. Apron and slat-bonnet hung on
nails behind the kitchen door, and on a shelf adjoining were her trowels, shears and other such tools,
including always a huge ball of twine. My brother
Charlie and I, as we got on toward school age, were
drafted to help with the weeding, but neither of us
could ever make out any difference between weeds
and non-weeds, so we were presently transferred to
the front of the house, where every plant that came
up between the cobblestones of Hollins street was
indubitably verminous. The crop there was always
large, and keeping it within bounds was not an
easy job. We usually tackled it with broken

kitchen knives, and often cut our hands. We disliked it so much that it finally became convict labor. That is to say, it was saved up for use as punishment. I recall only that the maximum penalty
was one hour, and that this was reserved for such
grave offenses as stealing ginger-snaps, climbing
in the pear-tree, hanging up the cat by its hind leg,
or telling lies in a gross and obvious manner.

Charlie was somewhat sturdier than I, and a
good deal fiercer. During most of our childhood he
could lick me in anything approximating a fair
fight, or, at all events, stall me. Civil war was forbidden in Hollins street, but my Grandfather
Mencken, who lived in Fayette street, only three
blocks away, had no apparent objection to it, save
of course when he was taking his afternoon nap. I
remember a glorious day when eight or ten head of
his grandchildren called on him at once, and began
raising hell at once. The affair started as a more
or less decorous pillow-fight, but proceeded quickly
to much more formidable weapons, including even
bed-slats. It ranged all over the house, and must
have done a considerable damage to the bric-a-brac,
which was all in the Middle Bismarck mode. My
grandmother and Aunt Pauline, fixed by my
grandfather's pale blue eye, pretended to be
amused by it for a while, but when a large china
thunder-mug came bouncing down the third-story
stairs and a black hair-cloth sofa in the parlor lost
a leg they horned in with loud shrieks and lengths

of stove-wood, and my grandfather called time.

Charlie and I were very fond of Aunt Pauline, who was immensely hospitable, and the best doughnut cook in all the Baltimores. When the creative urge seized her, which was pretty often, she would make enough doughnuts to fill a large tin wash-boiler, and then send word down to Hollins street that there was a surprise waiting in Fayette street. It was uphill all the way, but Charlie and I always took it on the run, holding hands and pretending that we were miraculously dashing car-horses. We returned home an hour or so later much more slowly, and never had any appetite for supper. The immemorial tendency of mankind to concoct rituals showed itself in these feasts. After Charlie had got down his first half dozen doughnuts, and was taking time out to catch his breath and scrape the grease and sugar off his face, Aunt Pauline would always ask " How do they taste? " and he would always answer " They taste like more." Whether this catechism was original with the high contracting parties or had been borrowed from some patent-medicine almanac or other reference-work I don't know, but it never varied and it was never forgotten.

There were no kindergartens, playgrounds or other such Devil's Islands for infants in those innocent days, and my brother and I roved and rampaged at will until we were ready for school. Hollins street was quite safe for children, for there was little traffic on it, and that little was slow-moving, and a cart approaching over the cobblestones could be heard a block away. The backyard was enough for us during our earliest years, with the cellar in reserve for rainy days, but we gradually worked our way into the street and then across it to Union Square, and there we picked up all the games then prevailing. A few years ago, happening to cross the square, I encountered a ma'm in horn-rimmed spectacles teaching a gang of little girls ring-around-a-rosy. The sight filled me suddenly with so black an indignation that I was tempted to grab the ma'm and heave her into the goldfish pond. In the days of my own youth no bossy female on the public payroll was needed to teach games to little girls. They taught one another — as they had been doing since the days of Neanderthal Man.

Nevertheless, there was a constant accretion of novelty, at least in detail. When we boys chased Indians we were only following the Sumerian boys who chased Akkadians, but the use of hatchets was certainly new, and so was the ceremony of scalping; moreover, our fiends in human form, Sitting Bull and Rain-in-the-Face, had been as unknown and unimagined to the Sumerian boys as Henry Ward Beecher or John L. Sullivan. The group songs we sang were mainly of English provenance, but they had all degenerated with the years. Here, precisely, is what we made of " King William " in Hollins street, *circa* 1885:

> King William was King James's son;
> Upon a ri' a race he won;
> Upon his breast he wore a star,
> The which was called the life of war.

What a *ri'* was we never knew and never inquired, nor did we attach any rational concept to *the life of war*. A favorite boys' game, called " Playing Se*bast*apool " (with a heavy accent on the *bast*), must have been no older in its outward form than the Crimean War, for Sebastapool was plainly Sevastopol, but in its essence it no doubt came down from Roman times. It could be played only when building or paving was going on in the neighborhood, and a pile of sand lay conveniently near. We would fashion this sand into circular ramparts in some friendly gutter, and then bristle the ramparts with gaudy tissue-paper flags, always home-made. Their poles were slivers of firewood, and their tissue-paper came from Newton's toy-store at Baltimore and Calhoun streets, which served the boys and girls of West Baltimore for seventy years, and did not shut down at last until the Spring of 1939. The hired girls of the block cooked flour paste to fasten the paper to the poles.

To the garrison of a Sebastapool all the smaller boys contributed tin soldiers, including Indians. These soldiers stood in close and peaceful ranks, for there was never any attempt at attack or defense. They were taken in at night by their owners, but the flags remained until rain washed the

Sebastapool away, or the milkman's early morning horse squashed it There were sometimes two or three in a block. Girls took a hand in making the flags, but they were not allowed to pat the ramparts into shape, or to touch the tin soldiers. Indeed, for a little girl of that era to show any interest in military affairs would have been as indecorous as for her to play leap-frog or chew tobacco. The older boys also kept rather aloof, though they stood ready to defend a Sebastapool against raiders. Tin soldiers were only for the very young. The more elderly were beyond such inert and puerile simulacra, which ranked with rag dolls and paper boats. These elders fought in person, and went armed.

In the sacred rubbish of the family there is a specimen of my handwriting dated 1883 — two signatures on a sheet of paper now turned a dismal brown, the one small and rather neat and the other large and ornamented with flourishes. They seem somehow fraudulent, for I was then but three years old, but there they are, and the date, which is in my mother's hand, is very clear. Maybe she guided my stubby fingers. In the same collection there is another specimen dated January 1, 1887. It shows a beginning ease with the pen, though hardly much elegance. My mother also taught me many other humble crafts — for example, how to drive a nail, how to make paper boats, and how to sharpen a lead pencil. She even taught me how to thread a

needle, and for a time I hoped to take over darning my own stockings and patching the seats of my
own pants, but I never managed to master the use
of the thimble, and so I had to give up. Tying
knots was another art that stumped me. To this
day I can't tie a bow tie, though I have taken lessons over and over again from eminent masters, including such wizards as Joe Hergesheimer and
Paul Patterson. When I go to a party someone has
to tie my tie for me. Not infrequently I arrive with
the ends hanging, and must appeal to my hostess.

This incapacity for minor dexterities has pursued me all my life, often to my considerable embarrassment. In school I could never learn to hold
a pen in the orthodox manner: my handwriting sat-
isfied the professors, but my stance outraged them,
and I suffered some rough handling until they finally resigned me to my own devices. In later life
I learned bricklaying, and also got some fluency
in rough carpentering, but I could never do anything verging upon cabinet-work. Thus I inher-
ited nothing of the skill of my Grandfather Abhau.
All my genes in that field came from my father, who
was probably the most incompetent man with his
hands ever seen on earth. I can't recall him teaching me anything in my infancy, not even marbles.
He would sometimes brag of his youthful virtuosity at all the customary boys' games, but he always added that he had grown so old (he was
thirty-one when I was six) and suffered so much

from dead beats, noisy children and ungrateful cigarmakers, drummers and bookkeepers that he had lost it. Nor could he match the endless stories that my mother told me in the years before I could read, or the many songs. The only song I ever heard him sing was this one:

Rain forty days,
Rain forty nights,
Sauerkraut sticking out the smokestack.

Apparently there were additional words, but if so he never sang them. The only *Märchen* in his répertoire had to do with a man who built a tin bridge. I recall nothing of this tale save the fact that the bridge was of tin, which astonished my brother and me all over again every time we heard of it. We tried to figure out how such a thing was possible, for the mention of tin naturally made us think of tomato-cans. But we never learned.

II

The Caves of
Learning

My first day in school I have forgotten as I have
forgotten my first day on earth, but my second I
remember very well, for I etched it on my cortex by
getting lost, along with my cousin Pauline, who
lived next door in Hollins street.

Pauline and I were of an age, and hence entered
the caves of learning together. They were situate
in the very heart of old Baltimore, a good mile and
a half from Hollins street, and the business of getting to them involved a long journey by the Balti-
more-street horse-car, with a two-block walk to follow. On the first day we were taken over the route
by Pauline's father, my uncle Henry, who gave us
careful sailing directions along the way, pointing
out all salient lights and landfalls — the City Hall

dome, the *Sun* Iron Building, Oehm's Acme Hall (which specialized in boys' pants with double seats), and so on. On the second day, launched on our own, we recalled enough of this instruction to board the horse-car going in the right direction, and even enough to get off correctly at Holliday street, but after that our faculties failed us, and we set out afoot toward the right instead of the left.

The result was that we presently found ourselves in Pratt street, an inferno of carts and trucks, with the sluggish Back Basin, which smelled like the canals of Venice, confronting us on the far side. The Basin looked immense to us, and unmistakably sinister. Over its dark, greasy waters a score of Chesapeake Bay packets were in motion, churning up the slime with their paddles and blowing their sirens ferociously. It was a fascinating spectacle, but terrifying, and in a little while we began to blubber, and a crowd of Aframerican dock-wallopers gathered around us, and a cop was soon pushing his way through it, inquiring belligerently what in hell the trouble was now. We must have managed to tell him the name of our school, though that part of it is a blank, for he delivered us only a few minutes late to the principal and proprietor thereof, Professor Friedrich Knapp, and got a shot of Boonekamp bitters for his pains.

This was my introduction (barring that obliterated first day) to F. Knapp's Institute, a seminary that catered to the boys and girls of the Baltimore bourgeoisie for more than sixty years. It was already beginning, in 1886, to feel the competition of the public schools, but Professor Knapp was not alarmed, for he believed firmly, and often predicted, that the public schools would collapse soon or late under the weight of their own inherent and incurable infamy. They were fit, he argued freely, only for dealing with boys too stupid, too lazy, too sassy or too dirty to be admitted to such academies as his own, and it was their well-deserved destiny to be shut down eventually by the police, if not by actual public violence. As for sending girls to them, he simply could not imagine it; as well shame and degrade the poor little angels by cutting off their pigtails or putting them into pants.

The professor discoursed on the obscene subject very often, and with special heat whenever another boy left him to tackle the new and cheaper learning. He always hinted that he had really kicked the traitor out, and sometimes he followed with a homily on parents who neglected the upbringing of their children, and so bred forgers, footpads and assassins. The worst punishment he ever threatened against a boy who came to school with his hair uncombed, or supernormal shadows behind his ears, was expulsion with a certificate so unfavorable that only the public schools would take him. Every time there was a hanging at the city jail (which was pretty often in those days when psychiatrists still confined themselves to running madhouses), he referred to the departed, not by his crime but by his education, which was invariably in the public schools. No authentic graduate of F. Knapp's Institute, he let it be known, had ever finished on the gallows.

Otherwise, the professor was a very mild and even amiable man, and much more diligent at praise than at blame. He was a Suabian who had come to Baltimore in 1850, and he still wore, nearly forty years afterward, the classical uniform of a German schoolmaster — a long-tailed coat of black alpaca, a boiled shirt with somewhat fringey cuffs, and a white lawn necktie. The front of his coat was dusty with chalk, and his hands were so caked with it that he had to blow it off every time he took snuff. He was of small stature but large diameter, and wore closely-clipped mutton-chop whiskers. His hands had the curious softness so often observed in pedagogues, barbers, and Y.M.C.A. secretaries. This impressed itself on me the first time he noticed me wiggling a loose milk-tooth with my tongue, and called me up to have it out. He watched for such manifestations sharply, and pulled, I should say, an average of six teeth a week. It was etiquette in the school for boys to bear this barbarity in silence. The girls could yell, but not the boys. Both, however, were free to howl under the bastinado, which was naturally applied to the girls much more lightly and less often than to the boys.

The professor viewed the pedagogical art with

great pride, and was a man of some eminence in the town. He was on easy terms with the Mayor, General Ferdinand C. Latrobe, who once got us an hour's release from learning by dropping in from the City Hall across the street to harangue us darkly on civic virtue. The old professor, in the days when I knew him, had begun to restrict his personal teaching to a few extra abstruse subjects, *e.g.*, fractions, but he always lined up all the boys for inspection in the morning, and he led both boys and girls in the singing that opened every day's session. For this last purpose all hands crowded into the largest classroom. The professor conducted with his violin, and his daughter Bertha helped out at a parlor organ. The songs, as I recall them, were chiefly German favorites of his youth — " Goldene Abend Sonne," " Winter, Adieu!," " Fuchs, du hast die Gans gestohlen," " Hurrah, Hurrah, Hurra-la-la-la-la!," and so on. Most of the pupils knew very little German, though they were taught it fiercely, but they all managed to sing the songs.

As I have said, the institute had already begun to wither around the edges when I first knew it. In 1879 (so I gather from a faded announcement in an old Baltimore directory) it had had a teaching staff of twelve savants, and offered instruction in French, Latin and Hebrew, not to mention German and English, but by my time the staff had evaporated down to six or seven, and French and Latin

had been abandoned. There was still, however, a
class in Hebrew for the accommodation of a dozen
or more Jewish boys, and I sat in on its proceedings
(which went on in the same classroom with less ex-
otic proceedings) long enough to learn the Hebrew
alphabet. This must have been in my ninth year.
By the time I left Knapp's for the Polytechnic the
class had been shut down, and I had forgotten all
the letters save *aleph, beth, vav, yodh* and *resh.*
These I retain more or less to the present day, and
whenever I find myself in the society of an orthodox
rabbi I always show them off. On other Jews I do
not waste them, for other Jews seldom recognize
them.

There was no enmity between the Chosen and
the *Goyim* in the old professor's establishment, and
no sense of difference in his treatment of them,
though he was in the habit, on bursting into a classroom that was disorderly, to denounce it violently
as a *Judenschule.* He used this word, not because
it was invidious, but simply because it described
precisely the thing he complained of, and was
sound colloquial German. He was also fond of using a number of Hebrew loan-words, for example,
tokos (backside), *schlemihl* (oaf), *kosher* (clean)
and *mashuggah* (crazy), most of which have since
come into American. The Jewish boys of Baltimore, in that innocent era, were still palpably and
unashamedly Jews, with Hittite noses, curly hair,
and such given names as Aaron, Leon, Samuel and

Isaac. I never encountered one named Irving, Sidney, Malcolm or Wesley, nor even Charles or William. The old professor and his aides labored hard to teach these reluctant Yiddo-Americans the principles of their sacred tongue, but apparently with very little success, for the only textbook I ever saw in use was an elementary *Fibel*, with letters almost as large as those in the top line of an oculist's chart. All its victims were of German-Jewish origin, and came of well-to-do families, for in those days Eastern Jews were still rare in Baltimore, and whenever we boys passed one on the street we went Bzzzzzzzz in satirical homage to his beard. I must add in sorrow that the Jewish boys at Knapp's were unanimously *Chazirfresser*.

There was also in the school a group of students, all male, from Latin America, chiefly Cubans and Demerarans. I recall that their handkerchiefs were always well doused with perfume, and that they willingly paid tops, marbles and slate-pencils for the seats nearest the stove in Winter. There was one Cuban whose father had been captured by brigands and carved in a dreadful manner: his detailed description of the paternal wounds was very graphic, and made him something of a hero. For the rest, the student-body included German-Americans, Irish-Americans, French-Americans, Italian-Americans and even a few American-Americans. There was never any centrifugence on racial lines, and the only pupil I can remember who had a nickname hinting at anything of the sort was a husky German girl, lately arrived in the Republic, who went under the style or appellation of Germany-On-Wheels. She had a fist like a pig's foot and was not above clouting any boy who annoyed her. Moreover, she was a mistress of all the German declensions, and hence unpopular. The old professor treated these diverse tribes and species with uniform but benevolent suspicion — all, that is, save the American-Americans, whom he plainly regarded as intellectually underprivileged, to say the least. I also heard him hint more than once that their fathers were behind with their tuition fees.

The Institute, in its heyday, had specialized in German, but by my time all its teaching was in English. I must have learned some German in it, for to this day I can rattle off the German alphabet in par, and reading the Gothic type of a German newspaper is almost as easy to me as reading the Lateinisch. Also, I retain a few declensions in poll-parrot fashion, and can recite them with fearful fluency, especially under malt-and-hops power. Again, I can still write a very fair German script, though reading the script of actual Germans often stumps me. Yet again, I always get the curious feeling, hearing German spoken, that it is not really a foreign language, for all its sounds seem quite natural to me, including even the *ch* of *ich*. But the professor and his goons certainly never taught me to speak German, or even to read it with any ease. They tried to ram it into their pupils as they rammed in the multiplication table — by endless repetition, usually in chorus. To this day I know the conjugation of *haben* down to *Sie würden gehabt haben*, though I couldn't write even a brief note in Hoch Deutsch without resort to a grammar and a dictionary. What little of the language I actually acquired in my youth I picked up mainly from the German hired girls who traipsed through the Hollins street kitchen during the eighties — corralled at the Norddeutscher-Lloyd pier at Locust Point by my father (who spoke next to no German, but knew the chief inspector of immigrants), and then snatched away, after a year or so, by some amorous ice-man, beer-man or ashman. One actually married a saloonkeeper, learned bartending, survived him, and died rich. My mother complained bitterly that these husky Kunigundas, Käthes, Ottilies and Charlöttchens were hardly house-broken before they flitted away, but some of them, and especially the Bavarians, were prime cooks, and all of them were ready to feed my brother Charlie and me at any moment, and to lie us out of scrapes.

My father, whose mother had been British-born, had a firm grasp upon only the more indecorous expletives of German, so the language was not used in the house. But my mother knew it well enough to palaver with the hired girls, and with the German marketmen, plumbers, tinners, beermen and grocery boys who were always in and out. When her father dropped in he would speak to her in German, but she would usually talk back, for some reason that I never learned, in English. Such bilingual dialogues sometimes went on for hours, to the fascination of my brother and me. We tried to figure out what the old man had said on the basis of what my mother answered. Maybe this taught us some German, but probably not much. One of the family anecdotes has to do with my efforts as a small child to dredge out of this grandfather an explanation of the puzzling differences between his language and ours. " Grandpa," I asked him, " if the German for *kiss* is *Kuss,* why isn't the German for *fish Fush?* " He knew English well enough, but this mystery he could not explain. My brother and I concocted a dreadful dialect for communicating with the German hired girls in their pre-English stages. Its groundwork was a crudely simplified English, but it included many pseudo-German words based on such false analogies as the one I have just mentioned, for example, *Monig* for *money* (from *Honig-honey*) and *Ratz* for *rat* (from *Katz-cat*). How we arrived at *Roch* for *(cock)roach* (pronounced in the German manner, to rhyme with *Loch*) I can't tell you: it must have been a sheer inspiration. To this day, alas, my

German is dreadful (though not quite as bad as my Sanskrit and Old Church Slavonic), and it always amuses me to encounter the assumption that I am a master of it, and even a scholar.

Professor Knapp, to return to him, spent most of his day moseying in and out of his classrooms at the institute, observing the technic of his agents and doing drum-head justice on boys of an evil nature. He was a virtuoso with the rattan, and chose his tool for a given caning with apparent care. He had an arsenal as large as a golfer's bag of clubs, and carried it with him from class to class. But the routine of the operation was always the same, and every boy knew it as familiarly as he knew the rules of run-a-mile or catty. The condemned would be beckoned politely to the place of execution beside the teacher's desk, and at the word *Eins* from the professor he would hold up his hands. At *Zwei* he would lower them until they stuck out straight from his shoulders, and at *Drei* he would bend over until his finger-tips touched his ankles. The punitive swooshes *a posteriori* would follow — sometimes two, three or even four, but more often only one. As I have said, it was etiquette for the condemned to make an outcry. He was also allowed and even expected to massage his *gluteus maximus* violently as he pranced back to his bench. This always led the professor to remark sagely: " You can't rub it out." Criminal girls were punished more gently, with smacks from a ruler on the open palm. They consoled themselves by hugging the insulted hand under the opposite arm.

The professor showed very little moral indignation when he carried on such exercises, and I never heard of a victim denouncing them as unjust. Whenever they took place the whole class seemed to be convinced that they were sound in law and equity, and necessary to peace and civilization. No doubt this was because the professor always took much more visible delight in rewards than in punishments. When, listening in on a recitation, he noted a boy or girl who did well, he grinned like a Santa Claus, and halted the proceedings long enough to give the worthy one a " merit." A merit was simply a card inscribed with the date and the recipient's name, and signed by the professor. Teachers could also award them, but we naturally liked the professor's best. A pupil who accumulated fifty in the course of a year received a book at the close of school, with his parents present to swell with pride. I received my first on June 28, 1888. It was a copy of Grimms' Fairy Tales, horribly translated by a lady of the name of Mrs. H. B. Paull. I got it, as the inscription notifies, " for industry and good deportment." I have it still, and would not part with it for gold and frankincense.

These merits were not plain cards, but works of art in the *Gartenlaube* manner, and very elegant in our eyes. They were lithographed in full color, and commonly showed a spray of flowers, a cat playing with a ball of wool, or a Winter scene in the Black Forest, with the snow represented by powdered mica. Sometimes the art took the form of a separate hand, embossed as well as colored. The hand was anchored to the card at the cuff, which was always laced, and one got at the inscription by turning back the fingers. Merits with hands were especially esteemed, though they had no greater exchange value than the plain ones. One of them still survives as a bookmark in the copy of Grimms' Fairy Tales aforesaid. On my withdrawal from these scenes it will go to the League of Nations.

There were teachers at the institute who came and went mysteriously and have been forgotten, but I remember very clearly all the members of the permanent staff — the old professor's daughter, Miss Bertha; his niece, Miss Elvina; his son, Mr. Willie; his chief-of-staff, Mr. Fox; and his slave, Mr. Paul. Mr. Paul was a tall, smooth-shaven, saturnine German who always wore a long black coat, and was greatly given to scenting himself with *Kölnischeswasser*. There was no science of ventilation in those days, and schoolrooms were kept hermetically sealed. Mr. Paul's powerful aroma thus served admirably as a disinfectant, but toward the end of a laborious day it sometimes made us more or less giddy. He lived at the school, taking part of his emolument in board and lodging, and I heard years later, from a fellow pupil who

was a great hand at the keyhole, that his maximum
salary in cash was never above $10 a week.

This fact was no doubt responsible for his generally subversive frame of mind, which led him to
an unhappy false step in 1888 or thereabout, almost fatal to his career. It took the form of an address to his class advocating the eight-hour day,
then an anarchistic novelty in the world, and almost
as alarming to the bourgeoisie as the downright
confiscation of tax-free securities would be today.
Worse, he recited a slogan in support of it, running as follows:

> Eight hours for work;
> Eight hours for sleep;
> Eight hours for what you will.

The boys could make nothing of his argument,
but quickly learned the slogan. I did so myself and
one evening recited it proudly to my father, looking confidently for his applause. Instead, he leaped
from his chair, turned pale, and began to swear
and splutter in a fearful manner. I made off in
alarm, and it was years afterward before I learned
from him why he was so indignant, and what followed from his dudgeon.

It appeared then that he had been convinced in
conscience, and was still convinced in conscience,
that the eight-hour day was a project of foreign
nihilists to undermine and wreck the American Republic. In his own cigar factory nearly all work

was piece-work, so he really didn't care how long his men kept at it, but he conceived it to be his duty to holler against the heresy in the interest of other employers. This he did, it appeared, on the very next day, and to Professor Knapp. The professor, who had also heard from other fathers, was much upset, and had Mr. Paul on the carpet. From that time on we heard nothing more of the subject. Mr. Paul applied himself with undivided diligence to his chosen branches — penmanship, free-hand drawing, mathematics up to the multiplication table, and deportment — and discreetly avoided all politico-economic speculations.

He was a kindly man, with some gifts as a draftsman. He taught me to draw complicated, fantastic, incredible flowers with both pen and pencil, and on lazy afternoons he would often suspend his teaching and entertain the boys and girls by covering the blackboard with images of birds carrying letters in their bills, and their plumage bulging out into elaborate curlicues. This art, now in decay, was greatly esteemed in those days. In penmanship Mr. Paul followed classical models. Every downstroke had to be good and thick, and every upstroke as thin as a spider's web.

At Christmas time all the boys and girls were put to writing canned letters of filial duty to their parents. Fancy four-page blanks were provided for this purpose, with the first page lithographed in full color. The text was written on the blackboard, all inkwells were cleaned and refilled, and new pens of great fineness were provided. The first boy who made a blot tasted the rattan, and after that everyone was very careful. As I recall it, the business of concocting these letters occupied the better part of a day. The professor himself dropped in from time to time to praise the young penmen who were doing well, and to pull the ears of those who were making messes. When an error was detected his son, Mr. Willie, was sent for to scratch it out with a sharp penknife. Too many errors caused the whole blank to be condemned and torn up, and the offender had to buy another at a cost of ten cents. We were always glad when this agony was over.

Mr. Willie, when I first knew him, was in his middle thirties. He was short and stocky, wore the silky mustache of the period, and combed his hair in oyster-shell style. He was much more worldly than Mr. Paul, and often entertained us with tales of his adventures. One of his favorite stories recounted his observations and sensations on seeing a surgeon cut off a man's leg. This happened somewhere in the West, where he had served for a year or two as a disbursing agent of the General Land Office. The boys liked the story, and encouraged him to improve its horrors, but the girls clapped their hands over their ears whenever he began it, and professed to shiver. He was also fond of telling about the hazards of navigating the Missouri river, which he had traversed during the seventies to the southern frontier of what is now South Dakota. In one of his stories he told how the river-packets of the time, when they ran aground on a sandbar, put out stilts operated by steam, and lifted themselves over it. Not a boy in the school believed this story, and I myself was nearly forty years old before I discovered that it was really true. But one of Mr. Willie's actual stretchers I swallowed without a shadow of doubt. He was discoursing one day on the immense number of books in the world, and their infinite variety. " On the single subject of the eye of the dog," he said, " enough has been written to fill this classroom." We all believed that one.

The dean or first mate of F. Knapp's Institute was Mr. Fox, a tall Pennsylvanian with a goatish beard, greatly resembling the late Admiral Winfield Scott Schley. He ran the school store, and carried it about with him in a large black dispatch-box. The boys believed that he made a large income selling them pens, slate-pencils, pads of scratch-paper, and other such supplies. They also believed that he made a great deal of additional money by serving as the secretary of a lodge of Freemasons. The business of this lodge occupied him on dull afternoons, when recitations degenerated into singsong, and there was no rattaning to be done. He would spend hours addressing postcards to the members, notifying them of initiations, oyster-roasts, funerals, and the like. While he plugged away he would solemnly chew his beard. We boys marvelled that it never grew any shorter.

Mr. Fox assisted the old professor as lord high executioner, and did most of the minor fanning of the wicked. He employed a frayed rattan of small percussive powers, and was but little feared. One day in 1889 I saw demonstrated before him the truth of Oscar Wilde's saying that nature always imitates art. The comic papers of the time had among their stock characters a boy who put a slate, a shingle or a book in his pants to protect himself from justice. This was actually done in my sight by a very small boy whose name, as I recall it, was Johnnie Horlamus. When Mr. Fox turned him over, the seat of his pants bulged out into an incredible square, and Mr. Fox halted the proceedings to investigate. His search produced a third grade geography-book. When he pulled it out the whole class roared, and he had to bite his beard hard to keep from roaring himself. He let Johnnie off with a single very gentle clout.

Mr. Fox was no virtuoso like the professor. He rattaned conscientiously, but without any noticeable style. The professor not only adorned the science, but made a notable contribution to it. This was the invention of mass caning, the use of which was confined to his morning inspection in the schoolyard. It often happened that he would detect three, four or even five boys with unshined shoes or unwashed ears. He would order them to step forward a few paces, and then line them up very precisely. When they had all got into the position called for by his command of *Drei* he would try to fetch their fundaments simultaneously with one swoop of an extra-long rattan. Sometimes he succeeded, and sometimes he failed. The favorite spot in the line was naturally the one nearest him, for the boy who had it got the thick part of the rattan, swinging through a small arc, and was hence but little hurt. The boy at the far end got the thin and poisonous tip, swinging over an orbit long enough to give it the speed of a baseball and the bite of an adder's fang.

The professor believed that he was responsible for the policing and sanitation of his pupils from the time they left home in the morning until they returned there safely in the afternoon. It was a felony by the school code for a boy to hook a ride on a horse-truck. Culprits were detected by the simple fact that such trucks, being dirty, commonly left marks on the knees of stockings or seats of pants or both, but the boys preferred to believe that they were betrayed by stooges among the girls. Many an innocent girl had her pigtail severely yanked on that charge. This yanking was itself a felony, but the victim seldom complained, for if she did so her pigtail would be surely yanked again, and with a yo-heave-ho so hearty that it just fell short of scalping her.

The most serious of all crimes, of course, was fighting on the streets. When detected, it not only brought a Class A rattaning, but also a formal threat of banishment to the Gehenna of the public schools. But the institute's statutes, like the canon law of Holy Church, always provided for exceptions and dispensations. In this case the pummeling, clubbing and even (if it could be imaginably achieved) strangling and dismemberment of a boy from Scheib's School was dismissed as venial. Scheib's was so close to F. Knapp's that the two were separated only by the narrow channel of Orange alley. Professor Knapp and Pastor Scheib were ostensibly on the most fraternal footing, and always spoke of each other in flattering terms, but there was a great deal of pupil-snatching to and fro, and deep down in their chalky pedagogical hearts they were a Guelph and a Ghibelline.

III

The Baltimore of
the Eighties

THE CITY into which I was born in 1880 had a
reputation all over for what the English, in their
real-estate advertising, are fond of calling the
amenities. So far as I have been able to discover
by a labored search of contemporary travel-books,
no literary tourist, however waspish he may have
been about Washington, Niagara Falls, the prai-
ries of the West, or even Boston and New York,
ever gave Baltimore a bad notice. They all agreed,
often with lubricious gloats and gurgles, (*a*) that
its indigenous victualry was unsurpassed in the
Republic, (*b*) that its native Caucasian females
of all ages up to thirty-five were of incomparable
pulchritude, and as amiable as they were lovely,
and (*c*) that its home-life was spacious, charming,

full of creature comforts, and highly conducive to the facile and orderly propagation of the species.

There was some truth in all these articles, but not, I regret to have to add, too much. Perhaps the one that came closest to meeting scientific tests was the first. Baltimore lay very near the immense protein factory of Chesapeake Bay, and out of the bay it ate divinely. I well recall the time when prime hard crabs of the channel species, blue in color, at least eight inches in length along the shell, and with snow-white meat almost as firm as soap, were hawked in Hollins street of Summer mornings at ten cents a dozen. The supply seemed to be almost unlimited, even in the polluted waters of the Patapsco river, which stretched up fourteen miles from the bay to engulf the slops of the Baltimore canneries and fertilizer factories. Any poor man could go down to the banks of the river, armed with no more than a length of stout cord, a home-made net on a pole, and a chunk of cat's meat, and come home in a couple of hours with enough crabs to feed his family for two days. Soft crabs, of course, were scarcer and harder to snare, and hence higher in price, but not much. More than once, hiding behind my mother's apron, I helped her to buy them at the door for two-and-a-twelfth cents apiece. And there blazes in my memory like a comet the day when she came home from Hollins market complaining with strange and bitter indignation that the fishmongers there — including old Harris, her favorite — had begun to *sell* shad roe. Hitherto, stretching back to the first settlement of Baltimore Town, they had always thrown it in with the fish. Worse, she reported that they had now entered upon an illegal combination to lift the price of the standard shad of twenty inches — enough for the average family, and to spare — from forty cents to half a dollar. When my father came home for lunch and heard this incredible news, he predicted formally that the Republic would never survive the Nineteenth Century.

Terrapin was not common eating in those days, any more than it is in these, but that was mainly because few women liked it, just as few like it today. It was then assumed that their distaste was due to the fact that its consumption involved a considerable lavage with fortified wines, but they still show no honest enthusiasm for it, though Prohibition converted many of them into very adept and eager boozers. It was not, in my infancy, within the reach of the proletariat, but it was certainly not beyond the bourgeoisie. My mother, until well past the turn of the century, used to buy pint jars of the picked meat in Hollins market, with plenty of rich, golden eggs scattered through it, for a dollar a jar. For the same price it was possible to obtain *two* wild ducks of respectable if not royal species — and the open season ran gloriously from the instant the first birds wandered in from Labrador to the time the last stragglers set sail for Brazil.

So far as I can remember, my mother never bought any of these ducks, but that was only because the guns, dogs and eagle eye of my uncle Henry, who lived next door, kept us oversupplied all Winter.

Garden-truck was correspondingly cheap, and so was fruit in season. Out of season we seldom saw it at all. Oranges, which cost sixty cents a dozen, came in at Christmas, and not before. We had to wait until May for strawberries, asparagus, fresh peas, carrots, and even radishes. But when the huge, fragrant strawberries of Anne Arundel county (pronounced Ann'ran'l) appeared at last they went for only five cents a box. All Spring the streets swarmed with hucksters selling such things: they called themselves, not hucksters, but Arabs (with the first *a* as in *day*), and announced their wares with loud, raucous, unintelligible cries, much worn down by phonetic decay. In Winter the principal howling was done by colored men selling shucked oysters out of huge cans. In the dark backward and abysm of time their cry must have been simply " Oysters! ", but generations of Aframerican larynxes had debased it to " Awn-eeeeeee! ", with the final *e*'s prolonged until the vendor got out of breath. He always wore a blue-and-white checked apron, and that apron was also the uniform of the colored butlers of the Baltimore gentry when engaged upon their morning work — sweeping the sidewalk, scouring the white marble front steps, polishing up the handle of the big front door, and bragging about their white folks to their colleagues to port and starboard.

Oysters were not too much esteemed in the Baltimore of my youth, nor are they in the Baltimore of today. They were eaten, of course, but not often, for serving them raw at the table was beyond the usual domestic technic of the time, and it was difficult to cook them in any fashion that made them consonant with contemporary ideas of elegance. Fried, they were fit only to be devoured at church oyster-suppers, or gobbled in oyster-bays by drunks wandering home from scenes of revelry. The more celebrated oyster-houses of Baltimore — for example, Kelly's in Eutaw street — were patronized largely by such lamentable characters. It was their playful custom to challenge foolish-looking strangers to wash down a dozen raw Chincoteagues with half a tumbler of Maryland rye: the town belief was that this combination was so deleterious as to be equal to the kick of a mule. If the stranger survived, they tried to inveigle him into eating another dozen with sugar sprinkled on them: this dose was supposed to be almost certainly fatal. I grew up believing that the only man in history who had ever actually swallowed it and lived was John L. Sullivan.

There is a saying in Baltimore that crabs may be prepared in fifty ways and that all of them are good. The range of oyster dishes is much narrower, and they are much less attractive. Fried oysters I have just mentioned. Stewed, they are undoubtedly edible, but only in the sorry sense that oatmeal or boiled rice is edible. Certainly no Baltimorean not insane would argue that an oyster stew has any of the noble qualities of the two great crab soups — shore style (with vegetables) and bisque (with cream). Both of these masterpieces were on tap in the old Rennert Hotel when I lunched there daily (years after the term of the present narrative) and both were magnificent. The Rennert also offered an oyster pot-pie that had its points, but the late Jeff Davis, manager of the hotel (and the last public virtuoso of Maryland cookery), once confessed to me that its flavor was really due to a sly use of garlic. Such concoctions as panned and scalloped oysters have never been eaten in my time by connoisseurs, and oyster fritters (always called flitters in Baltimore) are to be had only at free-for-all oyster-roasts and along the wharves. A roasted oyster, if it be hauled off the fire at the exact instant the shell opens, is not to be sniffed at, but getting it down is a troublesome business, for the shell is too hot to be handled without mittens. Despite this inconvenience, there are still oyster-roasts in Baltimore on Winter Sunday afternoons, and since the collapse of Prohibition they have been drawing pretty good houses. When the Elks give one they hire a militia armory, lay in a thousand kegs of beer, engage 200 waiters, and prepare for a mob. But the mob is not attracted by the oysters alone; it comes mainly to eat hot-dogs, barbecued beef and sauerkraut and to wash down these lowly victuals with the beer.

The greatest crab cook of the days I remember was Tom McNulty, originally a whiskey drummer but in the end sheriff of Baltimore, and the most venerated oyster cook was a cop named Fred. Tom's specialty was made by spearing a slice of bacon on a large fork, jamming a soft crab down on it, holding the two over a charcoal brazier until the bacon had melted over the crab, and then slapping both upon a slice of hot toast. This titbit had its points, I assure you, and I never think of it without deploring Tom's too early translation to bliss eternal. Fred devoted himself mainly to oyster flitters. The other cops rolled and snuffled in his masterpieces like cats in catnip, but I never could see much virtue in them. It was always my impression, perhaps in error, that he fried them in curve grease borrowed from the street railways. He was an old-time Model T flat-foot, not much taller than a fire-plug, but as big around the middle as a load of hay. At the end of a busy afternoon he would be spattered from head to foot with blobs of flitter batter and wild grease.

It was the opinion of my father, as I have recorded, that all the Baltimore beers were poisonous, but he nevertheless kept a supply of them in the house for visiting plumbers, tinners, cellar-inspectors, tax-assessors and so on, and for Class D social callers. I find by his bill file that he paid $1.20 for a case of twenty-four bottles. His own favorite malt liquor was Anheuser-Busch, but he also made occasional experiments with the other brands that were then beginning to find a national market: some of them to survive to this day, but the most perished under Prohibition. His same bill file shows that on December 27, 1883, he paid Courtney, Fairall & Company, then the favorite fancy grocers of Baltimore, $4 for a gallon of Monticello whiskey. It retails now for from $3 to $3.50 a *quart*. In those days it was always straight, for the old-time Baltimoreans regarded blends with great suspicion, though many of the widely-advertised brands of Maryland rye were of that character. They drank straight whiskey straight, disdaining both diluents and chasers. I don't recall ever seeing my father drink a high-ball; the thing must have existed in his day, for he lived on to 1899, but he probably regarded its use as unmanly and ignoble. Before every meal, including breakfast, he ducked into the cupboard in the diningroom and poured out a substantial hooker of rye, and when he emerged he was always sucking in a great whiff of air to cool off his tonsils. He regarded this appetizer as necessary to his well-being. He said that it was the best medicine he had ever found for toning up his stomach.

How the stomachs of Baltimore survived at all in those days is a pathological mystery. The standard evening meal tended to be light, but the other two were terrific. The répertoire for breakfast, beside all the known varieties of pancake and porridge, included such things as ham and eggs, broiled mackerel, fried smelts, beef hash, pork chops, country sausage, and even — God help us all! — what would now be called Welsh rabbit. My father, save when we were in the country, usually came home for lunch, and on Saturdays, with no school, my brother Charlie and I sat in. Our favorite Winter lunch was typical of the time. Its main dishes were a huge platter of Norfolk spots or other pan-fish, and a Himalaya of corn-cakes. Along with this combination went succo-tash, buttered beets, baked potatoes, string beans, and other such hearty vegetables. When oranges and bananas were obtainable they followed for dessert — sliced, and with a heavy dressing of grated cocoanut. The calorie content of two or three helpings of such powerful aliments probably ran to 3000. We'd all be somewhat subdued afterward, and my father always stretched out on the dining-room lounge for a nap. In the evening he seldom had much appetite, and would usually complain that cooking was fast going downhill in Baltimore, in accord with the general decay of human society. Worse, he would warn Charlie and me against eating too much, and often he undertook to ration us. We beat this sanitary policing by laying in a sufficiency in the kitchen before sitting down to table. As a reserve against emergencies we kept a supply of ginger snaps, mushroom crackers, all-day suckers, dried apricots and solferino taffy in a cigar-box in our bedroom. In fear that it might spoil, or that mice might sneak up from the cellar to raid it, we devoured this stock at frequent intervals, and it had to be renewed.

The Baltimoreans of those days were complacent beyond the ordinary, and agreed with their envious visitors that life in their town was swell. I can't recall ever hearing anyone complain of the fact that there was a great epidemic of typhoid fever every Summer, and a wave of malaria every Autumn, and more than a scattering of smallpox, especially among the colored folk in the alleys, every Winter. Spring, indeed, was the only season free from serious pestilence, and in Spring the communal laying off of heavy woolen underwear was always followed by an epidemic of colds. Our house in Hollins street, as I first remember it, was heated by Latrobe stoves, the invention of a Baltimore engineer. They had mica windows (always called isinglass) that made a cheery glow, but though it was warm enough within the range of that glow on even the coldest Winter days, their flues had little heat to spare for the rooms upstairs. My brother and I slept in Canton-flannel nightdrawers with feathers above us and underneath, but that didn't help us much on January mornings when all the windows were so heavily frosted that we couldn't see outside. My father put in a steam-heating plant toward the end of the eighties — the first ever seen in Hollins street —, but such things were rare until well into the new century. The favorite central heating device for many years was a hot-air furnace that was even more inefficient than the Latrobe stove. The only heat in our bath-room was supplied from the kitchen, which meant that there was none at all until the hired girl began to function below. Thus my brother and I were never harassed by suggestions of morning baths, at least in Winter. Whenever it was decided that we had reached an intolerable degree of grime, and measures were taken to hound us to the bathroom, we went into the vast old zinc-lined tub together, and beguiled the pains of getting clean by taking toy boats along. Once we also took a couple of goldfish, but the soap killed them almost instantly.

At intervals of not more than a month in Winter a water-pipe froze and burst, and the whole house was cold and clammy until the plumbers got through their slow-moving hocus-pocus. Nothing, in those days, seemed to work. All the house ma-chinery was constantly out of order. The roof sprang a leak at least three times a year, and I recall a day when the cellar was flooded by a broken water-main in Hollins street, and my brother and I had a grand time navigating it in wooden wash-tubs. No one, up to that time, had ever thought

of outfitting windows with fly-screens. Flies over-
ran and devoured us in Summer, immense swarms
of mosquitoes were often blown in from the swamps
to the southwest, and a miscellany of fantastic
moths, gnats, June-bugs, beetles, and other in-
sects, some of them of formidable size and pug-
nacity, buzzed around the gas-lights at night.

We slept under mosquito canopies, but they were
of flimsy netting and there were always holes in
them, so that when a mosquito or fly once got in
he had us all to himself, and made the most of it.
It was not uncommon, in Summer, for a bat to
follow the procession. When this happened my
brother and I turned out with brooms, baseball bats
and other weapons, and pursued the hunt to a kill.
The carcass was always nailed to the backyard
fence the next morning, with the wings stretched
out as far as possible, and boys would come from
blocks around to measure and admire it. Whenever an insect of unfamiliar species showed up we
tried to capture it, and if we succeeded we kept it
alive in a pill-box or baking-powder can. Our
favorite among pill-boxes was the one that held
Wright's Indian Vegetable Pills (which my father
swallowed every time he got into a low state), for
it was made of thin sheets of wood veneer, and was
thus more durable than the druggists' usual card-
board boxes.

Every public place in Baltimore was so furiously
beset by bugs of all sorts that communal gather-

ings were impossible on hot nights. The very cops
on the street corners spent a large part of their
time slapping mosquitoes and catching flies. Our
pony Frank had a fly-net, but it operated only
when he was in motion; in his leisure he was as
badly used as the cops. When arc-lights began
to light the streets, along about 1885, they attracted so many beetles of gigantic size that their
glare was actually obscured. These beetles at once
acquired the name of electric-light bugs, and it
was believed that the arc carbons produced them
by a kind of spontaneous generation, and that their
bite was as dangerous as that of a tarantula. But
no Baltimorean would ever admit categorically that
this Congo-like plague of flying things, taking one
day with another, was really serious, or indeed a
plague at all. Many a time I have seen my mother
leap up from the dinner-table to engage the swarming flies with an improvised punkah, and heard her
rejoice and give humble thanks simultaneously that
Baltimore was not the sinkhole that Washington
was.

These flies gave no concern to my brother Charlie
and me; they seemed to be innocuous and even
friendly compared to the chiggers, bumble-bees
and hornets that occasionally beset us. Indeed,
they were a source of pleasant recreation to us,
for very often, on hot Summer evenings, we would
retire to the kitchen, stretch out flat on our backs
on the table, and pop away at them with sling-

shots as they roosted in dense clumps upon the ceiling. Our favorite projectile was a square of lemon-peel, roasted by the hired girl. Thus prepared, it was tough enough to shoot straight and kill certainly, but when it bounced back it did not hurt us. The hired girl, when she was in an amiable mood, prepared us enough of these missiles for an hour's brisk shooting, and in the morning she had the Red Cross job of sweeping the dead flies off the ceiling. Sometimes there were hundreds of them, lying dead in sticky windrows. When there were horse-flies from the back alley among them, which was not infrequently, they leaked red mammalian blood, which was an extra satisfaction to us. The stables that lined the far side of the alley were vast hatcheries of such flies, some of which reached a gigantic size. When we caught one we pulled off its wings and watched it try idiotically to escape on foot, or removed its legs and listened while it buzzed in a loud and futile manner. The theory taught in those days was that creatures below the warm-blooded level had no feelings whatever, and in fact rather enjoyed being mutilated. Thus it was an innocent and instructive matter to cut a worm into two halves, and watch them wriggle off in opposite directions. Once my brother and I caught a turtle, chopped off its head, and were amazed to see it march away headless. That experience, in truth, was so astonishing as to be alarming, and we never monkeyed with turtles thereafter. But we got a good deal of pleasure, first and last, out of chasing and butchering toads, though we were always careful to avoid taking them in our hands, for the juice of their kidneys was supposed to cause warts.

At the first smell of hot weather there was a tremendous revolution in Hollins street. All the Brussels carpets in the house were jimmied up and replaced by sleazy Chinese matting, all the hair-cloth furniture was covered with linen covers, and every picture, mirror, gas bracket and Rogers group was draped in fly netting. The carpets were wheelbarrowed out to Steuart's hill by professional carpet beaters of the African race, and there flogged and flayed until the heaviest lick yielded no more dust. Before the mattings could be laid all the floors had to be scrubbed, and every picture and mirror had to be taken down and polished. Also, the lace curtains had to come down, and the ivory-colored Holland shades that hung in Winter had to be changed to blue ones, to filter out the Summer sun. The lace curtains were always laundered before being put away — a formidable operation involving stretching them on huge frameworks set up on trestles in the backyard. All this uproar was repeated in reverse at the ides of September. The mattings came up, the carpets went down, the furniture was stripped of its covers, the pictures, mirrors and gas brackets lost their netting, and the blue Holland shades were displaced by the ivory ones. It always turned out, of course, that the flies of Summer had got through the nettings with ease, and left every picture peppered with their calling cards. The large pier mirror between the two windows of the parlor usually got a double dose, and it took the hired girl half a day to renovate it, climbing up and down a ladder in the clumsy manner of a policeman getting over a fence, and dropping soap, washrags, hairpins and other gear on the floor.

The legend seems to prevail that there were no sewers in Baltimore until after the World War, but that is something of an exaggeration. Our house in Hollins street was connected with a private sewer down the alley in the rear as early as I have any recollection of it, and so were many other houses, especially in the newer parts of the town. But I should add that we also had a powder-room in the backyard for the accommodation of laundresses, whitewashers and other visiting members of the domestic faculty, and that there was a shallow sink under it that inspired my brother and me with considerable dread. Every now and then some child in West Baltimore fell into such a sink, and had to be hauled out, besmeared and howling, by the cops. The one in our yard was pumped out and fumigated every Spring by a gang of colored men who arrived on a wagon that was called an O.E.A. — *i.e.*, odorless excavating apparatus. They discharged this social-minded duty with great fervor and dispatch, and achieved non-odoriferousness, in the innocent Aframerican way, by burning buckets of rosin and tar. The whole neighborhood choked on the black, greasy, pungent smoke for hours afterward. It was thought to be an effective preventive of cholera, smallpox and tuberculosis.

All the sewers of Baltimore, whether private or public, emptied into the Back Basin in those days, just as all those of Manhattan empty into the North and East rivers to this day. But I should add that there was a difference, for the North and East rivers have swift tidal currents, whereas the Back Basin, distant 170 miles from the Chesapeake capes, had only the most lethargic. As a result it began to acquire a powerful aroma every Spring, and by August smelled like a billion polecats. This stench radiated all over downtown Baltimore, though in Hollins street we hardly ever detected it. Perhaps that was due to the fact that West Baltimore had rival perfumes of its own — for example, the emanation from the Wilkins hair factory in the Frederick road, a mile or so from Union Square. When a breeze from the southwest, bouncing its way over the Wilkins factory, reached Hollins street the effect was almost that of poison gas. It happened only seldom, but when it happened it was surely memorable. The householders of the vicinage always swarmed down to the City Hall the next day and raised blue hell, but they

never got anything save promises. In fact, it was
not until the Wilkinses went into the red and shut
down their factory that the abomination abated
— and its place was then taken, for an unhappy
year or two, by the degenerate cosmic rays projected from a glue factory lying in the same general direction. No one, so far as I know, ever argued that these mephitic blasts were salubrious,
but it is a sober fact that town opinion held that
the bouquet of the Back Basin was. In proof
thereof it was pointed out that the clerks who
sweated all Summer in the little coops of offices
along the Light street and Pratt street wharves
were so remarkably long-lived that many of them
appeared to be at least 100 years old, and that
the colored stevedores who loaded and unloaded
the Bay packets were the strongest, toughest,
drunkenest and most thieving in the whole port.

The Baltimore of the eighties was a noisy town,
for the impact of iron wagon tires on hard cobble-
stone was almost like that of a hammer on an anvil.
To be sure, there was a dirt road down the middle
of every street, kept in repair by the accumulated
sweepings of the sidewalks, but this cushioned track
was patronized only by hay-wagons from the
country and like occasional traffic: milk-men, grocery deliverymen and other such regulars kept to
the areas where the cobbles were naked, and so
made a fearful clatter. In every way, in fact, city
life was much noiser then than it is now. Children

at play were not incarcerated in playgrounds and policed by hired ma'ms, but roved the open streets, and most of their games involved singing or yelling. At Christmas time they began to blow horns at least a week before the great day, and kept it up until all the horns were disabled, and in Summer they began celebrating the Fourth far back in June and were still exploding fire-crackers at the end of July. Nearly every house had a dog in it, and nearly all the dogs barked more or less continuously from 4 a.m. until after midnight. It was still lawful to keep chickens in backyards, and many householders did so. All within ear range of Hollins street appeared to divide them as to sex in the proportion of a hundred crowing roosters to one clucking hen. My grandfather Mencken once laid in a coop of Guineas, unquestionably the noisiest species of *Aves* known to science. But his wife, my step-grandmother, had got in a colored clergyman to steal them before the neighbors arrived with the police.

In retired by-streets grass grew between the cobblestones to almost incredible heights, and it was not uncommon for colored rag-and-bone men to pasture their undernourished horses on it. On the steep hill making eastward from the Washington Monument, in the very heart of Baltimore, some comedian once sowed wheat, and it kept on coming up for years thereafter. Every Spring the Baltimore newspapers would report on the prospects of the crop, and visitors to the city were taken to see it. Most Baltimoreans of that era, in fact, took a fierce, defiant pride in the bucolic aspects of their city. They would boast that it was the only great seaport on earth in which dandelions grew in the streets in Spring. They believed that all such vegetation was healthful, and kept down chills and fever. I myself once had proof that the excess of litter in the streets was not without its value to mankind. I was riding the pony Frank when a wild thought suddenly seized him, and he bucked me out of the saddle in the best manner of a Buffalo Bill bronco. Unfortunately, my left foot was stuck in the stirrup, and so I was dragged behind him as he galloped off. He had gone at least a block before a couple of colored boys stopped him. If the cobblestones of Stricker street had been bare I'd not be with you today. As it was, I got no worse damage than a series of harsh scourings running from my neck to my heels. The colored boys took me to Reveille's livery-stable, and stopped the bloodshed with large gobs of spider web. It was the hemostatic of choice in Baltimore when I was young. If, perchance, it spread a little tetanus, then the Baltimoreans blamed the mercies of God.

IV

The Head of
the House

MY grandfather Mencken, in the days when I first
became aware of him, was approaching sixty, and
hence seemed to me to be a very old man. But
there was certainly nothing decrepit about him,
even though a broken leg dating from the Civil
War era had left him with a slight limp, for he
threw back his shoulders in a quasi-military fashion, he had a piercing eye of a peculiarly vivid
blue, and he presented to the world what I can
only describe as a generally confident and even
somewhat cocky aspect. His bald head rose in a
Shakespearean dome, and the hair that survived
over his ears was brushed forward stiffly. His
cheeks were shaven down to the neck, but he wore
a mustache of no particular kind, and allowed his

beard to sprout and hang down within the meridians of longitude marked off by his eyes. Whiskers of such irrational design were not uncommon in that age, which was immensely more hairy than the present glorious day. Many of the extant generals of the Civil War had sets of them, and so did many German forty-eighters. My grandfather, in a way of speaking, was a forty-eighter himself, for he shoved off for these shores from his native Saxony at almost the precise moment the German Vorparlament met at Frankfort-on-Main. But that was as far as his connection with democratic idealism ever went. In his later life he used to hint that he had left Germany, not to embrace the boons of democracy in this great Republic, but to escape a threatened overdose at home. In world affairs he was a faithful customer of Bismarck, and in his capacity of patriotic American he inclined toward the ironically misnamed Democratic party, which had fought a long war to save slavery and was still generally disreputable. His two sons, who were high tariff Republicans, finally managed, I believe, to induce him to vote against Grover Cleveland in 1884, but my father told me years later that they viewed his politics with some distrust to the end of his days.

I recall him best on his visitations to our house in Hollins street, which, though not very frequent, were carried out with considerable ceremonial. He lived in Fayette street, only a few blocks away, and usually arrived on foot. When the stomp-stomp of his tremendous shillelagh of a cane was heard, and he heaved into sight in his long-tailed black coat, his Gladstonian collar and his old-fashioned black cravat, a hush fell upon the house, my mother and father put on their best party manners, and my brother Charlie and I were given a last nervous inspection and cautioned to be good on penalty of the knout. Arrived, he deposited his hat on the floor beside his chair, mopped his dome meditatively, and let it be known that he was ready for the business of the day, whatever it might turn out to be, and however difficult and onerous. It covered, first and last, an immense range, running from infant feeding and the choice of wallpaper at one extreme to marriage settlements and the intricacies of dogmatic theology at the other. No man on this earth ever believed more innocently and passionately in the importance of the family as the basic unit of human society, or had a higher sense of duty to his own. As undisputed head of the American branch of the Menckenii he took jurisdiction over all its thirty members — his two sons, his three daughters, his two daughters-in-law, his three sons-in-law, and his twenty grandchildren — with his wife, my step-grandmother, thrown in as a sort of friendly alien. There was never, so far as I could learn afterward, any serious challenge of his authority, nor, I must add, did he ever exercise it in a harsh and offensive manner. He simply assumed as a matter of course — indeed, as an axiom so self-evident that the human mind could not conceive a caveat to it — that he was charged by virtue of his status and office with a long list of responsibilities, and he met them in the amiable and assured fashion of a man who knew his work in the world, and was ready to do it though the heavens fell.

My mother, in the years after his death, always defended the justice of his decisions, or, at all events, their strict legality, though more than once, by her own account, they went counter to her own judgment and desire. There was, for example, the matter of the christening of my younger brother, born in 1889. For some reason that I never learned she wanted to call him Albert, and for months that was actually his studio or stable name. Even my father, who was prejudiced against the name because the only Albert he knew was a dead-beat who owed him a bill of $135, nevertheless acquiesced, and all the cups, rattles, knitted jackets, belly-bands and velvet caps that came in for the baby were so engraved or embroidered. But my father yet hesitated strangely to send for a clergyman and have the business over, and one day the reason therefor appeared. It was a beautiful Sunday in early Spring and my grandfather chose it to set up his Court of King's Bench in the Summer-house in our backyard. Without any time-consuming preliminaries, he announced simply that the baby would have to be called August — plain August and nothing else, with no compromise on a second name that might convert him eventually into A. Albert, A. Bernard, A. Clarence . . . . . . or A. Zoroaster. August had been the name of his own father, and was the name of his first-born son, my father. It was a proud and (to his ears) mellifluous name, ancient in the Mencken family and going back, in one form or other, to the dawn of civilization. Since this erstwhile Albert was my mother's fourth child, and in all human probability would be her last, it was of paramount necessity, as a matter of family decency and decorum, that he should be August. And August he was, and is.

Why the name hadn't been given to me I don't know, and the fact that it wasn't shows a touch of the mysterious, for I was the *Stammhalter* and hence the object of my grandfather's special concern and solicitude. As the eldest son of his eldest son I'd someday enjoy, in the course of nature, the high dignities of head of the family, and it goes without saying that he must have given a great deal of consideration to my labeling. His reasons for deciding that I was to be named after his second son, my uncle Henry, I have never been able to discover, and for many years I wondered what source had provided my incongruous middle name of Louis. Then I learned that my grandfather's first wife and my own grandmother, Harriet McClellan, had borne and lost a son in 1862, and died

herself a few months later, and that this ill-starred
and forgotten infant had been named Louis after
one of her uncles. The old man never ceased to
mourn his poor Harriet. They had married when
she was but sixteen, and had been happy together
in years of hard struggle. My mother once told
me that he used to make surreptitious afternoon
visits to Hollins street in his declining years, to
talk about his lost love. His undying thought of
her greatly touched my mother, and was probably
mainly responsible for the affection and respect
that she always seemed to have for him. His judicial decisions as head of the house had more than
once gone against her, but she was nevertheless
staunchly for him, and liked to tell me about him.

One of his judgments I recall very clearly,
though it must have been handed down not later
than 1886. It had to do with the hairdressing of
my brother Charlie and me. We had been pa-
tronizing a neighborhood barber of the name of
Lehnert, and we liked him very much, for he cut
our hair in not more than three minutes by the
clock, and always gave us a horse-doctor's dose of
highly perfumed hair-oil. When we got back from
his atelier we let the admiring hired girl smell
our heads, which continued to radiate a suffocating
scent for days· afterward. But my grandfather
objected to Lehnert's free and far from well-con-
sidered use of the clippers, and one day issued an
order that he was to be notified the next time our

hair needed cutting. When the time came word was duly sent to him, and he appeared in Hollins street the following Sunday morning. My father vanished discreetly but my mother stood by for the operation, which was carried out in the side-yard. What I chiefly recall of it is that Charlie and I sat in a kitchen chair and were swathed in a bed-sheet, and that it seemed to us to take a dreadfully long while. Lehnert could have clipped a whole herd of boys in the same time. When the job was done at last my mother professed politely to admire the result, but there was very little enthusiasm in her tone. The next day my father took us both downtown, and had my grandfather's zigzag shear marks smoothed out by the head barber at the Eutaw House, a majestic man of color who claimed to have serviced not only all the principal generals of the Civil War, but also every Governor of Maryland back to colonial days. But when the time came to return to Lehnert for another clip he was warned to follow the model before him, and this he always did thereafter, to the relief and satisfaction of all concerned.

My grandfather, as I have said, wore a Gladstonian collar and a stock-like cravat of archaic design. Both had disappeared from the marts of commerce before my time, but my aunt Pauline had plans and specifications for them, and so enjoyed the honor of making them. She was the *châtelaine* of my grandfather's big house in Fayette street, for his wife, my step-grandmother, was in indifferent health. Aunt Pauline was already married, with two children of her own, but she never forgot her filial duty to her father, nor did he. When he arrived home for dinner, which was at about 2 p.m., the soup had to be ready to go on the table at the precise instant he hung up his hat in the hall. He had copious and complicated ideas about cooking and household management, as he had about medicine, law, moral theology, economics, interior decoration and the use of the spheres, and his public spirit, though it was not strong, nevertheless forbade him to keep them to himself. In his backyard in Fayette street he carried on extensive horticultural experiments, virtually all of which, I believe, failed. What I chiefly remember of them is his recurrent reports that cats had rolled in and ruined his strawberries, or that a storm had blown down his lima-beans, or that some other act of God had wrecked his effort to produce a strain of tobacco resistant to worms, high winds, and the irrational fluctuations of the market. But he seems to have had some luck with the *Curcurbitaceae*, for every year he presented all his daughters and daughters-in-law with gourds for use in darning stockings. Inasmuch as these gourds, though very light, had surfaces as hard as iron, they did not wear out, and so my mother, who never threw anything away if room could be found for it in the house, accumulated a large battery. Sometimes, when she was out shopping, my brother Charlie and I fought with them in the cellar, for when one of them collided with a human skull it made a loud, hollow, satisfying report, and yet did not cause death or even unconsciousness.

There is a document in the family archives, headed grandly "Halte im Gedächtniss Jesum Christum!", which certifies that my grandfather submitted to the rite of confirmation as a Christian of the Protestant sub-species in the church at Borna, Saxony, on March 20, 1842, but he had apparently lost his confidence in Jahveh by the time I became acquainted with him. Indeed, it would not be going too far to say that he was an outright infidel, though he always got on well with the rev. clergy, and permitted his three daughters to commune freely with the Protestant Episcopal Church, the American agency of his first wife's Church of England. It was in his character of skeptic that he subscribed toward the Baltimore crematorium in 1889, and ordered his two sons to subscribe too — so far as I know, the only example of overt social-mindedness that he ever showed. He belonged to no organization save a lodge of Free-masons, and held himself diligently aloof from the German societies that swarmed in Baltimore in the eighties. Their singing he regarded as a public disturbance, and their *Turnerei* as insane. Most of the German business men of Baltimore, in those days, had come from the Hansa towns, and as a

Saxon he was compelled to disdain them as *Platt-deutschen*, though his own remote forebears had been traders in Oldenburg. I somehow gathered the impression, even as a boy, that he was a rather lonely man, and my mother told me years later that she was of the same opinion. Left a widower at thirty-four, with four small children to care for and his roots in America still shaky, he had seen some hard and bitter years, and they had left their marks upon him. He showed none of the expansive amiability of his two sons, but was extremely reserved.

By the time I knew him his days of struggle were over and he was in easy waters, but he still kept a good deal to himself, and when he took me of an afternoon, as a small boy, on one of his headlong buggy-rides, he seldom paid a visit to anyone save the Xaverian Brothers at St. Mary's Industrial School, a bastile for problem boys about two miles from Hollins street. These holy men tried to teach their charges trades, and one of the trades they offered was that of the cigarmaker. My grandfather, who dealt in Pennsylvania leaf tobacco, sold them their raw materials, and my father and uncle undertook to market their output — in the end, an impossible matter, for the cheroots that the boys made were as hard as so many railroad spikes, and no one could smoke them. When my grandfather called upon the Xaverians the tobacco business was quickly disposed of, and he and they sat down to drink beer and debate theology. These discussions, as I recall them, seemed to last for hours, and while they were going on I had to sit in a gloomy hallway hung with gory religious paintings — saints being burned, broken on the wheel and disemboweled, the Flood drowning scores of cows, horses, camels and sheep, the Crucifixion against a background of hair-raising lightnings, and so on. I was too young, of course, to follow the argument; moreover, it was often carried on in German. Nevertheless, I gathered that it neither resulted in agreement nor left any hard feelings. The Xaverians must have put in two or three years trying to rescue my grandfather from his lamentable heresies, but they made no more impression upon him than if they had addressed a clothing-store dummy, though it was plain that he respected and enjoyed their effort. On his part, he failed just as dismally to seduce them from their oaths of chastity, poverty and obedience. I met some of them years afterward, and found that they still remembered him with affection, though he had turned their pastoral teeth.

The buggy that he used for his movements about town was an extraordinarily stout vehicle, and it had need to be, for when he got under way he paid no attention to the fact that the cobblestones of Baltimore were very rough. Where we went when I was aboard I didn't always know, for the top was always up and we elder grandchildren rode standing in the space between the seat and the back curtain. Sometimes he would jam in four or five of us, with a couple of juniors on the seat beside him and two or three more on hassocks on the floor. When, in his wild career over the cobbles, he struck one of the stepping-stones that used to run across the roadway at street corners, we all took a leap into the air, and came down somewhat mixed up. But somehow it never hurt us, and in the end we got so used to it that we rather liked it. In the last years of his life, after my brother Charlie and I had acquired a pony, my grandfather would drive out with us of an afternoon — he in his caterpillar-tread buggy and we in our cart. Once, proceeding out the Franklin road, we came in sight of a tollgate, and he ordered us to drive ahead of him. When the tollkeeper asked for his money we were to point to the buggy following, and say that the old man in it would pay for us. We did so as ordered, but when he came up he denied that he knew us. By that time, of course, we were out of the tollkeeper's reach. The old man thought it was a swell joke, and told my father and uncle about it as if expecting applause, but they failed to be amused. The next time we drove out the Franklin road the tollkeeper charged ten cents instead of five, and he kept on charging us ten cents instead of five until his professional wounds were healed.

My grandfather made frequent trips to Pennsylvania to buy tobacco, and was full of anecdotes of the singular innocence of the Pennsylvania Germans, whose ghastly dialect he had picked up. His favorite tale concerned a yokel of Lancaster county from whom he had bought a crop of tobacco for future delivery, offering a three-months' note in payment. The yokel declined the note on the ground that he needed nothing to help his memory: he would be on hand without fail when the time came to settle. " Keep it yourself," he said, " so you won't forget to pay me." My grandfather traded with these ill-assimilated *Bauern* for many years in complete amity, and had a high regard for them. He sold their tobacco all over. Some of it actually went to Key West, which was then assumed by most Americans to be foreign territory, using only Havana leaf in its celebrated cigars. In deference to the visitors who sometimes dropped in at the factories, the Pennsylvania leaf sent to them was repacked in empty Havana tobacco bales. My grandfather, as a moral theologian, admitted that there was something irregular about this transaction, but he consoled himself by saying that Key West was full of swindlers escaped from Cuba and points south, and that it was impossible to do any business with them at all without yielding something to their peculiar ethics.

The house in Fayette street was a wonderland

to us youngsters of Hollins street, for grandchildren are always indulged more than children,
and we had privileges in it that were unknown at
home. I have described in Chapter I a pillow-
fight that almost wrecked it. We always made a
formal call on Christmas morning — my brother
Charlie and I representing the Augustine line of
the family, and my cousins Pauline and John
Henry representing the Henrician. Ostensibly, of
course, our mission was to offer our duty to our
grandparents, but actually, we glowed with other
expectations. They were never disappointed. The
parlor in Fayette street had a much higher ceiling
than those in Hollins street, and so the Christmas
tree that flamed and coruscated there was larger
and more splendid. At its foot were piles of toys,
and among them there was always an express-
wagon — to haul the other things home. One year
this wagon was for my cousin John Henry, the
next it was for Charlie, the next it was for me, and
so *da capo*. After taking aboard a suitable re-
freshment of *Pfeffernüsse*, *Springele*, *Lebkuchen*
and other carbohydrates, and stuffing our pockets
with almonds, butternuts, walnuts, candy and
fruit, we loaded our cargo and started home at a
run, yelling and cavorting along the way. Christmas in those days was a gaudy festival, and my
Grandmother Mencken (or maybe it was my Aunt
Pauline) had a singular facility for choosing good
Christmas presents. Down to the middle of my

teens she always managed to find something for me that really delighted me, and many of the books that provided my earliest reading were her selections — including the " Chatterbox " that took me through my first full-length story. But of this, more hereafter.

V

The Training of
a Gangster

THE BALTIMORE of the eighties had lately got over
an evil (but proud) name for what the insurance
policies call civil commotion. Down to the Civil
War and even beyond its gangs were of such enter-
prise and ferocity that many connoisseurs ranked
them as the professional equals, if not actually the
superiors, of the gangs of New York, Marseilles
and Port Said. It was nothing for them to kidnap
a police sergeant, scuttle a tugboat in the harbor,
or set fire to a church, an orphan asylum or a
brewery. Once a mob made up of the massed gangs
of the town broke into the jail and undertook to
butcher a party of military gentlemen who had
sought refuge there after a vain effort to save an
unpopular newspaper from pillage. One of these

gentlemen, a doddering veteran of the Revolution named General James M. Lingan, was done to death with great barbarity, and another, General Light Horse Harry Lee, father of the immortal Robert E. Lee, was so badly used that he was never the same again.

At the opening of the Civil War, as every school-boy knows, another Baltimore mob attacked a Massachusetts regiment passing through the city on its way to save democracy at Bull Run, and gave it such a lacing that what it got in that battle three months later seemed almost voluptuous by comparison. This was in April, 1861. Before the end of the year the town proletariat had switched from the Confederate theology to the Federal, and devoted itself to tarring and feathering Southern sympathizers, and wrecking their houses. The war over, it continued its idealistic exercises until the seventies, and at the time I was born Baltimore was still often called Mob Town, though by then the honorific had begun to be only retrospective.

Thus it was necessary for every self-respecting boy of my generation to belong to a gang. No one, in fact, ever asked him if he wanted to join or not join; he was simply taken in when he came to the right ripeness, which was normally between the ages of eight and nine. There was, of course, some difference between the gangs of the proletariat and those of the more tender bourgeoisie. The former tried to preserve, at least to some extent, the grand tradition. They had quarters in empty houses or stable lofts, smoked clay pipes, rushed the can, carried lethal weapons, and devoted themselves largely to stoning cops and breaking into and looting the freight cars of the Baltimore & Ohio Railroad. The latter were a great deal milder and more elegant. They carried only clubs, and then only in times of danger; they never got any further along the road to debauchery than reading dime-novels and smoking cigarettes; and the only thing they ever stole (save, of course, ash-barrels and garbage-boxes on election night) was an occasional half-peck of apples, potatoes or turnips. These victuals were snatched on the run from the baskets that corner-grocers then set outside their stores, along with bundles of brooms, stacks of wooden kitchen-pails, and hog carcasses hanging from hooks.

I attained, by the age of eight, to a considerable proficiency in this larceny, and so did my brother Charlie. Our victim was usually Mr. Thiernau, a stout, bustling, sideburned man who operated a grocery-and-meat store at Gilmor and Baltimore streets, less than a block from our back gate. He wore invariably what was then the uniform of his calling — a long white apron stained with blood, a Cardigan jacket, and large cuffs made of some sort of straw. Around the little finger of his left hand ran a signet ring, and behind his right ear he carried his pencil. So far as I can remember, he never made any attempt to pursue the boys who looted him; in truth, I suspect that his baskets were set out as a kind of accommodation to them, with the aim of gaining their favor. Not infrequently they were delegated to buy supplies for their mothers, and on such occasions they always chose Mr. Thiernau's store, not that of the Knoops across the street. The Knoops, two brothers and a cousin, appear to have leaned toward Levirate ideas, for when the cousin died one of the brothers married his widow. They were Germans of large girth, gloomy aloofness and high commercial acumen, and they accumulated among them a considerable estate, but they never exposed anything that was edible on the sidewalk, and so the boys of the neighborhood were against them. Even Mr. Thiernau, I believe, kept his best vegetables to be sold inside his store, not stolen in front of it.

One day, after my brother Charlie and I had made a fine haul of sweet potatoes, my father came home unexpectedly and caught us roasting them on a fire in the backyard. He demanded to know where we had got them from, and our guilty looks betrayed us. He thereupon made a great uproar, declaring that he would drown us, ship us to the Indian country or even hand us over to the child-stealers rather than see us grow up criminals. I put all the blame on Charlie, for he had actually made the snatch while I bossed the job and watched, and my father ordered him to return the potatoes to Mr. Thiernau at once, half burned as they were. Charlie set off boo-hooing, threw the potatoes into a garbage-box in the alley, and came home prepared to report that Mr. Thiernau had taken them back with polite thanks. But he delayed on the way to watch the Thiernau colored driver unload a cargo of dead hogs, and by the time he returned my father had apparently forgotten the matter, for we heard no more from him about it. We discovered the next day, however, that the hired girl had orders to supply us with potatoes whenever the roasting fever was on us, and for a week or so we patronized her. But her stock never seemed to have the right flavor, though it came from the same Thiernau's, and we eventually resumed our larcenies. They were terminated a year or so later by Mr. Thiernau's sudden death, which was a great shock to us, and naturally turned us to moral considerations and made us uneasily Hell-minded.

The Hollins street gang functioned as a unit only on occasions of public ceremonial — for instance, at election time. It began lifting boxes and barrels for the election night bonfire two or three weeks before the great day, usually under command of a large, roomy boy named Barrel Fairbanks, and they were commonly stored in the stable behind his house. If we managed to collar a paint barrel it was a feat that cheered us, for paint barrels burned with a fierce flame and made a great

deal of smoke. The grocerymen and feed dealers
of the neighborhood, knowing that we were on the
prowl, tried to save their good boxes and barrels
by setting out their decrepit ones, and we always
accepted the suggested arrangement. It was only
when there was a real famine in fuel that we resorted to taking back gates off their hinges, and
even then we confined ourselves to gates that were
ready to fall off of their own motion.

The first election night bonfire that I remember
was built on the evening of that day in November,
1888, which saw the stuffings of Cleveland and
Thurman knocked out of them by Harrison and
Morton. The returns were published from the por-
tico of a Democratic ward club at Lombard and
Stricker streets, across Union Square from our
house, and the fire was kindled at the crossing of
Hollins and Stricker streets. As the sad news drib-
bled along the Democrats fell into a low state of
mind, and some of them actually went home before
the kegs of beer that they had laid in were empty;
but my father rejoiced, for as a high-tariff Republican he was bound in conscience to regard Cleveland as a fiend in human form. I recall him coming
down to the corner to see and applaud the fire,
which blazed higher than the houses along Hollins
street. The cops offered no objection to it, though
in those days they were all Democrats, for the flames
did no damage to the solid Baltimore cobblestones
that underlay them, and if they singed a few trees it

was only God's will. When the cobbles yielded to asphalt, long after I was a grown man, election-night bonfires were prohibited.

I recall one election night when the tough boys from the region of the Baltimore & Ohio repair-shops, having had bad luck in collecting material for their own fire, made an attempt to raid ours. They arrived just as it was kindled. They were armed with clubs, and made their attack from two sides, yelling like Indians. We of Hollins street were ordinarily no match for these ruffians, but that night there was an audience looking on, so we fought fiercely, and finally managed to drive them off. Some of them, retreating, carried off blazing boxes, but not many. I got a clout across the arm that night, and nursed it proudly for a week. I was in hopes that Dr. Wiley would order the arm into a sling, but when he dropped in the next day he could find nothing save a large blue bruise. When he began to show signs of taking a routine look at my tongue, I slipped away quickly, pleading an important engagement.

Every Baltimore boy, in those days, had to be a partisan of some engine company, or, as the phrase ran, to go for it. The Hollins street boys went for No. 14, whose house was in Hollins street three blocks west of Union Square. Whenever an alarm came in a large bell on the roof of the engine-house broadcast it, and every boy within earshot reached into his hip-pocket for his directory of alarm-boxes. Such directories were given out as advertisements by druggists, horseshoers, saloon-keepers and so on, and every boy began to tote one as soon as he could read. If the fire was nearby, or seemed to be close to a livery-stable, a home for the aged, or any other establishment promising lively entertainment, all hands dropped whatever was afoot and set off for it at a gallop. It was usually out by the time we reached the scene, but sometimes we had better luck. Once we saw a blaze in a slaughter-house, with a drove of squealing hogs cremated in a pen, and another time we were entranced by a fire in the steeple of a Baptist church. Unhappily, this last ended as a dud, for the firemen quickly climbed up their high ladders and put it out.

The duties of a boy who went for an engine were not onerous. The main thing was simply to go for it. At an actual fire he could not distinguish between his own firemen and those of some other and altogether abhorrent company, for they all wore the same scoop-tailed helmets and the same black rubber coats. But he was expected nevertheless to go for them through thick and thin. If, venturing into a strange neighborhood, he was halted by the local pickets and asked to say what engine he went for, he always answered proudly and truthfully, even though the truth might cost him a black eye. I never heard of a boy failing to observe this obligation of honor. Even the scoundrels who went for

No. 10, when we caught one of them in our territory, never tried to deceive us. The most they would do would be to retreat ten paces before letting off their clan cry. We would then proceed, as in duty bound, to hang them out, which is to say, to chase them off the soil of our Fatherland.

The frontiers of the various gangs in West Baltimore were known to all the boys denizened there, and it was not common for a boy to leave his own territory. If he did so, it was at the risk of being hung out, or maybe beaten. But fights between adjoining gangs were relatively rare, for the cops kept watch along the borders, and all hands avoided them diligently. Once the Hollins street gang, engaged in exploring Franklin Square, which was three blocks from Union Square, encountered a gang that went for No. 8 engine, and a battle was joined. But it had gone on for no more than a few minutes when a cop came lumbering up Calhoun street, and both armies at once fled northward, which is to say, into No. 8 territory. The No. 8 boys, though they were officially obliged to do us in at every chance, concealed us in their alleys until the cop gave up the chase, for in the presence of the common enemy gang differences sank to the level of the academic. Any boy in flight from a cop was sure of sanctuary anywhere. In fact, a favorite way of making a necessary journey through hostile lines was to do it at a run, yelling " Cheese it !

The cops! " Boys respected this outcry even when they knew it was fraudulent.

There was in West Baltimore a neutral territory that all gangs save the ruffians from the region of the B. & O. shops respected — and they seldom invaded it, for they had better hunting-grounds nearer their base. It was a series of open lots beginning at Fulton avenue and Baltimore street, three blocks from Union Square, and running westward until it was lost in a wilderness of lime-kilns, slaughter-houses and cemeteries. From east to west it must have been a mile long, and from south to north half a mile wide. It is now covered with long rows of the red brick, marble trimmed two-story houses that are so typical of Baltimore, but in my nonage it was wild country, with room enough for half a dozen baseball diamonds, not to mention huge thickets of Jimson weeds, nigger-lice, and other such nefarious flora. The lower end, at Fulton avenue, was much frequented by the colored men who made their livings beating carpets. They would erect poles, string them with washlines, hang the carpets, and then flog them by the hour, raising great clouds of dust. A little further to the westward other colored men pursued the art and mystery of the sod-cutter. They would load their rolled-up sods on wheelbarrows and push them down into the city, to refresh and adorn the backyards of the resident bourgeoisie.

We Hollins street boys spent many a pleasant afternoon roving and exploring this territory, which had the name of Steuart's Hill. We liked to watch the operation of the lime-kilns, all of them burning oyster shells, and the work of the carpet-beaters and sod-cutters. But best of all we liked to visit the slaughter-houses at the far western end. There was a whole row of them, and their revolting slops drained down into a deep gully that we called the Canyon. This Canyon was the Wild West of West Baltimore, and the center of all its romance. Whenever a boy came to the age when it became incumbent on him to defy God, the laws of the land and his father by smoking his first cigarette, he went out there for the operation. It was commonly a considerable ceremony, with a ring of older boys observing and advising. If the neophyte got sick he was laid out on one of the lower shelves of the Canyon until he recovered. If he began crying for his mother he was pelted with nigger-lice and clods of lime.

The Canyon was also a favorite resort of boys who read dime novels. This practice was regarded with horror by the best moral opinion of the time, and a boy who indulged it openly was given up as lost beyond hope. The best thing expected of him was that he would run away from home and go west to fight the Indians; the worst was that he would end on the gallows. In the more elderly years of my infancy I tried a few dime novels, trembling like a virgin boarding an airship for Hollywood, but I found them so dull that I could scarcely get through them. There were other boys, however, who appeared to be able to bear them, and even to like them, and these addicts often took them out to the Canyon to read in peace. No cops ever showed themselves in that vicinity, which was probably, in fact, outside the city limits of Baltimore. It was an Alsatia without laws, and tolerated every sort of hellment. I have seen a dozen boys stretched on the grass within a circumference of fifty feet, all of them smoking cigarettes and reading dime novels. It was a scene of inspiring debauchery, even to the most craven spectator.

One afternoon, having been left behind when the Hollins street gang made a trip to the Canyon, I set out alone to overtake it. Just west of Fulton avenue, which is to say, in full sight of householders and passers-by along Baltimore street, I was held up with perfect technic by three boys of a strange gang. One of them aimed a cap pistol at my head and ordered me to stick up my hands, and the other two proceeded to frisk me. They found a pocket-knife, a couple of sea-shells, three or four nails, two cigarette pictures, a dozen chewing-tobacco tags, a cork, a slate pencil, an almost fossil handkerchief, and three cents in cash. I remember as clearly as if it were yesterday their debate over the three cents. They were sorely tempted, for it appeared that they were flat broke, and needed money badly. But in the end they decided primly that taking it would be stealing. The other things they took without qualm, for that was only hooking.

When they turned me loose at last I ran all the way to the Canyon, and sounded the alarm. The gentlemen of the Hollins street gang were pleasantly engaged in throwing stones into a pool of hog blood that had formed beneath the scuppers of one of the slaughter-houses, but when they heard my story they started for the scene of the outrage at once, scooping up rocks on the way. They got there, of course, too late to capture the bandits, but they patrolled the vicinity for the rest of the afternoon, and revisited it every day for a couple of weeks, hoping to make a collar, and get me back my handkerchief, nails, slate pencil, and chewing-tobacco tags. I may say at once that they were never recovered, nor did I ever see the robbers again. They must have come from some remote part of West Baltimore. Or perhaps they were prisoners escaped from the House of Refuge.

This bastile was a mile westward, on the banks of Gwynn's Falls. It was a harsh granite building surrounded by sepulchral trees, and all the boys of West Baltimore feared it mightily. Its population consisted of boys who had become so onery that their own fathers resigned them to the cops. The general belief was that a rascal who once entered its gates was as good as lost to the world. If he ever got out at all, which was supposed to be very unusual, the cops were waiting to grab him again, and thereafter he made quick progress to the scaffold. I knew only one boy who ever actually sat in its dungeons. He was a lout of fourteen whose father kept an oyster-bay in Frederick avenue. The passion of love having seized him prematurely, he got into a fight over a girl, and stabbed the other fellow with an oyster-knife. I well recall the day the cops dragged him through Union Square to the watch-house in Calhoun street, and then hurried back to haul his victim to the University of Maryland hospital in a grocery-wagon.

This affair caused a great sensation in Hollins street, for it was the introduction of many of us to the hazards and terrors of amour. We crowded around the watch-house a day or two later, waiting to hear the result of the cutthroat's trial, and slunk away in silence when a colored malefactor we knew came out and reported that he had been doomed to the House of Refuge, or, as we always called it, the Ref. We assumed as a matter of course that he had been sentenced for life. If he ever got out I didn't hear of it, and for all I can tell you he may be there yet, though the Ref was long ago transformed into a storehouse for the Baltimore sewer department. No member of the Hollins street gang ever entered its door. We had our faults, as I freely admit, but the immemorial timorousness of the bourgeoisie restrained us from downright felony. Two of the boys I chased cats with in 1888 drank

themselves to death in their later years, two others
went into politics, one became a champion bicycle
racer, three became millionaires, and one actually
died an English baronet, but none, to my knowledge, ever got to the death-house, or even to the
stonepile.

In those days the nicknames of boys ran according to an almost invariable pattern, though all
boys, of course, did not have them. The example
of Barrel Fairbanks I have mentioned: he was too
fat to be called simply Fats and not quite fat
enough to be worthy the satirical designation of
Skinny, so he took the middle label of Barrel. Any
boy who happened to be lame was called Hop, anyone who had lost an eye was One-eye, and anyone
who wore glasses (which was then very unusual)
was Four-eyes. If a boy had a head of uncommon
shape he was always called Eggy. The victims of
such cruel nicknames never, so far as I can recall,
objected to them; on the contrary, they appeared
to be proud of their distinctions. Many nicknames
were derived from the professions of their bearers'
fathers. Thus the eldest son of a doctor was always
Doc, and if a boy's father had the title of Captain
— whether ship captain, fire captain, police captain, or military captain, it was all one — he was
himself known as Cap. The eldest sons of all policemen above the grade of patrolmen took their father's titles as a matter of course. A block or two up
Hollins street lived a sergeant whose son was called

Sarge, and when the father was promoted to a lieu-
tenancy the son became Loot. In case a boy's father had the military title of Major, which was not
unusual in those days, for West Baltimore swarmed
with householders who had been officers in the Civil
War, he was called Major himself. I never knew
a boy whose father was a colonel or general, but
those to be found elsewhere in Baltimore undoubtedly followed the rule. The eldest sons of pedagogues were all called Professor, and if a boy's
father was a professional gambler (there was such
a boy in Hollins street) he was apt to be called
either Colonel or Sport. Younger sons did not
share in these hereditary honors, which went by
primogeniture. The nicknames they bore, if they
had any at all, were based upon their own peculiarities.

The latter-day custom of calling boys by their
full given names was quite unknown. Every
Charles was Charlie, every William was Willie,
every Robert was Bob, every Richard was Dick and
every Michael was Mike. I never heard a boy
called Bill: the form was always Willie or Will.
Bill was reserved for adults of the lower ranks, for
example, ashcart drivers. My own stable-name, as
I have noted, was Harry, and my immediate relatives so hail me to this day. My father's brother
Henry, whose house was next door to ours in Hollins street, was Uncle Hen to us until the time of
the World War, when the changing fashion con-

verted him into the more decorous Uncle Henry. I
had two uncles with the same given name of John:
one was Uncle John to me and the other was Uncle
Johnnie, though Uncle Johnnie was the elder. I
had an uncle named William, but I still call him
Uncle Will, though his son, more than forty years
his junior, rates the formal William. My father
was Gus to his wife and all his friends, though his
sisters called him August, and his underlings called
him Mr. August. My mother's given name was
Anna, but my father always called her Annie, and
she was Aunt Annie to the cousins next door. One
of the rules of the time was that a boy named Albert
was always called Buck, never Al. Only a boy with
an unusual given name escaped these *Koseformen*.
The name of Theodore, for example, which was
seldom encountered in the pre-Roosevelt era, was
never supplanted by Teddy or Ted, but always
remained Theodore. There was a boy in Hollins
street named Seymour, and he remained Seymour
until he broke his leg, when he became Hop. But
most boys were Eddie, Johnnie, Bob, Dick or
Willie.

The humor of the young bourgeoisie males of
Baltimore, in those days, was predominantly skato-
logical, and there was no sign of the revolting
sexual obsession that Freudians talk of. The favorite jocosities had to do with horse apples,
O.E.A. wagons and small boys who lost control of
their sphincters at parties or in Sunday-school;

when we began to spend our Summers in the
country my brother and I also learned the comic
possibilities of cow flops. Even in the city a popular
ginger-and-cocoanut cake, round in contour and
selling for a cent, was called a cow flop, and little
girls were supposed to avoid it, at least in the presence of boys. Colored girls were fair game for any
prowling white boy, but there was never anything
carnal about hunting them; they were pursued
simply because it was believed that a nigger-louse
burr, entangled in their hair (we always kept stocks
at hand in the season), could not be removed without shaving their heads. Otherwise, the relations
between the races were very friendly, and it was not
at all unusual for a colored boy from the alley behind Hollins street to be invited to join a game of
one-two-three, or a raid on Mr. Thiernau's potatoes
and turnips. Many of the cooks in our block were
colored women, though our own were always Caucasians down to 1900 or thereabout. All surplus
victuals and discarded clothes were handed as a
matter of course to the neighboring blackamoors,
and they were got in for all sorts of minor jobs.
There have been no race riots in Baltimore to this
day, though I am by no means easy about the future, for a great many anthropoid blacks from the
South have come to town since the city dole began
to rise above what they could hope to earn at home,
and soon or late some effort may be made to chase
them back. But if that time ever comes the up-

rising will probably be led, not by native Baltimoreans, but by the Anglo-Saxon baboons from the West Virginia mountains who have flocked in for the same reason, and are now competing with the blacks for the poorer sort of jobs.

The Baltimore Negroes of the eighties had not yet emerged into the once-fine neighborhoods they now inhabit; they still lived, in the main, in alleys, or in obscure side-streets. We boys believed in all the traditional Southern lore about them — for example, that the bite of one with blue gums was poisonous, that those of very light skin were treacherous and dangerous, that their passion for watermelon was at least as powerful as a cat's for catnip, and that no conceivable blow on the head could crack their skulls, whereas even a light tap on the shin would disable them. Mr. Thiernau once set me to tussling with a colored boy in his store, and I made desperate efforts to reach his shins with my heel, but he was too agile for me, and so he got the better of the bout. When I reached home my mother sniffed at me suspiciously, and then ordered me to take a bath and change my clothes from the skin out. The alley behind our house had some colored residents who had lived there for many years, but most of its inhabitants came and went rather frequently, with the rent-collector assisting them. He always appeared on Saturday evening, and if the rent was not ready he turned out his tenant at once, without bothering to resort to legal means. The furniture that he thus set out on the sidewalk was often in a fantastic state of dilapidation, but it always included some of the objects of art that poor blackamoors of that era esteemed — a blue glass cup with the handle off, a couple of hand-painted but excessively nicked dinner-plates, a china shepherdess without a head, and so on. These things had come out of trash-cans, but they were fondly cherished. Behind the alley in the rear of our house, cutting off the Negro cabins from the houses in Baltimore street, ran a blind and very narrow sub-alley, perhaps not more than three feet wide. It was considered a good joke to inveigle a strange boy into it, for it was full of fleas. There were many such blind alleys in West Baltimore. One of them, running off Gilmor street, a block or so from our house, was called Child-stealers' alley, and we avoided it whenever possible. It was supposed to be the den of a monster who stole little children and carried them off to unknown but undoubtedly dreadful dooms. Such criminals were never spoken of as kidnappers, but always as child-stealers. So far as I can recall, none of them ever actually stole a child; indeed, none was ever seen in the flesh. But they were feared nevertheless.

Like all other boys, my brother Charlie and I were always in a condition of extreme insolvency. My mother had read an article in an early issue of the *Ladies' Home Journal* [1] arguing that children should not be given money freely but required to earn it, and this became the rule of the house. My brother and I alternated in shining our father's Congress gaiters of a morning, and received five cents for each shine, then the standard price in Baltimore. For other chores we were paid on the same scale, and in good weeks our joint income reached sixty or seventy cents, and sometimes even a dollar. But it was never enough, so we supplemented it by various forms of graft and embezzlement. When my mother sent me to Hollins market with two or three dollars in hand and a list of supplies to be bought, I always knocked down at least a nickel. My brother and I also got a little revenue from Sunday-school collection money, for when we were given dimes we put in only nickels, and when we were given nickels we put in only pennies. All the male scholars save a few milksops followed the same system. The teachers must have been aware of it, but they never did anything about it. We picked up more money by walking to and from school — a round trip of at least three miles — and pocketing the three-cent fare each way. Sometimes, when a car was crowded we managed to elude the conductor, and so rode without paying. On some cars there was no conductor, and the driver

---

[1] She had subscribed for it from its first issue, and continued to do so until her death in 1925. Once, when she somehow let her subscription lapse, she got a letter from Edward W. Bok, the editor, urging her not to desert him.

had to see to the fares. Inasmuch as he couldn't leave his horses, there were channels running down the sides of the car to carry to him the coins inserted by passengers. When a dozen boys got on a car together, it was usually possible for at least half of them to dodge paying fare. The driver always made a pother, but every boy swore that it was his money that had rolled down. The ensuing debate could be easily protracted until we were at our destination.

When all such devices failed, and Charlie and I faced actual bankruptcy, we had to resort to more desperate measures. Here, unhappily, we were cribbed, cabined and confined by the notions of dignity that prevailed among the West Baltimore bourgeoisie. We somehow understood without being told that it would be unseemly for us to run errands for Mr. Thiernau, or to carry the marketing of strange ladies returning home from Hollins market, or to shovel snow off sidewalks in Winter, or to help hostlers with their horses, or carriage-washers at their work. But there was one labor that, for some reason or other, was considered more or less elegant, though it was strictly forbidden by all parents, and that was selling newspapers. In 1889 or thereabout my brother Charlie and I undertook it in the hope of accumulating quickly enough funds to buy a cat-and-rat rifle. We had an air-rifle, but wanted a cat-and-rat rifle, which used real cartridges, and our father's harsh and profane prohibition of it only made us want it the more. So we hoofed down to the alley behind the old *Evening World* office in Calvert street — a good mile and a half from Hollins street — and laid in six *Worlds* at half a cent apiece. Leaping on horse-cars and howling " Paper! Paper! " was a grand adventure, but we soon found that a great many tougher, louder and more experienced boys were ahead of us, and when we counted up our profits at the end of two or three hours of hard work, and found that we had made but six cents between us, we decided that selling papers was far from what it had been cracked up to be. Incidentally, we never got that cat-and-rat rifle.

School took in in those days early in September, and ran on until the end of June. There were very few holidays save the Saturdays and Sundays, and boys had to depend for their major escapes from learning upon the appearance of measles or chicken-pox in the house. But there was one day that was always kept in Baltimore, and that was September 12, the anniversary of the Battle of North Point. This historic action was fought at the junction of the Chesapeake Bay and the Patapsco river in 1814, and as a result of it Baltimore escaped being burned by the British, as Washington was. Moreover, it produced two imperishable heroes in the shape of a pair of Baltimore boys, Wells and McComas, who hid in a tree and assassinated the British commander, General Robert

Ross. Yet more, Francis Scott Key, jugged on a British ship in Baltimore harbor, wrote "The Star-Spangled Banner" while the accompanying bombardment of Fort McHenry was going on. Thus September 12 was always celebrated in Baltimore, and all the boys got a day off from school, which was to me a matter of special rejoicing, for the day was my birthday. The last doddering veterans of the War of 1812 are dead now, and there is no longer a Defenders' Day parade, but September 12 remains a legal holiday in Maryland, and my birthday is still marked by blasts of patriotic rhetoric and artillery.

VI

Larval Stage of
a Bookworm

THE FIRST long story I ever read was " The Moose
Hunters," a tale of the adventures of four half-
grown boys in the woods of Maine, published in
Chatterbox for 1887. *Chatterbox*, which now seems
to be pretty well forgotten, was an English annual
that had a large sale, in those days, in the American
colonies, and " The Moose Hunters " seems to have
been printed as a sort of sop or compliment to that
trade, just as an English novelist of today lards his
narrative with such cheery native bait as " waal,
pardner," " you betcha " and " geminy-crickets."
The rest of the 1887 issue was made up of intensely
English stuff ; indeed, it was so English that, reading it and looking at the woodcuts, I sucked in an
immense mass of useless information about English

history and the English scene, so that to this day I know more about Henry VIII and Lincoln Cathedral than I know about Millard Fillmore or the Mormon Temple at Salt Lake City.

" The Moose Hunters," which ran to the length of a full-length juvenile, was not printed in one gob, but spread through *Chatterbox* in instalments. This was an excellent device, for literary fans in the youngest brackets do their reading slowly and painfully, and like to come up frequently for air. But writing down to them is something else again, and that error the anonymous author of " The Moose Hunters " avoided diligently. Instead, he wrote in the best journalese of the era, and treated his sixteen-year-old heroes precisely as if they were grown men. So I liked his story very much, and stuck to it until, in a series of perhaps twenty sessions, I had got it down.

This was in the Summer of 1888 and during hot weather, for I remember sitting with the volume on the high marble front steps of our house in Hollins street, in the quiet of approaching dusk, and hearing my mother's warnings that reading by failing light would ruin my eyes. The neighborhood apprentices to gang life went howling up and down the sidewalk, trying to lure me into their games of follow-your-leader and run-sheep-run, but I was not to be lured, for I had discovered a new realm of being and a new and powerful enchantment. What was follow-your-leader to fighting savage Canucks on the Little Magalloway river, and what was chasing imaginary sheep to shooting real meese? I was near the end of the story, with the Canucks all beaten off and two carcasses of gigantic meese hanging to trees, before the author made it clear to me that the word *moose* had no plural, but remained unchanged *ad infinitum.*

Such discoveries give a boy a considerable thrill, and augment his sense of dignity. It is no light matter, at eight, to penetrate suddenly to the difference between *to, two* and *too,* or to that between *run* in baseball and *run* in topographical science, or *cats* and *Katz.* The effect is massive and profound, and at least comparable to that which flows, in later life, out of filling a royal flush or debauching the wife of a major-general of cavalry. I must have made some effort to read *Chatterbox* at the time my Grandmother Mencken gave it to me, which was at Christmas, 1887, but for a while it was no go. I could spell out the shorter pieces at the bottoms of columns, but the longer stories were only jumbles of strange and baffling words. But then, as if by miracle, I found suddenly that I could read them, so I tackled " The Moose Hunters " at once, and stuck to it to the end. There were still, of course, many hard words, but they were no longer insurmountable obstacles. If I staggered and stumbled somewhat, I nevertheless hung on, and by the Fourth of July, 1888, I had blooded my first book.

An interval of rough hunting followed in Hollins street and the adjacent alleys, with imaginary Indians, robbers and sheep and very real tomcats as the quarry. Also, I was introduced to chewing tobacco by the garbageman, who passed me his plug as I lay on the roof of the ash-shed at the end of the backyard, watching him at his public-spirited work. If he expected me to roll off the roof, clutching at my midriff, he was fooled, for I managed to hold on until he was out of sight, and I was only faintly dizzy even then. Again, I applied myself diligently to practising leap-frog with my brother Charlie, and to mastering the rules of top-spinning, catty and one-two-three. I recall well how it impressed me to learn that, by boys' law, every new top had to have a license burned into it with a red-hot nail, and that no strange boy on the prowl for loot, however black-hearted, would venture to grab a top so marked. That discovery gave me a sense of the majesty of the law which still sustains me, and I always take off my hat when I meet a judge — if, of course, it is in any place where a judge is not afraid to have his office known.

But pretty soon I was again feeling the powerful suction of beautiful letters — so strange, so thrilling, and so curiously suggestive of the later suction of amour —, and before Christmas I was sweating through the translation of Grimms' Fairy Tales that had been bestowed upon me, " for industry and good deportment," at the closing exercises of F. Knapp's Institute on June 28. This vol-

ume had been put into lame, almost pathological
English by a lady translator, and my struggles
with it awoke in me the first faint gutterings of the
critical faculty. Just what was wrong with it I
couldn't, of course, make out, for my gifts had not
yet flowered, but I was acutely and unhappily conscious that it was much harder going than " The
Moose Hunters," and after a month or so of unpleasantly wrestling with it I put it on the shelf.
There it remained for more than fifty years. Indeed, it was not until the appearance of " Snow
White " as a movie that I took it down and tried it
again, and gagged at it again.

That second experiment convinced me that the
fault, back in 1888, must have been that of either
the brothers Grimm or their lady translator, but I
should add that there was also some apparent resistant within my own psyche. I was born, in
truth, without any natural taste for fairy tales, or,
indeed, for any other writing of a fanciful and unearthly character. The fact explains, I suppose,
my lifelong distrust of poetry, and may help to account for my inability to memorize even a few
stanzas of it at school. It probably failed to stick
in my mind simply because my mind rejected it as
nonsense — sometimes, to be sure, very jingly and
juicy nonsense, but still only nonsense. No doubt
the same infirmity was responsible for the feeble-
ness of my appetite for the hortatory and incredible juvenile fiction fashionable in my nonage —

the endless works of Oliver Optic, Horatio Alger, Harry Castlemon and so on. I tried this fiction more than once, for some of the boys I knew admired it vastly, but I always ran aground in it. So far as I can recall, I never read a single volume of it to the end, and most of it finished me in a few pages.

What I disliked about it I couldn't have told you then, and I can account for my aversion even now only on the theory that I appear to have come into the world with a highly literal mind, geared well enough to take in overt (and usually unpleasant) facts, but very ill adapted to engulfing the pearls of the imagination. All such pearls tend to get entangled in my mental *vibrissae*, and the effort to engulf them is as disagreeable to me as listening to a sermon or reading an editorial in a second-rate (or even first-rate) newspaper. I was a grown man, and far gone in sin, before I ever brought myself to tackle " Alice in Wonderland," and even then I made some big skips, and wondered sadly how and why such feeble jocosity had got so high a reputation. I am willing to grant that it must be a masterpiece, as my betters allege — but not to *my* taste, not for *me*. To the present moment I can't tell you what is in any of the other juvenile best-sellers of my youth, of moral and sociological hallucination all compact, just as I can't tell you what is in the Bhagavad-Gita (which Will Levington Comfort urged me to read in 1912 or thereabout), or in the works of Martin Tupper, or in the report of Vassar Female College for 1865. I tried dime-novels once, encouraged by a boy who aspired to be a train-robber, but they only made me laugh. At a later time, discovering the pseudo-scientific marvels of Jules Verne, I read his whole canon, and I recall also sweating through a serial in a boys' weekly called *Golden Days*, but this last dealt likewise with *savants* and their prodigies, and was no more a juvenile, as juveniles were then understood, than " Ten Thousand Leagues Under the Sea."

But before you set me down a prig, let me tell you the rest of it. That rest of it is my discovery of " Huckleberry Finn," probably the most stupendous event of my whole life. The time was the early part of 1889, and I wandered into Paradise by a kind of accident. Itching to exercise my newly acquired art of reading, and with " The Moose Hunters " exhausted and Grimms' Fairy Tales playing me false, I began exploring the house for print. The Baltimore *Sunpaper* and *Evening News*, which came in daily, stumped me sadly, for they were full of political diatribes in the fashion of the time, and I knew no more about politics than a chimpanzee. My mother's long file of *Godey's Lady's Book* and her new but growing file of the *Ladies' Home Journal* were worse, for they dealt gloomily with cooking, etiquette, the policing of children, and the design and construction of millinery, all of them sciences that still baffle me. Nor was there any pabulum for me in the hired girl's dog's-eared files of *Bow Bells* and the *Fireside Companion,* the first with its ghastly woodcuts of English milkmaids in bustles skedaddling from concupiscent baronets in frock-coats and cork-screw mustaches. So I gradually oscillated, almost in despair, toward the old-fashioned secretary in the sitting-room, the upper works of which were full of dismal volumes in the black cloth and gilt stamping of the era. I had often eyed them from afar, wondering how long it would be before I would be ripe enough to explore them. Now I climbed up on a chair, and began to take them down.

They had been assembled by my father, whose taste for literature in its purer states was of a generally low order of visibility. Had he lived into the days of my practice as a literary critic, I daresay he would have been affected almost as unpleasantly as if I had turned out a clergyman, or a circus clown, or a labor leader. He read every evening after dinner, but it was chiefly newspapers that he read, for the era was one of red-hot politics, and he was convinced that the country was going to Hell. Now and then he took up a book, but I found out long afterward that it was usually some pamphlet on the insoluble issues of the hour, say "Looking Backward," or "If Christ Came to Chicago," or "Life Among the Mormons." These works disquieted him, and he naturally withheld them from his innocent first-born. Moreover, he was still unaware that I could read — that is, fluently, glibly, as a pleasure rather than a chore, in the manner of grown-ups.

Nevertheless, he had managed somehow to bring together a far from contemptible collection of books, ranging from a set of Chambers' Encyclopedia in five volumes, bound in leather like the Revised Statutes, down to " Atlantis: the Antediluvian World," by Ignatius Donnelly, and " Around the World in the Yacht *Sunbeam*." It included a two-volume folio of Shakespeare in embossed morocco, with fifty-odd steel plates, that had been taken to the field in the Civil War by " William H. Abercrombie, 1st Lieut. Company H, 6th Regiment, Md. Vol. Inftr.," and showed a corresponding dilapidation. Who this gallant officer was I don't know, or whether he survived the carnage, or how his cherished text of the Bard ever fell into my father's hands. Also, there were Dickens in three thick volumes, George Eliot in three more, and William Carleton's Irish novels in a third three. Again, there were " Our Living World," by the Rev. J. G. Wood; " A History of the War For the Union," by E. A. Duyckinck; " Our Country," by Benson J. Lossing, LL.D., and " A Pictorial History of the World's Great Nations From the Earliest Dates to the Present Time," by Charlotte M. Yonge — all of them likewise in threes, folio, with lavish illustrations on steel, stone and wood, and smelling heavily of the book-agent. Finally, there were forty or fifty miscellaneous books, among them, as I recall, " Peculiarities of American Cities," by Captain Willard Glazier; " Our Native Land," by George T. Ferris; " A Compendium of Forms," by one Glaskell; " Adventures Among Cannibals " (with horrible pictures of missionaries being roasted, boiled and fried), " Uncle Remus," " Ben Hur," " Peck's Bad Boy," " The Adventures of Baron Münchhausen," " One Thousand Proofs That the Earth Is Not a Globe " (by a forgotten Baltimore advanced thinker named Carpenter), and a deadly-looking " History of Freemasonry in Maryland," by Brother Edward T. Schultz, 32°, in five coal-black volumes.

I leave the best to the last. All of the above, on my first exploration, repelled and alarmed me; indeed, I have never read some of them to this day. But among them, thumbing round, I found a series of eight or ten volumes cheek by jowl, and it appeared on investigation that the whole lot had been written by a man named Mark Twain. I had heard my father mention this gentleman once or twice in talking to my mother, but I had no idea who he was or what he had done: he might have been, for all I knew, a bartender, a baseball-player, or one of the boozy politicoes my father was always meeting in Washington. But here was evidence that he was a man who wrote books, and I noted at once that the pictures in those books were not of the usual funereal character, but light, loose and lively. So I proceeded with my inquiry, and in a little while I had taken down one of them, a green quarto, sneaked it to my bedroom, and stretched out on my bed to look into it. It was, as smarties will have guessed by now, " Huckleberry Finn."

If I undertook to tell you the effect it had upon me my talk would sound frantic, and even delirious. Its impact was genuinely terrific. I had not gone further than the first incomparable chapter before I realized, child though I was, that I had entered a domain of new and gorgeous wonders, and thereafter I pressed on steadily to the last word. My gait, of course, was still slow, but it became steadily faster as I proceeded. As the blurbs on the slip-covers of murder mysteries say, I simply couldn't put the book down. After dinner that evening, braving a possible uproar, I took it into the family sitting-room, and resumed it while my father searched the *Evening News* hopefully for reports of the arrest, clubbing and hanging of labor leaders. Anon, he noticed what I was at, and demanded to know the name of the book I was reading. When I held up the green volume his comment was " Well, I'll be durned! "

I sensed instantly that there was no reproof in this, but a kind of shy rejoicing. Then he told me that he had once been a great reader of Mark Twain himself — in his younger days. He had got hold of all the volumes as they came out — "The Innocents" in 1869, when he was still a boy himself; "Roughing It" in 1872, "The Gilded Age" in 1873, "Tom Sawyer" in 1876, "A Tramp Abroad" in 1880, the year of my birth, and so on down to date. (All these far from pristine firsts are still in the Biblioteca Menckeniana in Hollins street, minus a few that were lent to neighbor boys and never returned, and had to be replaced.) My father read them in the halcyon days before children, labor troubles and Grover Cleveland had begun to frazzle him, and he still got them down from the shelf on quiet evenings, after the first-named were packed off to bed. But a man of advancing years and cares had to consider also the sorrows of the world, and so he read in Mark less than aforetime.

As for me, I proceeded to take the whole canon at a gulp — and presently gagged distressfully. "Huckleberry Finn," of course, was as transparent to a boy of eight as to a man of eighty, and almost as pungent and exhilarating, but there were passages in "A Tramp Abroad" that baffled me, and many more in "The Innocents," and a whole swarm in "The Gilded Age." I well recall wrestling with the woodcut by W. F. Brown on page 113 of the "Tramp." It shows five little German girls swinging on a heavy chain stretched between two stone posts on a street in Heilbronn, and the legend under it is "Generations of Bare Feet." That legend is silly, for all the girls have shoes on, but what puzzled me about it was something quite different. It was a confusion between the word *generation* and the word *federation,* which latter was often in my father's speech in those days, for the American Federation of Labor had got under way only a few years before, and was just beginning in earnest to harass and alarm employers. Why I didn't consult the dictionary (or my mother, or my father himself) I simply can't tell you. At eight or nine, I suppose, intelligence is no more than a small spot of light on the floor of a large and murky room. So instead of seeking help I passed on, wondering idiotically what possible relation there could be between a gang of little girls in pigtails and the Haymarket anarchists, and it was six or seven years later before the " Tramp " became clear to me, and began to delight me.

It then had the curious effect of generating in me both a great interest in Germany and a vast contempt for the German language. I was already aware, of course, that the Mencken family was of German origin, for my Grandfather Mencken, in his care for me as *Stammhalter,* did not neglect to describe eloquently its past glories at the German universities, and to expound its connections to the most remote degrees. But my father, who was only half German, had no apparent interest in either the German land or its people, and when he spoke of the latter at all, which was not often, it was usually in sniffish terms. He never visited Germany, and never signified any desire to do so, though I recall my mother suggesting, more than once, that a trip there would be swell. It was "A Tramp Abroad" that made me German-conscious, and I still believe that it is the best guide-book to Germany ever written. Today, of course, it is archaic, but it was still reliable down to 1910, when I made my own first trip. The uproarious essay on "The Awful German Language," which appears at the end of it as an appendix, worked the other way. That is to say, it confirmed my growing feeling, born of my struggles with the conjugations and declensions taught at F. Knapp's Institute, that German was an irrational and even insane tongue, and not worth the sufferings of a freeborn American. These diverse impressions have continued with me ever since. I am still convinced that Germany, in the intervals of peace, is the most pleasant country to travel in ever heard of, and I am still convinced that the German language is of a generally preposterous and malignant character.

"Huck," of course, was my favorite, and I read it over and over. In fact, I read it regularly not less than annually down to my forties, and only a few months ago I hauled it out and read it once more — and found it as magnificent as ever. Only one other book, down to the beginning of my teens, ever beset me with a force even remotely comparable to its smash, and that was a volume called

"Boys' Useful Pastimes," by "Prof. Robert Griffith, A.M., principal of Newton High School." This was given to me by my Grandmother Mencken at Christmas, 1889, and it remained my constant companion for at least six years. The sub-title describes its contents: "Pleasant and profitable amusement for spare hours, comprising chapters on the use and care of tools, and detailed instructions by means of which boys can make with their own hands a large number of toys, household ornaments, scientific appliances, and many pretty, amusing and necessary articles for the playground, the house and out-of-doors." Manual training was still a novelty in those days, and I suspect that the professor was no master of it, for many of his plans and specifications were completely unintelligible to me, and also to all the neighborhood boys who dropped in to help and advise. I doubt, indeed, that any human being on earth, short of an astrophysicist, could have made anything of his directions for building boat models. But in other cases he was relatively explicit and understandable, and my brother Charlie and I, after long efforts, managed to make a steam-engine (or, more accurately, a steam-mill) according to his recipe. The boiler was a baking-powder tin, and the steam, issuing out of a small hole in the top, operated a sort of fan or mill-wheel. How we provided heat to make steam I forget, but I remember clearly that my mother considered the process dangerous, and ordered us to take the engine out of the cellar and keep it in the backyard.

I had no more mechanical skill than a cow, but I also managed to make various other things that the professor described, including a what-not for the parlor (my mother professed to admire it, but never put it into service), a rabbit-trap (set in the backyard, it never caught anything, not even a cat), and a fancy table ornamented with twigs from the pear tree arranged in more or less geometrical designs. " Boys' Useful Pastimes " was printed by A. L. Burt on stout paper, and remains extant to this day — a rather remarkable fact, for other boys often borrowed it, and sometimes they kept it on their work-benches for a long while, and thumbed it diligently. One of those boys was Johnnie Sponsler, whose father kept a store in the Frederick road, very near Hollins street. Johnnie was vastly interested in electricity, as indeed were most other boys of the time, for such things as electric lights, motors, telephones and doorbells were just coming in. He thus made hard use of Professor Griffith's Part VII, which was headed " Scientific Apparatus and Experiments," and included directions for making a static machine, and for electroplating door-keys. He later abandoned the sciences for the postal service, and is now, I believe, retired. " Boys' Useful Pastimes," and my apparent interest in it, may have been responsible for my father's decision to transfer me from F.

Knapp's Institute to the Baltimore Polytechnic in 1892. If so, it did me an evil service in the end, for my native incapacity for mechanics made my studies at the Polytechnic a sheer waste of time, though I managed somehow to pass the examinations, even in such abysmal subjects as steam engineering.

The influence of " Huck Finn " was immensely more powerful and durable. It not only reinforced my native aversion to the common run of boys' books; it also set me upon a systematic exploration of all the volumes in the old secretary, and before I finished with them I had looked into every one of them, including even Brother Schultz's sombre history of Freemasonry in Maryland. How many were actually intelligible to a boy of eight, nine, ten? I should say about a fourth. I managed to get through most of Dickens, but only by dint of hard labor, and it was not until I discovered Thackeray, at fourteen, that the English novel really began to lift me. George Eliot floored me as effectively as a text in Hittite, and to the present day I have never read " Adam Bede " or " Daniel Deronda " or " The Mill on the Floss," or developed any desire to do so. So far as I am concerned, they will remain mere names to the end of the chapter, and as hollow and insignificant as the names of Gog and Magog.

But I plowed through Chambers' Encyclopedia relentlessly, beginning with the shortest articles and gradually working my way into the longer ones. The kitchen-midden of irrelevant and incredible information that still burdens me had its origins in those pages, and I almost wore them out acquiring it. I read, too, the whole of Lossing, nearly all of Charlotte M. Yonge, and even some of Duyckinck, perhaps the dullest historian ever catalogued by faunal naturalists on this or any other earth. My brother Charlie and I enjoyed " Our Living World " chiefly because of the colored pictures, but I also read long stretches of it, and astonished my father by calling off the names of nearly all the wild beasts when the circus visited Baltimore in 1889. Finally, I recall reading both " Life Among the Mormons " and " One Thousand Proofs That the Earth Is Not a Globe."

Thus launched upon the career of a bookworm, I presently began to reach out right and left for more fodder. When the Enoch Pratt Free Library of Baltimore opened a branch in Hollins street, in March, 1886, I was still a shade too young to be excited, but I had a card before I was nine, and began an almost daily harrying of the virgins at the delivery desk. In 1888 my father subscribed to *Once-a-Week*, the predecessor of *Collier's*, and a little while later there began to come with it a long series of cheap reprints of contemporary classics, running from Tennyson's poems to Justin M'Carthy's " History of Our Own Times " ; and simultaneously there appeared from parts unknown a similar series of cheap reprints of scientific papers, including some of Herbert Spencer. I read them all, sometimes with shivers of puzzlement and sometimes with delight, but always calling for more. I began to inhabit a world that was two-thirds letterpress and only one-third trees, fields, streets and people. I acquired round shoulders, spindly shanks, and a despondent view of humanity. I read everything that I could find in English, taking in some of it but boggling most of it.

This madness ran on until I reached adolescence, and began to distinguish between one necktie and another, and to notice the curiously divergent shapes, dispositions and aromas of girls. Then, gradually, I began to let up.

But to this day I am still what might be called a reader, and have a high regard for authors.

VII

Strange Scenes and Far Places

To my brother Charlie and me our father seemed to be a tremendous traveler — indeed, almost a Marco Polo. His trips to buy tobacco ranged from New York State and Connecticut in the North to Cuba in the South, and from the wilds of the Pennsylvania Dutch in the East to Wisconsin in the West, and he also made at least one journey a year to some national potlatch of the Freemasons. In this last mysterious order he never attained to any eminent degree or held any office, but he was enrolled in both of its more sportive and expensive sub-divisions, the Knights Templar and the Shriners. At the orgies of the Knights Templar he appears to have arrayed himself in a uniform resembling that of a rear-admiral, for in the wardrobe

that he took with him there were a long-tailed blue
coat with brass buttons, a velvet chapeau with a
black feather, a silk baldric, and a sword. With
them he carried the red fez that marked him a member of the Ancient Arabic Order of the Nobles of
the Mystic Shrine. Whether or not the Shriners
and the Knights met jointly I don't know, but every time he returned from a muster of either the one
or the other or both he brought back souvenirs of
the convention and the convention town, and these
entertained Charlie and me in a very agreeable way,
and gave us considerable credit, when they were
exhibited, among the boys of the neighborhood.
Other such objects of art and instruction flowed in
from his tobacco-buying trips, so that the house
was always well supplied. I recall especially some
ornate fans from Havana, some jars of guava jelly
from the same place, a large book illustrating the
objects of interest in St. Louis, a photograph of
the bar of the Palmer House in Chicago, showing
(not very clearly) its floor of silver dollars, and a
book of views along the French Broad river in
North Carolina, apparently a souvenir of a visit
to Asheville. My father's traveler's tales were full
of thrills to Charlie and me, especially those that
had to do with bullfighting in Cuba. My mother always protested against them as horrifying and
brutalizing, but we never got enough of them. Or
of his accounts of strange victuals devoured and
enjoyed in far places. I well remember his return

from Kansas City, probably in 1889 or thereabout, with the first news that had ever reached Hollins street of a dessert called floating-island, then apparently a novelty in the world. We made him describe it over and over again, and in the end some effort was made to concoct it in the family kitchen, but that effort came to naught.

Our own travels, down to the end of the eighties, had been very meagre. I had been to Washington often, and Charlie rather less often, but neither of us had ever been far enough from home to have to stay overnight, and neither of us had ever eaten in a dining-car or slept in a sleeper. It was thus a gaudy piece of news when, in the first days of 1891, my grandfather Abhau let it be known that he had some long-neglected relatives in faraway Ohio, and was of a mind to pay them a visit, and take me along. These relatives were new to me, and even my mother had only the vaguest idea of them. They were the descendants, it appeared, of my grandfather's elder sister, who had been so much his senior that she might have been his aunt. On arriving in the United States at some undetermined time in the past, they had bought a lottery ticket on the dock, won a substantial prize (my grandfather's estimate of it ranged up to $20,000), and used the money to buy a couple of fine farms on the borders of the Western Reserve in Ohio, not far from Toledo. My grandfather now proposed to wait upon them, and to stop on the way to see some friends in Cleveland. Himself of no experience as a land traveler (though he had made some sea voyages as a youth), he wanted companionship for the journey, and as his oldest grandchild I got the nomination. It was to me as exciting a surprise as being appointed hostler to Maud S. or president of the Foos candy factory down the alley behind Hollins street.

The preparations for the journey took a couple of weeks, at least. There was, first of all, the matter of my trousseau. What was the climate of Northern Ohio in Winter? No one seemed to know, so my mother proceeded on the assumption that it must be pretty terrible. I thus drew a new and well-padded overcoat from Oehm's Acme Hall, and a new Winter cap with ear-flaps from Mr. Garrigues, the Bible-searching hatter in Baltimore street. Simultaneously, my mother began assembling a large stock of extra-heavy stockings and underclothes, and a great battery of mufflers, mittens and pulse-warmers, and to it was added a pair of massive goloshes. All these things had to be tried on, and some of them were broken in by being worn on my daily journeys to F. Knapp's Institute, for the weather in Baltimore had conveniently turned very cold. But I had no appetite in days so electric for the proceedings at F. Knapp's Institute, and for the first and last time in my school life I came home at the end of January with bad marks. Of the many sciences taught there that month, the only one that I really paid any attention to was geography, and in geography my studies were confined to the State of Ohio. I learned to my satisfaction that Toledo was very near its western frontier, and hence within handy reach of the spot where Sitting Bull had just been killed; that the village we were bound for was only a few miles from Lake Erie, which was twice as large as Chesapeake Bay and probably jammed to the brim with oysters, crabs and shad-fish; and that Cleveland was celebrated all over the world for the magnificence of its Euclid avenue, lined with the *palazzi* of Christian millionaires.

My father entered the picture in the closing days of our preparations. He came home one day with the tickets, including the Pullman tickets, and proceeded to instruct me in the technic of getting to bed at night and up again the next morning on a sleeper. He said that he would see us off at Camden Station, Baltimore, and, if there was time enough, make sure that we were properly stowed, but on the chance that the train would not halt more than a few minutes, he would also request his Washington agent, Mr. Cross, to take a look at us when we reached Washington. We were to travel, of course, by Baltimore & Ohio, and the route ran through Washington and Pittsburgh. I recall nothing of our actual departure, nor of Mr. Cross's inspection in Washington, but I remember very well my father's last-minute fears that I might not have enough money for possible expenses. My grandfather was the treasurer of the expedition, but inasmuch as he was an ancient of sixty-four there was always the chance that he might stray off and get lost, or fall into the hands of bunco-steerers, or succumb to amnesia, or lose his faculties otherwise, so it was necessary for me to be financed on my own. Every time my father thought of another of these contingencies he gave me another dollar bill, and urged me to store it safely. By the time we finally shoved off I had them secreted all over my person, and on our return two weeks later I managed to omit a couple from my settlement of accounts. With these, after a discreet interval, my brother Charlie and I bought a new air-rifle. The marks of its darts are still in the door of a cupboard on the third floor of Hollins street.

My grandfather and I changed trains at Pittsburgh in the morning, and I had my first glimpse of a quick-lunch counter. The appearance of a white waiter behind it was a piquant novelty to me, for all the restaurants I knew in Baltimore and Washington were served by blackamoors. I remember that the white coat of this Caucasian appeared to show a certain lack of freshness, but I forgot the fact when he shoved a huge stack of wheat cakes before me, with a large pitcher of syrup beside it, and then politely turned his back. At home the syrup pitcher was rigorously policed, and emptying it over a pancake brought a reprimand, if not a box of the ears, but in Pittsburgh there seemed to be no rules, so I fell to in a large and freehand way. Once or twice I noticed my grandfather looking at me uneasily, and making as if to speak, but he actually said nothing, and by the time we had to rush for our train the wheat cakes were all gone, and so was most of the syrup. There was also a plate of bread on the table, but I never touched it. As we left I saw the waiter return the slices to a pile on a shelf behind the counter. This gave me a considerable shock, and set me to wondering if the wheat cakes had also passed over some other plate before they reached mine. But I was too full of them to worry much, and after what seemed a very brief ride through country covered with snow, we reached Cleveland and were met by my grandfather's friend, Mr. Landgrebe.

Mr. Landgrebe turned out to be a very pleasant man, and when we got to his house he produced a young son, Karl, slightly older than I, who was agreeable too. How long we stayed in Cleveland I don't know, but it must have been no more than two days. But though the time was short, Mr. Landgrebe showed us all the marvels of the town, including not only the millionaires' elegantly hand-tooled castles along Euclid avenue, with every lawn peopled by a whole herd of cast-iron deers, dogs, cupids and Civil War soldiers, but also the infernal valley wherein the oil of these millionaires was processed and barreled, and a lunatic asylum in which, presumably, the victims of their free competition were confined. My grandfather, a man of tender heart, was much upset by the carryings-on of the Napoleons, George Washingtons and Pontius Pilates in the wards, and shushed me with some asperity whenever I ventured to giggle. It was my first visit to a lunatic asylum, and I enjoyed it in the innocent and thankful manner of any normal boy of ten. There was one poor maniac who entertained me particularly, for his aberration took the form of rolling up thin cylinders of paper and sticking them in his nose and ears. When I got home and told my brother Charlie about the wonderful things I had seen on my travels, he pronounced this lunatic the most wonderful of all. My own first choice, after mature reflection, was the trolley-car that ran past the Landgrebe house in Cleveland. There had been one in Baltimore for six months, but its route lay far from Hollins street, so I knew nothing about it. What struck me especially about the Cleveland car was the loud, whistling buzz that its trolley made as it came down the street. This buzz could be heard *before* the noise of the car itself was detectable — a marvelous indicator, to me, of the unearthly powers of electricity. But Charlie, who was less than nine years old, stuck to the lunatic.

When we finally got to the farms of my grandfather's kinfolk the snow had melted and the whole countryside was an ocean of mud, but by the next morning I had forgotten it, for by that time I was

on easy terms with the boys and girls of the two
houses, and thereafter they showed me what, in
those days, was called an elegant time. I had already spent two Summers at the Vineyard, and
was thus more or less familiar with rural scenes,
but the Vineyard, after all, was only ten miles as
the bird flies from Baltimore, and we were only
Summer sojourners. Here were real farms inhab-
ited by real farming people, and in their daily life
there was something every minute that was new to
me, and full of fascination. I got to know cows and
hogs familiarly, and learned to esteem them. I
helped the younger Almroths (it was at their house
that we stayed) to crack walnuts in the barn, to
fetch up apples from the cellar, and to haul wood
for the great egg-stoves that kept us warm. The
enormous country dinners and suppers, with their
pyramids of fried chicken and their huge platters
of white home-cured hog-meat, swimming in grease,
stoked and enchanted my vast appetite, and I rolled
and wallowed at night in the huge feather-beds.
It was pleasant to go out of a morning with Mr.
Almroth, and watch him (from a safe distance)
blow out stumps with sticks of dynamite. It was
even more pleasant to go into the woods with his
two older sons, and help stack the firewood that
they cut. One day I labored so diligently at this
task that I got into a lather and picked up a sore
throat, and the next day Mrs. Almroth cured it
with a mixture of honey and horse-radish — a pre-

scription that went far beyond anything Dr. Wiley ever ordered. The days ran by as fast as the Cleveland trolley-car, and the evenings around the egg-stove in the parlor were trips to a new and romantic world. The youngsters and I stuffed doughnuts, tortured the house dogs and swapped riddles out of Dr. Ayers' Almanac while my grandfather and the elders searched the remotest reaches of their genealogy, and the village schoolma'm (who boarded out during the term, and was the Almroths' guest that Winter) sat by the lamp on the table reading a book that seemed to me to be the thickest on earth. Before we left I sneaked a look at its title, and when we got back to Baltimore I borrowed it from the branch of the Pratt Library in Hollins street, but I never managed to get beyond its first chapter. It was " St. Elmo," by Mrs. Augusta Jane Evans Wilson.

The Almroths, it appeared, were professing Christians, and on the Sunday following our arrival they took my grandfather and me to their church, which stood in the midst of a slough in the village, and was, as I recall, of some branch or other of the Lutheran communion. We got in late and my grandfather diffidently declined to go forward to the Almroth pew, but slipped into a seat near the door and dragged me with him. But if he thought to escape the glare of notoriety by that device he was badly fooled, for at the close of the proceedings an officer arose near the pulpit and read a report on the attendance for the day. When he came to " Number of visitors present: two " the whole congregation arose as one Christian and rubber-necked East, West, North and South until we had been located. There was indeed such a hubbub that my grandfather was induced to arise and make a bow. As we were passing out afterward he was introduced to the pastor and all the notables of the congregation, including many who welcomed him in German, for the whole Lake Erie littoral was full of Germans. The pastor eyed me speculatively and seemed about to try me out on the Catechism, but just then a female customer began to whoop up his sermon in high, astounding terms, and I escaped under cover of his grateful thanks.

But of all the incidents of that memorable journey to the Wild West the one that sticks in my recollection most firmly was the last, for it was aided in gaining lodgment by an uneasy conscience. My grandfather and I, on our return, were hardened travelers, and dealt with train conductors, Pullman porters and such-like functionaries in a casual and confident manner. We arrived at Washington very early in the morning, and my father's plenipotentiary, Mr. Cross, was there to meet us. His face, when we sighted him on the platform, was very grave, and he approached us in the manner of a man charged with an unhappy duty. It took the form of handing us a telegram. My grandfather blanched when he saw it, and passed it to me without reading it, for telegrams always alarmed him. I opened it at his nod, and then proceeded to read it to him in a chastened whisper, as follows:

Frank Cross,   Baltimore, February 26, 1891
    Aug. Mencken & Bro.,
      Seventh and G streets, N.W.,
        Washington, D.C.

          Mr. B. L. Mencken is dead.
                    Habighurst.

Mr. Habighurst was my father's bookkeeper, and Mr. B. L. Mencken was my other grandfather, the progenitor, chief justice and captain general of all the American Menckenii. My grandfather Abhau was silent on the short trip back to Baltimore, and remained silent as we boarded a horsecar at Camden Station and rode out to Hollins street, our bags piled beside the driver. We got off at Stricker and Lombard streets, and made for the house across Union Square. As we came to the fishpond in the center of the square I saw that there was a black crêpe on the handle of the doorbell, in token of filial respect to the dead patriarch. The sight made me feel creepy, for that was the first crêpe I had ever seen on a Mencken doorbell. But I was only ten years old, and the emotions of boys of that age are not those of philosophers. For a brief instant, I suppose, I mourned my grandfather, but before we had crossed the cobblestones of Hollins street a vagrom and wicked thought ran through my head. I recognized its enormity instantly, but simply could not throttle it. The day was a Thursday — and they'd certainly not bury the old man until Sunday. No school tomorrow!

FROM

NEWSPAPER DAYS

1899 - 1906

VIII

Allegro
Con Brio

My father died on Friday, January 13, 1899, and was buried on the ensuing Sunday. On the Monday evening immediately following, having shaved with care and put on my best suit of clothes, I presented myself in the city-room of the old Baltimore *Morning Herald*, and applied to Max Ways, the city editor, for a job on his staff. I was eighteen years, four months and four days old, wore my hair longish and parted in the middle, had on a high stiff collar and an Ascot cravat, and weighed something on the minus side of 120 pounds. I was thus hardly a spectacle to exhilarate a city editor, but Max was an amiable fellow and that night he was in an extra-amiable mood, for (as he told me afterward) there was a good dinner under his belt, with a couple of globes of malt to wash it down, and all of his reporters, so far as he was aware, were transiently sober. So he received me very politely, and even cordially. Had I any newspaper experience? The reply, alas, had to be no. What was my education? I was a graduate of the Baltimore Polytechnic. What considerations had turned my fancy toward the newspaper business? All that I could say was that it seemed to be a sort of celestial call: I was busting with literary ardors and had been writing furiously for what, at eighteen, was almost an age — maybe four, or even five years. Writing what — prose or verse? Both. Anything published? I had to play dead here, for my bibliography, to date, was confined to a couple of anonymous poems in the Baltimore *American* — a rival paper, and hence probably not admired.

Max looked me over ruminatively — I had been standing all the while — and made the reply that city editors had been making to young aspirants since the days of the first Washington hand-press. There was, unhappily, no vacancy on the staff. He would take my name, and send for me in case some catastrophe unforeseen — and, as I gathered, almost unimaginable — made one. I must have drooped visibly, for the kindly Max at once thought of something better. Did I have a job? Yes, I was working for my Uncle Henry, now the sole heir and assign of my father's old tobacco firm of Aug. Mencken & Bro. Well, I had better keep that job, but maybe it might be an idea for me to drop in now and then of an evening, say between seven thirty and seven forty-five. Nothing, of course, could be promised; in fact, the odds against anything turning up were appalling. But if I would present myself at appropriate intervals there might be a chance, if it were God's will, to try me out, soon or late, on something commensurate with my undemonstrated talents. Such trial flights, it was unnecessary to mention, carried no emolument. They added a lot to a city editor's already heavy cargo of cares and anxieties, and out of the many that were called only a few were ever chosen.

I retired nursing a mixture of disappointment and elation, but with the elation quickly besting the disappointment — and the next night, precisely at seven thirty-one, I was back. Max waved me away without parley: he was busy jawing an office-boy. The third night he simply shook his head, and so on the fourth, fifth, sixth and seventh. On the eighth — or maybe it was the ninth or tenth — he motioned me to wait while he finished thumbing through a pile of copy, and then asked suddenly: " Do you ever read the *Herald*? " When I answered yes, he followed with " What do you think of it? " This one had all the appearance of a trap, and my heart missed a couple of beats, but the holy saints were with me. " I think," I said, " that it is much better written than the *Sunpaper*." I was to learn later that Max smelled something artful here, but, as always, he held himself well, and all I could observe was the faint flutter of a smile across his face. At length he spoke. " Come back," he said, " tomorrow night."

I came back, you may be sure — and found him missing, for he had forgotten that it was his night off. The next night I was there again — and found him too busy to notice me. And so the night following, and the next, and the next. To make an end, this went on for four weeks, night in and night out, Mondays, Tuesdays, Wednesdays, Thursdays, Fridays, Saturdays and Sundays. A tremendous blizzard came down upon Baltimore, and for a couple of days the trolley-cars were stalled, but I hoofed it ever hopefully to the *Herald* office, and then hoofed it sadly home. There arrived eventually, after what seemed a geological epoch by my calendar, the evening of Thursday, February 23, 1899. I found Max reading copy, and for a few minutes he did not see me. Then his eyes lifted, and he said casually: " Go out to Govanstown, and see if anything is happening there. We are supposed to have a Govanstown correspondent, but he hasn't been heard from for six days."

The percussion must have been tremendous, for I remember nothing about getting to Govanstown. It is now a part of Baltimore, but in 1899 it was only a country village, with its own life and tribulations. No cop was in sight when I arrived, but I found the volunteer firemen playing pinochle in their engine-house. The blizzard had blockaded their front door with a drift fifteen feet high, but they had dug themselves out, and were now lathering for a fire, though all the water-plugs in the place were still frozen. They had no news save their hopes. Across the glacier of a street I saw two lights — a bright one in a drugstore and a dim one in a funeral parlor. The undertaker, like nearly all the rest of Govanstown, was preparing to go to bed, and when I routed him out and he came downstairs in his pants and undershirt it was only to say that he had no professional business in hand. The druggist, hugging a red-hot egg-stove behind his colored bottles, was more productive. The town cop, he said, had just left in a two-horse buggy to assist in a horse-stealing case at Kingsville, a long drive out the Belair pike, and the Improved Order of Red Men had postponed their oyster-supper until March 6. When I got back to the *Herald* office, along toward eleven o'clock, Max instructed me to forget the Red Men and write the horse-stealing. There was a vacant desk in a far corner, and at it, for ten minutes, I wrote and tore up, wrote and tore up. Finally there emerged the following:

A horse, a buggy and several sets of harness, valued in all at about $250, were stolen last night from the stable of Howard Quinlan, near Kingsville. The county police are at work on the case, but so far no trace of either thieves or booty has been found.

Max gave only a grunt to my copy, but as I was leaving the office, exhausted but exultant, he called me back, and handed me a letter to the editor demanding full and friendly publicity, on penalty of a boycott, for an exhibition of what was then called a kinetoscope or cineograph. "A couple of lines," he said, "will be enough. Nearly everybody has seen a cineograph by now." I wrote:

At Otterbein Memorial U.B. Church, Roland and Fifth avenues, Hampden, Charles H. Stanley and J. Albert Loose entertained a large audience last night with an exhibition of war scenes by the cineograph.

I was up with the milkman the next morning to search the paper, and when I found both of my pieces, exactly as written, there ran such thrills through my system as a barrel of brandy and 100,-000 volts of electricity could not have matched. Somehow or other I must have done my duty by Aug. Mencken & Bro., for my uncle apparently noticed nothing, but certainly my higher cerebral centers were not focussed on them. That night I got to the *Herald* office so early that Max had not come back from dinner. When he appeared he looked me over thoughtfully, and suggested that it might be a good plan to try my talents on a village adjacent to Govanstown, Waverly by name. It was, he observed, a poor place, full of Methodists and Baptists who seldom cut up, but now and then a horse ran away or a pastor got fired. Reaching it after a long search in the snow, and raking it from end to end, I turned up two items — one an Epworth League entertainment, and the other a lecture for nearby farmers, by title (I have the clipping before me), "Considering the Present Low Price of Hay, Would It Not Be Advisable to Lessen the Acreage of Hay for Market?" Max showed no enthusiasm for either, but after I had finished writing them he handed me an amateur press-agent's handout about a new Quaker school and directed me to rewrite it. It made twenty-eight lines in the paper next morning, and lifted me beyond the moon to Orion. On the night following Max introduced me to two or three reporters, and told them that I was a youngster trying for a job. My name, he said, was Macon. They greeted me with considerable reserve.

Of the weeks following I recall definitely but one thing — that I never seemed to get enough sleep. I was expected to report at the cigar factory of Aug. Mencken & Bro. at eight o'clock every morning, which meant that I had to turn out at seven. My day there ran officially to five thirty, but not infrequently my uncle detained me to talk about family affairs, for my father had died intestate and his estate was in process of administration, with two sets of lawyers discovering mare's nests from time to time. Thus it was often six o'clock before I escaped, and in the course of the next hour or so I had to get home, change my clothes, bolt my dinner, and return downtown to the *Herald* office. For a couple of weeks Max kept me at my harrying of the remoter suburbs — a job, as I afterward learned, as distasteful to ripe reporters as covering a fashionable church-wedding or a convention of the W.C.T.U. I ranged from Catonsville in the far west to Back River in the east, and from Tuxedo Park in the north to Mt. Winans in the south. Hour after hour I rode the suburban trolleys, and one night, as I recall uncomfortably over all these years, my fares at a nickel a throw came to sixty cents, which was more than half my day's pay from Aug. Mencken & Bro. Max had said nothing about an expense account, and I was afraid to ask. Once, returning from a dismal village called Gardenville, a mile or two northeast of the last electric light, I ventured to ask him how far my diocese ran in that direction. "You are supposed to keep on out the road," he said, "until you meet the Philadelphia reporters coming in." This was an ancient Baltimore newspaper wheeze, but it was new to me, and I was to enjoy it a great deal better when I heard it worked off on my successors.

But my exploration of the fringes of Baltimore, though it came near being exhaustive, was really not long drawn out, for in a little while Max began to hand me city assignments of the kind that no one else wanted — installations of new evangelical pastors, meetings of wheelmen, interviews with bores just back from Europe, the Klondike or

Oklahoma, orgies of one sort or another at the Y.M.C.A., minor political rallies, concerts, funerals, and so on. Most of my early clippings perished in the great Baltimore fire of 1904, but a few survived, and I find from them that I covered a number of stories that would seem as antediluvian today as a fight between two brontosauri — for example, the showing of a picture-play by Alexander Black (a series of lantern-slides with a thin thread of banal recitative), and a chalk-talk by Frank Beard. When it appeared that I knew something of music, I was assigned to a long series of organ recitals in obscure churches, vocal and instrumental recitals in even more obscure halls, and miscellaneous disturbances of the peace in lodge-rooms and among the German singing societies. Within the space of two weeks I heard one violinist, then very popular in Baltimore, play Raff's Cavatina no less than eight times. The *Herald's* music critic in those days, an Englishman named W. G. Owst, was a very indolent fellow, and when he discovered that I could cover such uproars without making any noticeable bulls, he saw to it that I got more and more of them. Finally, I was entrusted with an assault upon Mendelssohn's " Elijah " by the Baltimore Oratorio Society — and suffered a spasm of stage fright that was cured by dropping into the Pratt Library before the performance, and doing a little precautionary reading.

Thus the Winter ran into Spring, and I began

to think of myself as almost a journalist. So far, to be sure, I had been entrusted with no spot news, and Max had never sent me out to help a regular member of the staff, but he was generous with his own advice, and I quickly picked up the jargon and ways of thought of the city-room. In this acclimatization I was aided by the device that had helped me to fathom Mendelssohn's " Elijah " and has always been my recourse in time of difficulty: what I couldn't learn otherwise I tried to learn by reading. Unhappily, the almost innumerable texts on journalism that now serve aspirants were then still unwritten, and I could find, in fact, only one formal treatise on the subject at the Pratt Library. It was " Steps Into Journalism," by E. L. Shuman of the Chicago *Tribune*, and though it was a primitive in its class it was very clearly and sensibly written, and I got a great deal of useful information out of it. Also, I read all of the newspaper fiction then on paper — for example, Richard Harding Davis's " Gallegher and Other Stories," Jesse Lynch Williams's " The Stolen Story and Other Stories," and Elizabeth G. Jordan's " Tales of the City-Room," the last two of which had but lately come out.[1]

How I found time for this reading I can't tell

1 It must have been a little later that I read " With Kitchener to Khartoum," " From Capetown to Ladysmith " and the other books of George W. Steevens, of the London *Mail*. They made a powerful impression on me, and I still believe that Steevens was the greatest newspaper reporter who ever lived.

you, for I was kept jumping by my two jobs, but find it I did. One night, sitting in the city-room waiting for an assignment, I fell asleep, and the thoughtful Max suggested that I take one night off a week, and mentioned Sunday. The next Sunday I stayed in bed until noon, and returned to it at 8 p.m., and thereafter I was ready for anything. As the Spring drifted on my assignments grew better and better, and when the time came for high-school commencements I covered all of them. There were five in those days, beginning with that of the City College and ending with that of the Colored High-school, and I heard the Mayor of Baltimore unload precisely the same speech at each. Max, who knew the man, complimented me on making his observations sound different every time, and even more or less intelligent, and I gathered the happy impression that my days as an unpaid volunteer were nearing their end. But a city editor of that costive era, at least in Baltimore, could take on a new man only by getting rid of an old one, and for a month or so longer I had to wait. Finally, some old-timer or other dropped out, and my time had come. Max made a little ceremony of my annunciation, though no one else was present. My salary, he said, would be $7 a week, with the hope of an early lift to $8 if I made good. I would have the use of a book of passes on the trolley-cars, and might turn in expense-accounts to cover any actual outlays. There was, at the moment, no typewriter available for me, but he had hopes of extracting one from Nachman, the business manager, in the near future. This was followed by some good advice. *Imprimis*, never trust a cop: whenever possible, verify his report. *Item*, always try to get in early copy: the first story to reach the city-desk has a much better chance of being printed in full than the last. *Item*, be careful about dates, names, ages, addresses, figures of every sort. *Item*, keep in mind at all times the dangers of libel. Finally, don't be surprised if you go to a house for information, and are invited to lift it from the *Sun* of the next morning. "The *Sun* is the Bible of Baltimore, and has almost a monopoly on many kinds of news. But don't let that fact discourage you. You can get it too if you dig hard enough, and always remember this: any *Herald* reporter who is worth a damn can write rings around a *Sun* reporter."

This last was very far from literally true, as I was to discover when I came to cover stories in competition with such *Sun* reporters as Dorsey Guy and Harry West, but there was nevertheless a certain plausibility in it, for the *Sun* laid immense stress upon accuracy, and thus fostered a sober, matter-of-fact style in its men. The best of them burst through those trammels, but the rank and file tended to write like bookkeepers. As for Max, he greatly favored a more imaginative and colorful manner. He had been a very good reporter himself, with not only a hand for humor but also a trick of pathos, and he tried to inspire his slaves to the same. Not many of them were equal to the business, but all of them save a few poor old automata tried, and as a result the *Herald* was rather briskly written, and its general direction was toward the New York *Sun*, then still scintillating under the impulse of Charles A. Dana, rather than toward the Baltimore *Sun* and the *Congressional Record*. It was my good fortune, during my first week on the staff, to turn up the sort of story that Max liked especially — the sudden death of a colored street preacher on the street, in the midst of a hymn. I was not present at the ringside, and had to rely on the cops for the facts, but I must have got a touch of drama into my report, for Max was much pleased, and gave me, as a reward, a pass to a performance of Rose Sydell's London Blondes.

I had gathered from the newspaper fiction mentioned a few pages back that the typical American city editor was a sort of cross between an ice-wagon driver and a fire-alarm, " full of strange oaths " and imprecations, and given to firing whole files of men at the drop of a hat. But if that monster actually existed in the Republic, it was surely not in the Baltimore *Herald* office. Max, of course, was decently equipped for his art and mystery: he could swear loudly enough on occasion and had a pretty hand for shattering invective, but most of the time, even when he was sorely tried, he kept to good humor and was polite to one and all. Whenever I made a mess of a story, which was certainly often enough, he summoned me to his desk and pointed out my blunders. When I came in with a difficult story, confused and puzzled, he gave me quick and clear directions, and they always straightened me out. Observing his operations with the sharp eyes of youth, I began to understand the curious equipment required of a city editor. He had to be an incredible amalgam of army officer and literary critic, diplomat and jail warden, psychologist and fortune-teller. If he could not see around corners and through four or five feet of brick he was virtually blind, and if he could not hear overtones audible normally only to dogs and children he was almost deaf. His knowledge of his town, as he gathered experience, combined that of a police captain, an all-night hackman, and a priest in a rowdy parish. He was supposed to know the truth about everyone and everything, even though he seldom printed it, and one of his most useful knowledges — in fact, he used it every day — was his knowledge of the most probable whereabouts of every person affected with a public interest, day or night.

Max had these skills, and many more. How he would have made out on the larger papers of a later period, with their incessant editions, I do not attempt to guess, but in his time and place he was a very competent man, and had the respect as well as the affection of his staff. In person he was of middle height, with light hair that was beginning to fall out, and an equator that had already begun to bulge. What remained of his hair he wore longish, in what was then called the football style. He affected rolling collars, and sometimes wore a Windsor tie. His colored shirts, in the manner of the day, were ironed to shine like glass, and his clothes were of somewhat advanced cut. We younger reporters modelled ourselves upon him in dress as in mien. The legends that played about him were mainly not of a professional nature, but romantic. He was a bachelor, and was supposed to be living in sin with a beautiful creature who occasionally took a drop too much, and exposed him to the embarrassment of her caterwauling. Whether or not that creature had any actual existence I can't tell you: all I can say is that I never saw her, and that the only time I ever visited Max in his quarters (he was laid up with pink-eye) I found him living *a cappella* upstairs of a French restaurant, and waited on by the proprietor's well-seasoned and far from aphrodisiac wife.[2]

It was a pleasant office that I found myself en-

[2] When he quit the *Herald* Max went into politics, and lived to be one of the Democratic bosses of Baltimore. But the first time he ran for elective office he was beaten, mainly, so it was reported, because many voters assumed from his name that he was a Jew, and others suspected that he might even be a Chinaman. He was actually of Scotch-Irish, Welsh, English and Pennsylvania German stock. He later married the charming secretary of the Governor of Maryland, and became the father of a son and a daughter who followed him into the newspaper business. He died in 1923.

tering. Many of the reporters, to be sure, were rummy old-timers who were of small ability and no diligence, but they were all at least amiable fellows, and working beside them were some youngsters of superior quality. The *Herald* Building was new, and its fifth-floor city-room was one of the most comfortable and convenient that I have ever seen, even to this day. But in many respects it would seem primitive now: it had, for example, but two telephones — one belonging to each of the two companies that then fought for subscribers in Baltimore. Both were Paleozoic instruments attached to the wall, and no one ever used them if it could be avoided. There was no telephone on the city editor's desk until my own time in that office, beginning in 1903. The office library, save for a dog's-eared encyclopedia with several volumes missing, was made up wholly of government reports, and the only man who ever used it was an old fellow who had the job of compiling cattle and provision prices. He finished work every day at about 5 p.m. and spent an hour reading in the encyclopedia. There was no index of the paper, and no office morgue. The city editor kept a clipping file of his own, and when it failed him he had to depend upon the shaky memories of the older reporters.

The city staff, save for such early birds as the court reporter, came to work at half an hour after noon, and every man was responsible for his bailiwick until 11 at night. The city editor himself began work an hour earlier and worked an hour or so later. There were no bulldogs or other early editions. The first mail edition did not close until after midnight. In consequence, there was no hurry about getting stories on paper, except very late ones. Rewrite men were unheard of. Every reporter, no matter how remote the scene of his story, came back to the office and wrote it himself. If he lagged, his copy was taken from him page by page, and he was urged on by the grunting and growling of the city editor, who was his own chief copy-reader, and usually wrote the head on the leading local story of the night. A great deal of copy was still written by hand, for there were not enough typewriters in the office to go round, and every time Nachman, the business manager, was asked to buy another he went on like a man stabbed with poniards. But every reporter had a desk, and every desk was equipped with a spittoon. This was a great convenience to me, for I had acquired the sinful habit of tobacco-chewing in my father's cigar factory, and am, in fact, still more or less in its loathsome toils.

The office was kept pretty clean by Bill Christian, a barber who had got the job of building superintendent because Colonel Cunningham, the managing editor, liked his tonsorial touch. Bill was allergic to work himself, but he rode herd diligently on his staff of colored scavengers, and the whole editorial floor was strangely spick and span for that time. Even the colonel's own den was excavated at least twice a month, and its accumulation of discarded newspapers hauled out. Bill failed, however, to make any progress against the army of giant cockroaches that had moved in when the building was opened, three or four years before. On dull nights the copy-readers would detail office-boys to corral half a dozen of these monsters, and then race them across the city-room floor, guiding them with walking-sticks. The sport required some skill, for if a jockey pressed his nag too hard he was apt to knock off its hind legs.

IX

Drill for a
Rookie

My first regular assignment as a reporter was
South Baltimore, or, to speak technically, the
Southern police district. It was, as I shall remark
again in Chapter XIII, a big territory, and there
was always something doing in it, but though my
memories of it are copious and melodramatic, I
must have spent only a few weeks in it, for by the
end of the Spring, as I find by a promenade
through the *Herald's* files, I was covering Aframerican razor-parties in the Northwestern, which
was almost as black as Mississippi, and making occasional dips into the Western, which embraced
the largest and busiest of Baltimore's five Tender-
loins.

In those days a reporter who had durable legs

and was reasonably sober tended to see a varied service, for it was not unusual for one of his elders to succumb to the jug and do a vanishing act. More than once during my first weeks, after turning in my own budget of assaults, fires, drownings and other such events from the Southern, I was sent out at eleven o'clock at night to find a lost colleague of the Eastern or Northeastern, and pump his news out of him, if he had any. It was by the same route, in July, that I found myself promoted to the Central, which was the premier Baltimore district, journalistically speaking, for it included the busiest of the police courts, a downtown hospital, police headquarters, the city jail, and the morgue. The regular man there had turned up at the office one noon so far gone in rum that Max relieved him of duty, and I was gazetted to his place as a means of shaming him, for I was still the youngest reporter in the office. When he continued in his cups the day following I was retained as his *locum tenens,* and when he went on to a third day he was reduced to the Northern police district, the Siberia of Baltimore, and I found myself his heir.

This man, though we eventually became good friends, resented his demotion so bitterly that for weeks he refused to speak to me, but I was too busy in my new bailiwick to pay any attention to him. Its police court was the liveliest in town, and had the smartest and most colorful magistrate, Gene Grannan by name. He was always willing to help the press by developing the dramatic content of the cases before him, and during my first week he thus watered and manured for me a couple of stories that delighted Max, and boosted my own stock. Such stories were almost a *Herald* monopoly, for *Sun* reporters were hobbled by their paper's craze for mathematical accuracy, and most *American* reporters were too stupid to recognize good stuff when they saw it. Max helped by inventing likely minor assignments for me, and one of them I still remember. It was a wedding in a shabby street given over to second-hand shops run by Polish Jews and patronized by sailors. The bride had written in demanding publicity, and I was sent to see her — partly as a means of gently hazing a freshman, but also on the chance that there might be a picturesque story in her. In the filthy shop downstairs her father directed me to the second floor, and when I climbed the stairs I found her in process of being dressed by her mother. She was standing in the middle of the floor with nothing on save a diaphanous vest and a flouncy pair of drawers. Never having seen a bride so close to the altogether before, I was somewhat upset, but she and her mother were quite calm, and loaded me with all the details of the impending ceremony. I wrote the story at length, but Max stuck it on his " If " hook, and there it died.

But such romantic interludes were not frequent. My days, like those of any other police reporter, were given over mainly to harsher matters — murders, assaults and batteries, street accidents, robberies, suicides, and so on. I well recall my first suicide, for the victim was a lovely young gal who had trusted a preacher's son too far, and then swallowed poison: she looked almost angelic lying on her parlor floor, with a couple of cops badgering her distracted mother. I remember, too, my first autopsy at the morgue — a most trying recreation for a hot Summer day —, and my first palaver with a burglar, and my first ride with the cops in a patrol-wagon, but for some reason or other my first murder has got itself forgotten. The young doctors at the City Hospital (now the Mercy Hospital) were always productive, for they did a heavy trade in street and factory accidents, and a very fair one in attempted suicides. In those days carbolic acid was the favorite drug among persons who yearned for the grave, just as bichloride of mercury was to be the favorite of a decade later, and I saw many of its customers brought in — their lips swollen horribly, and their eyes full of astonishment that they were still alive. Also, I saw people with their legs cut off, their arms torn off, their throats cut, their eyes gouged out. It was shocking for a little while, but then no more. Attached to the City Hospital was the first Pasteur Institute ever set up in America, and to it came patients from all over the South. It was in charge of an old doctor named Keirle, and usually he managed to save them, but now and then one of them reached him too late, and died of rabies in frightful agony. He let me in on several of these death scenes, with the poor patient strapped to the bed and the nurses stepping warily. When the horror became unendurable the old doctor would take over with his hypodermic. He was a humane and admirable man, one of the few actual altruists that I have ever known, and I marvel that the Baltimore which has monuments to the founder of the Odd Fellows and to the president of a third-rate railroad has never thought to honor itself by erecting one to his memory.

On July 28, 1899, when I was precisely eighteen years, ten months and sixteen days old, I saw my first hanging; more, it was a hanging of the very first chop, for no less than four poor blackamoors were stretched at once. When I was assigned to it as legman for one of the older reporters I naturally suffered certain unpleasant forebodings, but the performance itself did not shake me, though one of the condemned lost his black cap in going through the trap, and the contortions of his face made a dreadful spectacle. The affair was staged in the yard of the city jail, and there was a large gathering of journalists, some of them from other cities, for quadruple hangings, then as now, were fancy goods. I went through the big iron gate at 5 a.m., and found that at least a dozen colleagues had been on watch all night. Some of them had sustained themselves with drafts from a bottle, and were already wobbling. When, after hours of howling by relays of colored evangelists, the four candidates were taken out and hanged, two of these bibbers and six or eight other spectators fell in swoons, and had to be evacuated by the cops. The sheriff of Baltimore was required by law to spring the trap, and he had prepared himself for that office by resorting to a bottle of his own. When it was performed he was assisted out of the jail yard by his deputies, and departed at once for Atlantic City, where he dug in for a week of nightmare.

I saw a good many hangings after that, some in Baltimore and the rest in the counties of Maryland. The county sheriffs always took aboard so much liquor for the occasion that they were virtually helpless: they could, with some help, pull the trap, but they were quite unable to tie the knot, bind the candidate, or carry off the other offices of the occasion. These were commonly delegated to Joe Heine, a gloomy German who had been chief deputy sheriff in Baltimore for many years, and was such a master of all the technics of his post that no political upheaval could touch him. So far as I know, Joe never actually put a man to death in his life, for that was the duty of the sheriff, but he traveled the counties tying knots and making the condemned ready, and there was never a slip when he officiated. I missed the great day of his career, which fell in 1904 or thereabout, for I was becoming bored with hangings by that time, and when a nearby county sheriff invited me to one as his private guest and well-wisher, I gave my ticket to my brother Charlie. This was Charlie's first experience and he saw a swell show indeed, for the candidate, a colored giant, fought Joe and the sheriff on the scaffold, knocked out the county cops who came to their aid, leaped down into the bellowing crowd, broke out of the jail yard, and took to an adjacent forest. It was an hour or more before he was run down and brought back. By that time all the fight had oozed out of him, and Joe and the sheriff turned him off with quiet elegance.

But a reporter chiefly remembers, not such routine themes of his art as hangings, fires and murders, which come along with dispiriting monotony, but the unprecedented novelties that occasionally inspire him, some of them gorgeous and others only odd. Perhaps the most interesting story I covered in my first six months had to do with the purloining of a cadaver from a medical college. The burglar was the head *Diener* of the dissecting-room, and he packed the body in a barrel and shipped it to a colleague in the upper Middle West, where there was a shortage of such provisions at the time. Hot weather coming on *en route*, it was discovered, and for a week we had a gaudy murder mystery. When the *Diener* shut off the uproar by confessing, it turned out that the maximum punishment he could be given, under the existing Maryland law, passed in 1730, was sixty days in the House of Correction. On his return to duty the medical students welcomed him with a beer party that lasted forty-eight hours, and he boasted that he had been stealing and shipping bodies for years. But the cops, discouraged, did nothing about it.

At a somewhat later time, after I had forsaken police reporting, the moral inadequacy of the ancient Maryland statutes was revealed again. This time the culprit was a Methodist clergyman who operated one of the vice crusades that then afflicted all the big cities of the East. The cops, of course, were violently against him, for they could see nothing wrong about honest women making honest livings according to their talents. When the pastor charged that they pooh-poohed him because they were taking bribes from the girls they determined to get him, and to that end sneaked a spy into the Y.M.C.A. One night soon afterward the pastor visited the place with a Christian young man, and the spy, concealed in a cupboard, caught the two in levantine deviltries. The former was collared at once, and the State's attorney sent for. Unhappily, he had to advise the poor cops that the acts they laid to their prisoner were not forbidden by Maryland law, which was singularly tolerant in sexual matters. The maximum penalty it then provided for adultery, however brutal and deliberate, was $10 fine, with no alternative of imprisonment, and there was no punishment at all for forni-

cation, or for any of its non-Euclidian variations.
The cops were thus stumped, but they quickly
resolved their dilemma by concealing it from the
scared pastor, and giving him two hours to get out
of town. He departed leaving a wife and five children behind him, and has never been heard from
since. The Legislature being in session, the cops
then went to Annapolis and begged it to sharpen
the laws. It responded by forbidding, under heavy
penalties, a list of offenses so long and so bizarre
that some of them are not even recorded in Krafft-
Ebing.

I myself, while still assigned to the Central district, covered a case that well illustrated the humanity of the old Maryland statute. The accused
was a man who had run away from Pittsburgh with
another man's wife, and they had come to Baltimore in the drawing-room of a sleeper. The lady's
husband, having got wind of their flight, wired
ahead, asking the cops to arrest the pair on their
arrival. The cops refused to collar an apparently
respectable female on any such charge, but they
brought in the man, and he was arraigned before
Gene Grannan. As a matter of law, his guilt had
to be presumed, for the Court of Appeals of Maryland had decided only a little while before that
when a man and a woman went into a room together
and locked the door it would be insane to give them
the benefit of the doubt. Moreover, the prisoner,
advised by a learned police-station lawyer, ad-

mitted the charge freely, and confined his defense
to swearing that the crime had not been committed
until after the train crossed the Maryland line. If
he were sent back to Pennsylvania for trial he
would be in serious difficulties, for the penalty for
adultery there was almost as drastic as that for
arson or piracy, but in Maryland, as I have said,
it was a mere misdemeanor, comparable to breaking a window or spitting on the sidewalk. Grannan
doubted the truth of the defense, but decided that a
humane judge would have to accept it, so he fined
the culprit $2, and the pair resumed their honey-
moon with loud hosannas. When a Pennsylvania
cop showed up the next day with extradition papers he was baffled, for the man had been tried and
punished, and could not be put in jeopardy again.

Grannan held a session of his court every afternoon, and I always attended it. It was seldom, indeed, that he did not turn up something that made
good copy. He had been, before his judicial days,
chief of the Baltimore & Ohio's railroad police, and
thus had a wide acquaintance among professional
criminals, especially yeggmen, and held the professional respect of the cops. In that remote era
there was no file of finger-prints at Washington,
and even the Bertillon system was just coming into
use. The cops, in consequence, sometimes picked
up an eminent felon without knowing who he was.
But if he came before Grannan he was identified at
once, and started through a mill that commonly

landed him in the Maryland Penitentiary. That institution, which occupied a fine new building near the city jail, then had as its warden a reformed politician named John Weyler. He had been a tough baby in his day, and was even suspected of a hand in a homicide, but when I knew him he had said goodbye to all that, and was an excellent officer. I dropped in on him two or three times a week, and usually picked up something worth printing. He had a strange peculiarity: he never came outside the prison walls save when it was raining. Then he would wander around for hours, and get himself soaked to the skin, for he never used an umbrella. Once a month his board of visitors met at the Penitentiary, and he entertained the members at dinner. These dinners gradually took on lavishness and gaiety, and during one of them a member of the board, searching for a place marked " Gents," fell down the main staircase of the place and had to be sent to hospital. After that Weyler limited the drinks to ten or twelve a head.

Another good source of the kind of news that Max Ways liked was an old fellow named Hackman, the superintendent of the morgue. The morgue was housed in an ancient building at the end of one of the city docks, and Hackman seldom left it. There was a sort of derrick overhanging the water, and on it the harbor cops would pull up the floaters that they found, and let them dry. Some of them were covered with crabs and barnacles when they were brought in, and Hackman had a long pole for knocking such ornaments off. How greatly he loved his vocation was shown when a new health commissioner fired him, and he refused to give up his keys. The health commissioner thereupon called for a squad of cops, and went down to the morgue to take possession by force, followed by a trail of reporters. But Hackman was defiant, and when firemen were sent for to aid the cops, he barricaded himself among his clients, and declared that he would never be taken alive.

The ensuing battle went on all afternoon, and was full of thrills. The cops refused to resort to firearms and the firemen refused to knock down the door with their hose, so Hackman seemed destined to hold out forever. Every now and then he would open the door for a few inches, and howl fresh defiance at the health commissioner. Finally, one of the reporters, Frank R. Kent, of the *Sun*, sneaked up along the wall, and thrust in his foot the next time the door was opened. Before Hackman could hack Kent's foot off the cops rushed him, and the morgue was taken. The poor old fellow burst into tears as he was being led away. The morgue, he wailed, was his only solace, almost his only life; he had devoted years to its upkeep and improvement, and was proud of its high standing among the morgues of Christendom. Moreover, many of the sponges, cloths and other furnishings within, including the pole he used to delouse floaters, were his personal property, and he was being robbed of them. The health commissioner promised to restore them, and so Hackman faded from the scene, a victim to a Philistine society that could not fathom his peculiar ideals.

There were press-agents in those days as in these, and though they had not reached the dizzy virtuosity now on tap they nevertheless showed a considerable ingenuity and daring. One of the best I encountered in my first years remains unhappily nameless in my memory, though I well recall some of his feats. He slaved for Frank Bostock, a big, blond, tweedy, John Bullish Englishman who had leased an old cyclorama in Baltimore and put in a wild animal show. Even before the doors were open the agent bombarded the local newspapers with bulletins worthy the best tradition of Tody Hamilton, press-agent for P. T. Barnum — battles between tigers and boa constrictors, the birth of infant giraffes and kangaroos, the sayings of a baboon who could speak Swahili, and so on. When, after the opening, business turned out to be bad, he spit on his hands, and turned off some masterpieces. The one I remember best was the hanging of a rogue elephant, for I was assigned to cover it. This elephant, we were informed, had become so onery that he could be endured no longer, and it was necessary to put him to death. Ordinarily, he would be shot, but Bostock, as a patriotic and law-abiding Englishman, preferred hanging, and would serve as executioner himself.

The butchery of the poor beast — he looked very mangey and feeble — was carried out one morning in the Bolton street railroad yards. First his legs were tied together, and then a thick hawser was passed around his neck and pulled tight, and the two ends were fastened to the hook of a railroad crane. When Bostock gave the signal the crane began to grind, and in a few minutes the elephant was in the air. He took it very quietly, and was pronounced dead in half an hour. A large crowd saw the ceremony, and after that business at the Bostock zoo picked up. The press-agent got rid of the S.P.C.A. by announcing that the elephant had been given six ounces of morphine to dull his sensations. His remains were presented to the Johns Hopkins Medical School for scientific study, but no one there was interested in proboscidean anatomy, so they finally reached a glue factory.

Six months later the Bostock zoo gave the Baltimore newspapers a good story without any effort by its press-agent. On a cold Winter night, with six inches of sleet in the streets, it took fire, and in a few minutes all its major inmates were burned to death and the small fry were at large. The pursuit of the latter went on all night and all the next day, and the cops turned up an occasional frost-bitten monkey as much as a week later. No really dangerous animal got loose, but the town was in a state of terror for weeks, and many suburban dogs, mistaken for lions or tigers, were done to death by vigilantes. I recall picking up a powerful cold by wallowing around the night of the fire in the icy slush.

But the best of all the Baltimore press-agents of that age was a volunteer who worked for the sheer love of the science. His name was Frank Thomas, and he was the son of a contractor engaged in building a new courthouse. There were to be ten or twelve huge marble pillars in the façade of the building, and they had to be brought in from a quarry at Cockeysville, fourteen miles away. The hauling was done on trucks drawn by twenty horses. One day a truck lost a wheel and the pillar aboard was broken across the middle. Frank announced at once that a fossil dog had been found in the fracture, and supported the tale by having a crude dog painted on it and the whole photographed. That photograph made both the *Herald* and the *American*, though the suspicious *Sunpaper* sniffed at it. It took the geologists at the Johns Hopkins a week to convince the town that there could be no canine fossils in sedimentary rocks. A bit later Frank made it known that the new courthouse would be fitted with a contraption that would suck up all sounds coming in from the streets, and funnel them out through the sewers. In his handout he described eloquently the comfort of judges and juries protected against the noises of traffic and trade, and the dreadful roar of the accumulated sounds as they emerged from the sewers along the waterfront. Frank indulged himself in many other inventions, and I handled most of them for the *Herald*, for the courthouse was in my parish. When the building was finished at last he published an illustrated souvenir book on it, and I wrote the 8000 words of its text. My honorarium was $25.

His days, alas, were not all beer and skittles, for putting up a large building in the heart of a busy city is a job shot through with cephalalgia. While it was under way a high board fence surrounded it, and on that fence were all the usual advertising signs, most of them hideous. The *Herald* started a violent crusade against them, arguing that they disgraced the courthouse and affronted all decent people. I was assigned by Max Ways to write some of the indignant stories we printed, and thus I met Frank in the dual rôle of friend of his fancy and enemy of his fence. So far as I could make out, the *Herald's* crusade had no support whatsoever in public sentiment — in fact, it became more and more difficult to find anyone to endorse it — but it roared on for months. The fence came down at last at least three or four weeks later than it would have come down if there had been no hullabaloo, for Frank had iron in him as well as imagination, and held out defiantly as long as he could.

It was a crusading time, with uplifters of a hundred schools harrying every major American city, and every newspaper of any pretensions took a hand in the dismal game. I recall crusades against sweat-shops, against the shanghaiing of men for the Chesapeake oyster fleet, and against dance-halls that paid their female interns commissions on the drinks sold. I had a hand in all of them, and if they filled me with doubts they also gave me some exhilarating experiences. With the cops I toured the bastiles of the waterfront crimps, and examined the jails that they maintained for storing their poor bums, and with health department inspectors I saw all the worst sweat-shops of the town, including one in which a huge flock of hens was kept hard at work laying eggs in a filthy cellar. In the war upon bawdy dance-halls I became a witness, unwillingly, against the cops, for I was put on the stand to testify that I had seen two detectives in one of them, and that the detectives must have been aware of what was going on. The poor flatfeet were unquestionably guilty, for I had discussed the matter with them in the place, but I managed to sophisticate my testimony with so many ifs and buts that it went for nothing, and they were acquitted by the police board. That was my first and last experience as an active agent of moral endeavor. I made up my mind at once that my true and natural allegiance was to the Devil's party, and it has been my firm belief ever since that all persons who devote themselves to forcing virtue on their fellow men deserve nothing better than kicks in the pants. Years later I put that belief into a proposition which I ventured to call Mencken's Law, to wit:

Whenever A annoys or injures B on the pretense of saving or improving X, A is a scoundrel.

The moral theologians, unhappily, have paid no heed to this contribution to their science, and so Mencken's Law must wait for recognition until the dawn of a more enlightened age.

X

The Days of the Giants

Not infrequently I am asked by young college folk, sometimes male and sometimes female, whether there has been any significant change, in my time, in the bacchanalian virtuosity of the American people. They always expect me, of course, to say that boozing is now at an all-time high, for they are a proud generation, and have been brought up to believe that Prohibition brought in refinements unparalleled on earth since the fall of Babylon. But when I speak for that thesis it is only to please them, for I know very well that the facts run the other way. My actual belief is that Americans reached the peak of their alcoholic puissance in the closing years of the last century. Along about 1903 there was a sudden and marked letting up — partly due, I suppose, to the accelerating pace and hazard of life in a civilization growing more and more mechanized, but also partly to be blamed on the lugubrious warnings of the medical men, who were then first learning how to reinforce their hocus-pocus with the alarms of the uplift.

In my early days as a reporter they had no more sense of civic responsibility than so many stockbrokers or policemen. A doctor of any standing not only had nothing to say against the use of stimulants; he was himself, nine times out of ten, a steady patron of them, and argued openly that they sustained him in his arduous and irregular life. Dr. Z. K. Wiley, our family practitioner, always took a snifter with my father when he dropped in to dose my brother Charlie and me with castor oil, and whenever, by some unusual accident of his heavy practise, he had any free time afterward, he and my father gave it over to quiet wrestling with the decanters. His favorite prescription for a cold was rock-and-rye, and he believed and taught that a shot of Maryland whiskey was the best preventive of pneumonia in the *R* months. If you object here that Dr. Wiley was a Southerner, then I answer at once that Dr. Oliver Wendell Holmes was a Yankee of the Yankees, and yet held exactly the same views. Every schoolboy, I suppose, has heard by this time of Dr. Holmes's famous address before the Massachusetts Medical

Society on May 30, 1860, in which he argued that " if the whole materia medica, as now used, could be sunk to the bottom of the sea, it would be all the better for mankind — and all the worse for the fishes " ; but what the pedagogues always fail to tell their poor dupes is that he made a categorical exception of wine, which he ranked with opium, quinine, anesthetics and mercury among the sovereign and invaluable boons to humanity.

I was thus greatly surprised when I first heard a medical man talk to the contrary. This was in the Winter of 1899–1900, and the place was a saloon near a messy downtown fire. I was helping my betters to cover the fire, and followed them into the saloon for a prophylactic drink. The doctor, who was a fire department surgeon, thereupon made a speech arguing that alcohol was not a stimulant but a depressant, and advising us to keep off it until the fire was out and we were relaxing in preparation for bed. " You think it warms you," he said, sipping a hot milk, " but it really cools you, and you are seventeen point eight per cent. more likely to catch pneumonia at the present minute than you were when you came into this doggery." This heresy naturally outraged the older reporters, and they became so prejudiced against the doctor that they induced the Fire Board, shortly afterward, to can him — as I recall it, by reporting that he was always drunk on duty. But his words made a deep impression on my innocence, and continue to lurk in my mind to this day. In consequence, I am what may be called a somewhat cagey drinker. That is to say, I never touch the stuff by daylight if I can help it, and I employ it of an evening, not to hooch up my faculties, but to let them down after work. Not in years have I ever written anything with so much as a glass of beer in my system. My compositions, I gather, sometimes seem boozy to the nobility and gentry, but they are actually done as soberly as those of William Dean Howells.

But this craven policy is not general among the literati, nor was it to be noted among the journalists of my apprentice days. Between 1899 and 1904 there was only one reporter south of the Mason & Dixon Line who did not drink at all, and he was considered insane. In New York, so far as I could make out, there was not even one. On my first Christmas Eve on the *Herald* but two sober persons were to be found in the office — one of them a Seventh Day Adventist office-boy in the editorial rooms, and the other a superannuated stereotyper who sold lunches to the printers in the composing-room. There was a printer on the payroll who was reputed to be a teetotaler — indeed his singularity gave him the nickname of the Moral Element —, but Christmas Eve happened to be his night off. All the rest were full of what they called hand-set whiskey. This powerful drug was sold in a saloon next door to the *Herald* office, and was reputed to

be made in the cellar by the proprietor in person
— of wood alcohol, snuff, tabasco sauce, and coffin
varnish. The printers liked it, and got down a
great many shots of it. On the Christmas Eve I
speak of its effects were such that more than half
the linotype machines in the composing-room
broke down, and one of the apprentices ran his
shirt-tail through the proof-press. Down in the
press-room four or five pressmen got hurt, and the
city edition was nearly an hour late.

Nobody cared, for the head of the whole establishment, the revered managing editor, Colonel
Cunningham, was locked up in his office with a case
of Bourbon. At irregular intervals he would throw
a wad of copy-paper over the partition which separated him from the editorial writers, and when this
wad was smoothed out it always turned out to be
part of an interminable editorial against General
Felix Agnus, editor of the *American*. The General
was a hero of the Civil War, with so much lead in
his system that he was said to rattle as he walked,
but Colonel Cunningham always hooted at his war
record, and was fond of alleging — without any
ground whatsoever — that he had come to America
from his native France in the pussy-like character
of a barber. The editorial that he was writing that
Christmas Eve was headed, in fact, " The Barber
of Seville." It never got into the paper, for it was
running beyond three columns by press-time, and
the night editor, Isidor Goodman, killed it for fear

that its point was still to come. When the Colonel inquired about it two or three days afterward he was told that a truck had upset in the composing-room, and pied it.

The hero of the *Herald* composing-room in those days was a fat printer named Bill, who was reputed to be the champion beer-drinker of the Western Hemisphere. Bill was a first-rate linotype operator, and never resorted to his avocation in working-hours, but the instant his time was up he would hustle on his coat and go to a beer-house in the neighborhood, and there give what he called a setting. He made no charge for admission, but the spectators, of course, were supposed to pay for the beer. One night in 1902 I saw him get down thirty-two bottles in a row. Perhaps, in your wanderings, you have seen the same — but have you ever heard of a champion who could do it *without once retiring from his place at the bar?* Well, that is what Bill did, and on another occasion, when I was not present, he reached forty. Physiologists tell me that these prodigies must have been optical delusions, for there is not room enough in the coils and recesses of man for so much liquid, but I can only reply *Pfui* to that, for a record is a record. Bill avoided the door marked " Gents " as diligently as if he had been a débutante of the era, or the sign on it had been " For Ladies Only." He would have been humiliated beyond endurance if anyone had ever seen him slink through it.

In the year 1904, when the *Herald* office was destroyed in the great Baltimore fire, and we had to print the paper, for five weeks, in Philadelphia, I was told off to find accommodation for the printers. I found it in one of those old-fashioned $1-a-day hotels that were all bar on the first floor. The proprietor, a German with goat whiskers, was somewhat reluctant to come to terms, for he had heard that printers were wild fellows who might be expected to break up his furniture and work their wicked will upon his chambermaids, but when I told him that a beer-champion was among them he showed a more friendly interest, and when I began to brag about Bill's extraordinary talents his doubts disappeared and he proposed amiably that some Philadelphia foam-jumpers be invited in to make it a race. The first heat was run the very next night, and Bill won hands down. In fact, he won so easily that he offered grandly to go until he had drunk *twice* as much as the next best entry. We restrained him and got him to bed, for there had been some ominous whispering among the other starters, and it was plain that they were planning to call in help. The next night it appeared in the shape of a tall, knotty man from Allentown, Pa., who was introduced as the champion of the Lehigh Valley. He claimed to be not only a beer-drinker of high gifts, but also a member of the Bach Choir at Bethlehem; and when he got down his first dozen mugs — the boys were drinking from the wood — he cut

loose with an exultant yodel that he said was one
of Bach's forgotten minor works. But he might
very well have saved his wind, for Bill soon had
him, and at the end of the setting he was four or
five mugs behind, and in a state resembling suffo-
cation. The next afternoon I saw his disconsolate
fans taking him home, a sadder and much less melo-
dious man.

On the first two nights there had been only slim
galleries, but on the third the bar was jammed, and
anyone could see that something desperate was
afoot. It turned out to be the introduction of two
super-champions, the one a short, saturnine Welshman from Wilkes-Barré, and the other a hearty
blond young fellow from one of the Philadelphia
suburbs, who said that he was half German and
half Irish. The Welshman was introduced as the
man who had twice drunk Otto the Brewery Horse
under the table, and we were supposed to know who
Otto was, though we didn't. The mongrel had a
committee with him, and the chairman thereof offered to lay $25 on him at even money. The print-
ers in Bill's corner made up the money at once, and
their stake had grown to $50 in forty minutes by
the clock, for the hybrid took only that long to
blow up. The Welshman lasted much better, and
there were some uneasy moments when he seemed
destined to make history again by adding Bill to
Otto, but in the end he succumbed so suddenly that
it seemed like a bang, and his friends laid him out

on the floor and began fanning him with bar-towels.

Bill was very cocky after that, and talked grandiosely of taking on two champions at a time, in marathon series. There were no takers for several nights, but after that they began to filter in from the remoter wilds of the Pennsylvania Dutch country, and the whole *Herald* staff was kept busy guarding Bill by day, to make sure that he did not waste any of his libido for malt liquor in the afternoons. He knocked off twenty or thirty challengers during the ensuing weeks, including two more Welshmen from the hard-coal country, a Scotsman with an ear missing, and a bearded Dunkard from Lancaster county. They were mainly pushovers, but now and then there was a tough one. Bill did not let this heavy going interfere with the practise of his profession. He set type every night from 6 p.m. to midnight in the office of the *Evening Telegraph*, where we were printing the *Herald*, and never begar his combats until 12.30. By two o'clock he was commonly in bed, with another wreath of laurels hanging on the gas-jet.

To ease your suspense I'll tell you at once that he was never beaten. Germans, Irishmen, Welshmen and Scotsmen went down before him like so many Sunday-school superintendents, and he bowled over everyday Americans with such facility that only two of them ever lasted more than half an hour. But I should add in candor that he was out of service during the last week of our stay in Philadelphia. What fetched him is still a subject of debate among the pathologists at the Johns Hopkins Medical School, to whom the facts were presented officially on our return to Baltimore. The only visible symptom was a complete loss of speech. Bill showed up one night talking hoarsely, the next night he could manage only whispers, and the third night he was as mute as a shad-fish. There was absolutely no other sign of distress. He was all for going on with his derisive harrying of the Pennsylvania lushers, but a young doctor who hung about the saloon and served as surgeon at the bouts forbade it on unstated medical grounds. The Johns Hopkins experts in morbid anatomy have never been able to agree about the case. Some argue that Bill's potations must have dissolved the gummy coating of his pharyngeal plexus, and thus paralyzed his vocal cords; the rest laugh at this as nonsense savoring of quackery, and lay the whole thing to an intercurrent laryngitis, induced by insufficient bedclothes on very cold nights. I suppose that no one will ever know the truth. Bill recovered his voice in a couple of months, and soon afterward left Baltimore. Of the prodigies, if any, that marked his later career I can't tell you.

He was but one of a notable series of giants who flourished in Baltimore at the turn of the century, bringing the city a friendly publicity and causing the theory to get about that life there must be delightful. They appeared in all the ranks of society. The Maryland Club had its champions, and the cops had theirs. Some were drinkers pure and simple; others specialized in eating. One of the latter was an old man of easy means who lived at the Rennert Hotel, then the undisputed capital of gastronomy in the terrapin and oyster country. But for some reason that I can't tell you he never did his eating there; instead, he always took dinner at Tommy McPherson's eating-house, six or eight blocks away. He would leave the hotel every evening at seven o'clock, elegantly arrayed in a long-tailed black coat and a white waistcoat, and carrying a gold-headed cane, and would walk the whole way. Tommy's place was arranged in two layers, with tables for men only alongside the bar downstairs, and a series of small rooms upstairs to which ladies might be invited. The cops, goaded by vice crusaders, had forced him to take the doors off these rooms, but he had substituted heavy portières, and his colored waiters were instructed to make a noise as they shuffled down the hall, and to enter every room backward. The old fellow I speak of, though there were tales about his wild youth, had by now got beyond thought of sin, and all his eating was done downstairs. It consisted of the same dishes precisely every night of the week, year in and year out. First he would throw in three straight whiskeys, and then he would sit down to *two* double porterhouse steaks, with *two* large plates of peas, *two* of French fried potatoes, *two* of cole-slaw, and a mountain of rye-bread. This vast meal he would eat to the last speck, and not infrequently he called for more potatoes or bread. He washed it down with two quarts of Burgundy, and at its end threw in three more straight whiskeys. Then he would light a cigar, and amble back to the Rennert, to spend the rest of the evening conversing with the politicoes who made their headquarters in its lobby.

One day a report reached the *Herald* office that he was beginning to break up, and Max Ways sent me to take a look. He had, by then, been on his diet for no less than twelve years. When I opened the subject delicately he hooted at the notion that he was not up to par. He was, he told me, in magnificent health, and expected to live at least twenty years longer. His excellent condition, he went on to say, was due wholly to his lifelong abstemiousness. He ate only a sparing breakfast, and no lunch at all, and he had not been drunk for fifteen years — that is, in the sense of losing all control of himself. He told me that people who ate pork dug their graves with their teeth, and praised the Jews for avoiding it. He also said that he regarded all sea-food as poisonous, on the ground that it contained too much phosphorus, and that fowl was almost as bad. There was, in his view, only one perfectly safe and wholesome victual, and that was beef. It had everything. It was nourishing, palat-

able and salubrious. The last bite tasted as good
as the first. Even the bones had a pleasant flavor.
He ate peas and potatoes with it, he said, mainly
to give it some company: if he were ever cast on a
desert island he could do without them. The cole-
slaw went along as a sort of gesture of politeness
to the grass that had produced the beef, and he ate
rye-bread instead of wheat because rye was the
bone and sinew of Maryland whiskey, the most
healthful appetizer yet discovered by man. He
would not affront me by presuming to discuss the
virtues of Burgundy: they were mentioned in the
Bible, and all humanity knew them.

The old boy never made his twenty years, but
neither did he ever change his regimen. As the uplift gradually penetrated medicine various doctors
of his acquaintance began to warn him that he was
headed for a bad end, but he laughed at them in
his quiet way, and went on going to Tommy's place
every night, and devouring his two double porter-
houses. What took him off at last was not his eating, but a trifling accident. He was knocked down
by a bicycle in front of the Rennert, developed
pneumonia, and was dead in three days. The
resurrection men at both the Johns Hopkins and
the University of Maryland tried to get his body
for autopsy, and were all set to dig out of it a whole
series of pathological monstrosities of a moral tendency, but his lawyer forbade any knifeplay until
his only heir, a niece, could be consulted, and when

she roared in from Eufaula, Ala., it turned out
that she was a Christian Scientist, with a hate
against anatomy. So he was buried without yielding any lessons for science. If he had any real
rival, in those declining years of Baltimore gastronomy, it must have been John Wilson, a cop:
I have always regretted that they were never
brought together in a match. Once, at a cop party,
I saw John eat thirty fried hard crabs at a sitting
— no mean feat, I assure you, for though the claws
are pulled off a crab before it is fried, all the body-
meat remains. More, he not only ate the crabs, but
sucked the shells. On another occasion, on a bet,
he ate a ham and a cabbage in half an hour by the
clock, but I was not present at that performance.
When, a little later, he dropped dead in the old
Central station-house, the police surgeons laid it
to a pulmonary embolus, then a recent novelty in
pathology.

XI

Recollections of Notable Cops

SOME time ago I read in a New York paper that fifty or sixty college graduates had been appointed to the metropolitan police force, and were being well spoken of by their superiors. The news astonished me, for in my reportorial days there was simply no such thing in America as a book-learned cop, though I knew a good many who were very smart. The force was then recruited, not from the groves of Academe, but from the ranks of workingmen. The best police captain I ever knew in Baltimore was a meat-cutter by trade, and had lost one of his thumbs by a slip of his cleaver, and the next best was a former bartender. All the mounted cops were ex-hostlers passing as ex-cavalrymen, and all the harbor police had come up through the tugboat and garbage-scow branches of the merchant marine. It took a young reporter a little while to learn how to read and interpret the reports that cops turned in, for they were couched in a special kind of English, with a spelling peculiar to itself. If a member of what was then called " the finest " had spelled *larceny* in any way save *larsensy*, or *arson* in any way save *arsony*, or *fracture* in any way save *fraxr*, there would have been a considerable lifting of eyebrows. I well recall the horror of the Baltimore cops when the first board to examine applicants for places on the force was set up. It was a harmless body headed by a political dentist, and the hardest question in its first examination paper was " What is the plural of *ox?*," but all the cops in town predicted that it would quickly contaminate their craft with a great horde of what they called " professors," and reduce it to the level of letter-carrying or school-teaching.

But, as I have noted, their innocence of *literae humaniores* was not necessarily a sign of stupidity, and from some of them, in fact, I learned the valuable lesson that sharp wits can lurk in unpolished skulls. I knew cops who were matches for the most learned and unscrupulous lawyers at the Baltimore bar, and others who had made monkeys of the oldest and crabbedest judges on the bench, and were generally respected for it. Moreover, I knew cops who were really first-rate policemen, and loved their trade as tenderly as so many art artists or movie actors. They were badly paid, but they carried on their dismal work with unflagging diligence, and loved a long, hard chase almost as much as they loved a quick, brisk clubbing. Their one salient failing, taking them as a class, was their belief that any person who had been arrested, even on mere suspicion, was unquestionably and *ipso facto* guilty. But that theory, though it occasionally colored their testimony in a garish manner, was grounded, after all, on nothing worse than professional pride and *esprit de corps*, and I am certainly not one to hoot at it, for my own belief in the mission of journalism has no better support than the same partiality, and all the logic I am aware of stands against it.

In those days that pestilence of Service which torments the American people today was just getting under way, and many of the multifarious duties now carried out by social workers, statisticians, truant officers, visiting nurses, psychologists, and the vast rabble of inspectors, smellers, spies and bogus experts of a hundred different faculties either fell to the police or were not discharged at all. An ordinary flatfoot in a quiet residential section had his hands full. In a single day he might have to put out a couple of kitchen fires, arrange for the removal of a dead mule, guard a poor epileptic having a fit on the sidewalk, catch a runaway horse, settle a combat with table knives between husband and wife, shoot a cat for killing pigeons, rescue a dog or a baby from a sewer, bawl out a white-wings for spilling garbage, keep order on the sidewalk at two or three funerals, and flog half a dozen bad boys for throwing horse-apples at a blind man. The cops downtown, especially along the wharves and in the red-light districts, had even more curious and complicated jobs, and some of them attained to a high degree of virtuosity.

As my memory gropes backward I think, for example, of a strange office that an old-time roundsman named Charlie had to undertake every Spring. It was to pick up enough skilled workmen to effect the annual re-decoration and refurbishing of the Baltimore City Jail. Along about May 1 the warden would telephone to police headquarters that he needed, say, ten head of painters, five plumbers, two blacksmiths, a tile-setter, a roofer, a bricklayer, a carpenter and a locksmith, and it was Charlie's duty to go out and find them. So far as I can recall, he never failed, and usually he produced two or three times as many craftsmen of each category as were needed, so that the warden had some chance to pick out good ones. His plan was simply to make a tour of the saloons and stews in the Marsh Market section of Baltimore, and look over the drunks in congress assembled. He had a trained eye, and could detect a plumber or a painter through two weeks' accumulation of beard and dirt. As he gathered in his candidates, he searched them on the spot, rejecting those who had no union cards, for he was a firm believer in organized labor. Those who passed were put into storage at a police-station, and there kept (less the unfortunates who developed delirium tremens and had to be handed over to the resurrection-men) until the whole convoy was ready. The next morning Gene Grannan, the police magistrate, gave them two weeks each for vagrancy, loitering, trespass, committing a nuisance, or some other plausible misdemeanor, the warden had his staff of master-workmen, and the jail presently bloomed out in all its vernal finery.

Some of these toilers returned year after year, and in the end Charlie recognized so many that he could accumulate the better part of his convoy in half an hour. Once, I remember, he was stumped by a call for two electricians. In those remote days there were fewer men of that craft in practise than today, and only one could be found. When the warden put on the heat Charlie sent him a trolley-car motorman who had run away from his wife and was trying to be shanghaied for the Chesapeake oyster-fleet. This poor man, being grateful for his security in jail, made such eager use of his meagre electrical knowledge that the warden decided to keep him, and even requested that his sentence be extended. Unhappily, Gene Grannan was a pretty good amateur lawyer, and knew that such an extension would be illegal. When the warden of the House of Correction, which was on a farm

twenty miles from Baltimore, heard how well this
system was working, he put in a requisition for six
experienced milkers and a choir-leader, for he had
a herd of cows and his colored prisoners loved to
sing spirituals. Charlie found the choir-leader in
no time, but he bucked at hunting for milkers, and
got rid of the nuisance by sending the warden a
squad of sailors who almost pulled the poor cows
to pieces.

Gene had been made a magistrate as one of the
first fruits of the rising reform movement in Baltimore, and was a man of the chastest integrity, but
he knew too much about reformers to admire them,
and lost no chance to afflict them. When, in 1900,
or thereabout, a gang of snoopers began to tour
the red-light districts, seeking to harass and alarm
the poor working women there denizened, he instructed the gals to empty slops on them, and acquitted all who were brought in for doing it, usually on the ground that the complaining witnesses
were disreputable persons, and could not be believed on oath. One day, sitting in his frowsy
courtroom, I saw him gloat in a positively indecent
manner when a Methodist clergyman was led out
from the cells by Mike Hogan, the turnkey. This
holy man, believing that the Jews, unless they con-
sented to be baptized, would all go to Hell, had
opened a mission in what was then still called the
Ghetto, and sought to save them. The adults, of
course, refused to have anything to do with him,

but he managed, after a while, to lure a number of *kosher* small boys into his den, chiefly by showing them magic-lantern pictures of the Buffalo Bill country and the Holy Land. When their fathers heard of this there was naturally an uproar, for it was a mortal sin in those days for an orthodox Jew to enter a *Goy Schul.* The ritual for delousing offenders was an arduous one, and cost both time and money. So the Jews came clamoring to Grannan, and he spent a couple of hours trying to figure out some charge to lay against the evangelist. Finally, he ordered him brought in, and entered him on the books for " annoying persons passing by and along a public highway, disorderly conduct, making loud and unseemly noises, and disturbing religious worship." He had to be acquitted, of course, but Gene scared him so badly with talk of the penitentiary that he shut down his mission forthwith, and left the Jews to their post-mortem sufferings.

As I have noted in Chapter IX, Gene was a high favorite among us young reporters, for he was always good for copy, and did not hesitate to modify the course of justice in order to feed and edify us. One day an ancient German, obviously a highly respectable man, was brought in on the incredible charge of beating his wife. The testimony showed that they had been placidly married for more than 45 years, and seldom exchanged so much as a bitter word. But the night before, when the old man came home from the saloon where he played *Skat* every evening, the old woman accused him of having drunk more than his usual ration of eight beers, and in the course of the ensuing debate he gave her a gentle slap. Astounded, she let off an hysterical squawk, an officious neighbor rushed in, the cops came on his heels, and so the old man stood before the bar of justice, weeping copiously and with his wife weeping even more copiously beside him. Gene pondered the evidence with a frown on his face, and then announced his judgment. " The crime you are accused of committing," he said, " is a foul and desperate one, and the laws of all civilized countries prohibit it under heavy penalties. I could send you to prison for life, I could order you to the whipping-post [it still exists in Maryland, and for wife-beaters only], or I could sentence you to be hanged. [Here both parties screamed.] But inasmuch as this is your first offense I will be lenient. You will be taken hence to the House of Correction, and there confined for twenty years. In addition, you are fined $10,000." The old couple missed the fine, for at mention of the House of Correction both fainted. When the cops revived them, Gene told the prisoner that, on reflection, he had decided to strike out the sentence, and bade him go and sin no more. Husband and wife rushed out of the courtroom hand in hand, followed by a cop with the umbrella and market-basket that the old woman had forgotten. A week or two later news came in that she was ordering the old man about in a highly

cavalier manner, and had cut down his evenings of
Skat to four a week.

The cops liked and admired Gene, and when he
was in good form he commonly had a gallery of
them in his courtroom, guffawing at his whimsies.
But despite his popularity among them he did not
pal with them, for he was basically a very dignified,
and even somewhat stiff fellow, and knew how to
call them down sharply when their testimony before him went too far beyond the bounds of the
probable. In those days, as in these, policemen led
a social life almost as inbred as that of the justices
of the Supreme Court of the United States, and
outsiders were seldom admitted to their parties.
But reporters were exceptions, and I attended a
number of cop soirées of great elegance, with the
tables piled mountain-high with all the delicacies
of the season, and a keg of beer every few feet. The
graft of these worthy men, at least in my time, was
a great deal less than reformers alleged and the envious common people believed. Most of them, in
my judgment, were very honest fellows, at least
within the bounds of reason. Those who patrolled
the fish-markets naturally had plenty of fish to
eat, and those who manned the police-boats in the
harbor took a certain toll from the pungy captains
who brought up Baltimore's supplies of water-
melons, cantaloupes, vegetables, crabs and oysters
from the Eastern Shore of Maryland: indeed, this
last impost amounted to a kind of *octroi*, and at

one time the harbor force accumulated so much provender that they had to seize an empty warehouse on the waterfront to store it. But the pungy captains gave up uncomplainingly, for the pelagic cops protected them against the thieves and highjackers who swarmed in the harbor, and also against the land police. I never heard of cops getting anything that the donor was not quite willing and even eager to give. Every Italian who ran a peanut stand knew that making them free of it was good institutional promotion and the girls in the red-light districts liked to crochet neckties, socks and pulse-warmers for them. It was not unheard of for a cop to get mashed on such a girl, rescue her from her life of shame, and set her up as a more or less honest woman. I knew of several cases in which holy matrimony followed. But the more ambitious girls, of course, looked higher, and some of them, in my time, made very good marriages. One actually married a banker, and another died only a few years ago as the faithful and much respected wife of a prominent physician. The cops always laughed when reformers alleged that the wages of sin were death — specifically, that women who sold their persons always ended in the gutter, full of dope and despair. They knew that the overwhelming majority ended at the altar of God, and that nearly all of them married better men than they could have had any chance of meeting and roping if they had kept their virtue.

One dismal New Year's day I saw a sergeant lose an excellent chance to pocket $138.66 in cash money: I remember it brilliantly because I lost the same chance at the same moment. There had been the usual epidemic of suicides in the waterfront flop-houses, for the dawn of a new year turns the thoughts of homeless men to peace beyond the dissecting-room, and I accompanied the sergeant and a coroner on a tour of the fatal scenes. One of the dead men was lying on the fifth floor of a decaying warehouse that had been turned into ten-cent sleeping quarters, and we climbed up the long stairs to inspect him. All the other bums had cleared out, and the hophead clerk did not offer to go with us. We found the deceased stretched out in a peaceful attitude, with the rope with which he had hanged himself still around his neck. He had been cut down, but then abandoned.

The sergeant loosed the rope, and began a search of the dead man's pockets, looking for means to identify him. He found nothing whatever of that sort, but from a pants pocket he drew out a fat wad of bills, and a hasty count showed that it contained $416. A situation worthy of Scribe, or even Victor Hugo! Evidently the poor fellow was one of the Russell Sages that are occasionally found among bums. His money, I suppose, had been diminishing, and he had bumped himself off in fear that it would soon be all gone. The sergeant looked at the coroner, the coroner looked at me, and I looked at the sergeant. Then the sergeant wrapped up the money in a piece of newspaper lying nearby, and handed it to the coroner. " It goes," he said sadly, " to the State of Maryland. The son-of-a-bitch died intestate, and with no heirs."

The next day I met the coroner, and found him in a low frame of mind. " It was a sin and a shame," he said, " to turn that money over to the State Treasury. What I could have done with $138.67! (I noticed he made a fair split, but collared one of the two odd cents.) Well, it's gone now — damn the luck! I never *did* trust that flatfoot."

XII

A Girl from
Red Lion, P.A.

SOMEWHERE in his lush, magenta prose Oscar
Wilde speaks of the tendency of nature to imitate
art — a phenomenon often observed by persons
who keep their eyes open. I first became aware of
it, not through the pages of Wilde, but at the
hands of an old-time hack-driver named Peebles,
who flourished in Baltimore in the days of this history. Peebles was a Scotsman of a generally unfriendly and retiring character, but nevertheless
he was something of a public figure in the town.
Perhaps that was partly due to the fact that he had
served twelve years in the Maryland Penitentiary
for killing his wife, but I think he owed much more
of his eminence to his adamantine rectitude in
money matters, so rare in his profession. The very

cops, indeed, regarded him as an honest man, and said so freely. They knew about his blanket refusal to take more than three or four times the legal fare from drunks, they knew how many lost watches, wallets, stick-pins and walking-sticks he turned in every year, and they admired as Christians, though deploring as cops, his absolute refusal to work for them in the capacity of stool-pigeon.

Moreover, he was industrious as well as honest, and it was the common belief that he had money in five banks. He appeared on the hack-stand in front of the old Eutaw House every evening at nine o'clock, and put in the next five or six hours shuttling merrymakers and sociologists to and from the red-light districts. When this trade began to languish he drove to Union Station, and there kept watch until his two old horses fell asleep. Most of the strangers who got off the early morning trains wanted to go to the nearest hotel, which was only two blocks away, so there was not a great deal of money in their patronage, but unlike the other hackers Peebles never resorted to the device of driving them swiftly in the wrong direction and then working back by a circuitous route.

A little after dawn one morning in the early Autumn of 1903, just as his off horse began to snore gently, a milk-train got in from lower Pennsylvania, and out of it issued a rosy-cheeked young woman carrying a pasteboard suitcase and a pink parasol. Squired up from the train-level by a car-greaser with an eye for country beauty, she emerged into the sunlight shyly and ran her eye down the line of hacks. The other drivers seemed to scare her, and no wonder, for they were all grasping men whose evil propensities glowed from them like heat from a stove. But when she saw Peebles her feminine intuition must have told her that he could be trusted, for she shook off the car-greaser without further ado, and came up to the Peebles hack with a pretty show of confidence.

"Say, mister," she said, "how much will you charge to take me to a house of ill fame?"

In telling of it afterward Peebles probably exaggerated his astonishment a bit, but certainly he must have suffered something rationally describable as a shock. He laid great stress upon her air of blooming innocence, almost like that of a cavorting lamb. He said her two cheeks glowed like apples, and that she smelled like a load of hay. By his own account he stared at her for a full minute without answering her question, with a wild stream of confused surmises racing through his mind. What imaginable business could a creature so obviously guileless have in the sort of establishment she had mentioned? Could it be that her tongue had slipped — that she actually meant an employment office, the Y.W.C.A., or what not? Peebles, as he later elaborated the story, insisted that he had cross-examined her at length, and that she had not only reiterated her question in precise terms, but explained that she was fully determined to abandon herself to sin and looked forward confidently to dying in the gutter. But in his first version he reported simply that he had stared at her dumbly until his amazement began to wear off, and then motioned to her to climb into his hack. After all, he was a common carrier, and obliged by law to haul all comers, regardless of their private projects and intentions. If he yielded anything to his Caledonian moral sense it took the form of choosing her destination with some prudence. He might have dumped her into one of the third-rate bagnios that crowded a street not three blocks from Union Station, and then gone on about his business. Instead, he drove half way across town to the high-toned studio of Miss Nellie d'Alembert, at that time one of the leaders of her profession in Baltimore, and a woman who, though she lacked the polish of Vassar, had sound sense, a pawky humor, and progressive ideas.

I had become, only a little while before, city editor of the *Herald*, and in that capacity received frequent confidential communications from her. She was, in fact, the source of a great many useful news tips. She knew everything about everyone that no one was supposed to know, and had accurate advance information, in particular, about Page 1 divorces, for nearly all the big law firms of the town used her facilities for the manufacture of evidence. There were no Walter Winchells in that era, and the city editors of the land had to depend on volunteers for inside stuff. Such volunteers were moved (*a*) by a sense of public duty gracefully performed, and (*b*) by an enlightened desire to keep on the good side of newspapers. Not infrequently they cashed in on this last. I well remember the night when two visiting Congressmen from Washington got into a debate in Miss Nellie's music-room, and one of them dented the skull of the other with a spittoon. At my suggestion the other city editors of Baltimore joined me in straining journalistic ethics far enough to remove the accident to Mt. Vernon place, the most respectable neighborhood in town, and to lay the fracture to a fall on the ice.

My chance leadership in this public work made Miss Nellie my partisan, and now and then she gave me a nice tip and forgot to include the other city editors. Thus I was alert when she called up during the early afternoon of Peebles' strange adventure, and told me that something swell was on ice. She explained that it was not really what you could call important news, but simply a sort of human-interest story, so I asked Percy Heath to go to see her, for though he was now my successor as Sunday editor, he still did an occasional news story, and I knew what kind he enjoyed especially. He called up in half an hour, and asked me to join him. " If you don't hear it yourself," he said, "you will say I am pulling a fake."

A GIRL FROM RED LION, P.A.

When I got to Miss Nellie's house I found her sitting with Percy in a basement room that she used as a sort of office, and at once she plunged into the story.

" I'll tell you first," she began, " before you see the poor thing herself. When Peebles yanked the bell this morning I was sound asleep, and so was all the girls, and Sadie the coon had gone home. I stuck my head out of the window, and there was Peebles on the front steps. I said: ' Get the hell away from here! What do you mean by bringing in a drunk at this time of the morning? Don't you know us poor working people gotta get some rest? ' But he hollered back that he didn't have no drunk in his hack, but something he didn't know what to make of, and needed my help on, so I slipped on my kimono and went down to the door, and by that time he had the girl out of the hack, and before I could say ' scat ' he had shoved her in the parlor, and she was unloading what she had to say.

" Well, to make a long story short, she said she come from somewheres near a burg they call Red Lion, P.A., and lived on a farm. She said her father was one of them old rubes with whiskers they call Dunkards, and very strict. She said she had a beau in York, P.A., of the name of Elmer, and whenever he could get away he would come out to the farm and set in the parlor with her, and they would do a little hugging and kissing. She said Elmer was educated and a great reader, and he would bring her books that he got from his brother, who was a train butcher on the Northern Central, and him and her would read them. She said the books was all about love, and that most of them was sad. Her and Elmer would talk about them while they set in the parlor, and the more they talked about them the sadder they would get, and sometimes she would have to cry.

" Well, to make a long story short, this went on once a week or so, and night before last Elmer come down from York with some more books, and they set in the parlor, and talked about love. Her old man usually stuck his nose in the door now and then, to see that there wasn't no foolishness, but night before last he had a bilious attack and went to bed early, so her and Elmer had it all to their-self in the parlor. So they quit talking about the books, and Elmer began to love her up, and in a little while they was hugging and kissing to beat the band. Well, to make a long story short, Elmer went too far, and when she come to herself and kicked him out she realized she had lost her honest name.

" She laid awake all night thinking about it, and the more she thought about it the more scared she got. In every one of the books her and Elmer read there was something on the subject, and all of the books said the same thing. When a girl lost her honest name there was nothing for her to do excepting to run away from home and lead a life of shame. No girl that she ever read about ever done anything else. They all rushed off to the nearest city, started this life of shame, and then took to booze and dope and died in the gutter. Their family never knew what had became of them. Maybe they landed finally in a medical college, or maybe the Salvation Army buried them, but their people never heard no more of them, and their name was rubbed out of the family Bible. Sometimes their beau tried to find them, but he never could do it, and in the end he usually married the judge's homely daughter, and moved into the big house when the judge died.

"Well, to make a long story short, this poor girl lay awake all night thinking of such sad things, and when she got up at four thirty a.m. and went out to milk the cows her eyes was so full of tears that she could hardly find their spigots. Her father, who was still bilious, give her hell, and told her she was getting her just punishment for setting up until ten and eleven o'clock at night, when all decent people ought to be in bed. So she began to suspect that he may have snuck down during the evening, and caught her, and was getting ready to turn her out of the house and wash his hands of her, and maybe even curse her. So she decided to have it over and done with as soon as possible, and last night, the minute he hit the hay again, she hoofed in to York, P.A., and caught the milk-train for Baltimore, and that is how Peebles found her at Union Station and brought her here. When I asked her what in hell she wanted all she had to say was ' Ain't this a house of ill fame?', and it took me an hour or two to pump her story out of her. So now I have got her upstairs under lock and key, and as soon as I can get word to Peebles I'll tell him to take her back to Union Station, and start her back for Red Lion, P.A. Can you beat it? "

Percy and I, of course, demanded to see the girl, and presently Miss Nellie fetched her in. She was by no means the bucolic Lillian Russell that Peebles' tall tales afterward made her out, but she was certainly far from unappetizing. Despite her loss of sleep, the dreadful gnawings of her conscience and the menace of an appalling retribution, her cheeks were still rosy, and there remained a considerable sparkle in her troubled blue eyes. I never heard her name, but it was plain that she was of four-square Pennsylvania Dutch stock, and as sturdy as the cows she serviced. She had on her Sunday clothes, and appeared to be somewhat uncomfortable in them, but Miss Nellie set her at ease, and soon she was retelling her story to two strange and, in her sight, probably highly dubious men. We listened without interrupting her, and when she finished Percy was the first to speak.

" My dear young lady," he said, " you have been grossly misinformed. I don't know what these works of fiction are that you and Elmer read, but they are as far out of date as Joe Miller's Jest-Book. The stuff that seems to be in them would make even a newspaper editorial writer cough and scratch himself. It may be true that, in the remote era when they appear to have been written, the penalty of a slight and venial slip was as drastic as you say, but I assure you that it is no longer the case. The world is much more humane than it used to be, and much more rational. Just as it no longer burns men for heresy or women for witchcraft, so it has ceased to condemn girls to lives of shame and death in the gutter for the trivial dereliction you acknowledge. If there were time I'd get you some of the more recent books, and point out passages showing how moral principles have changed. The only thing that is frowned on now seems to be getting caught. Otherwise, justice is virtually silent on the subject.

" Inasmuch as your story indicates that no one knows of your crime save your beau, who, if he has learned of your disappearance, is probably scared half to death, I advise you to go home, make some plausible excuse to your pa for lighting out, and resume your care of his cows. At the proper opportunity take your beau to the pastor, and join him in indissoluble love. It is the safe, respectable and hygienic course. Everyone agrees that it is moral, even moralists. Meanwhile, don't forget to thank Miss Nellie. She might have helped you down the primrose way; instead, she has restored you to virtue and happiness, no worse for an interesting experience."

The girl, of course, took in only a small part of this, for Percy's voluptuous style and vocabulary were beyond the grasp of a simple milkmaid. But Miss Nellie, who understood English much better than she spoke it, translated freely, and in a little while the troubled look departed from those blue eyes, and large tears of joy welled from them. Miss Nellie shed a couple herself, and so did all the ladies of the resident faculty, for they had drifted downstairs during the interview, sleepy but curious. The practical Miss Nellie inevitably thought of money, and it turned out that the trip down by milk-train and Peebles' lawful freight of $1 had about exhausted the poor girl's savings, and she had only some odd change left. Percy threw in a dollar and I threw in a dollar, and Miss Nellie not only threw in a third, but ordered one of the ladies to go to the kitchen and prepare a box-lunch for the return to Red Lion.

Sadie the coon had not yet come to work, but Peebles presently bobbed up without being sent for, and toward the end of the afternoon he started off for Union Station with his most amazing passenger, now as full of innocent jubilation as a martyr saved at the stake. As I have said, he embellished the story considerably during the days following, especially in the direction of touching up the girl's pulchritude. The cops, because of their general confidence in him, swallowed his exaggerations, and I heard more than one of them lament that they had missed the chance to handle the case professionally. Percy, in his later years, made two or three attempts to put it into a movie scenario, but the Hays office always vetoed it.

How the girl managed to account to her father for her mysterious flight and quick return I don't know, for she was never heard from afterward. She promised to send Miss Nellie a picture post-card of Red Lion, showing the new hall of the Knights of Pythias, but if it was ever actually mailed it must have been misaddressed, for it never arrived.

XIII

———◆———

The Synthesis
of News

ONE of the first enemy reporters I came to terms
with in the days of my beginnings was an amiable,
ribald fellow with a pot belly and a pointed beard,
by name Leander J. de Bekker. He hailed from
Kentucky by way of Cincinnati and Chicago, and
was proud of the fact that he was of Dutch descent.
The Dutch, he told me at our first meeting, were
the champion beer-drinkers of Christendom, and
had invented not only free lunch but also the
growler, which got its name, so he said, from the
Dutch word *grauw*, signifying the great masses of
the plain people. This de Bekker and I made many
long and laborious treks together, for he was doing
South Baltimore for the *American* when Max
Ways sent me there to break in for the *Herald*,
and South Baltimore was a vast area of indefinite

boundaries and poor communications, with five or six miles of waterfront. At its upper end were the wharves used by the Chesapeake Bay packets, and at its lower end the great peninsula of Locust Point, given over mainly to railroad-yards and grain elevators, but adorned at its nose by Fort McHenry, the bombardment of which in 1814, allegedly by a B——h fleet, inspired Francis Scott Key to write " The Star-Spangled Banner."

There was always something doing in that expansive territory, especially for a young reporter to whom all the major catastrophes and imbecilities of mankind were still more or less novel, and hence delightful. If there was not a powder explosion at Fort McHenry, which was armed with smooth-bore muzzle-loaders dating from 1794, there was sure to be a collision between two Bay packets, and if the cops had nothing in the way of a homicide it was safe to reckon on a three-alarm fire. The blackamoors of South Baltimore were above the common in virulence, and the main streets of their ghetto — York street, Hughsie street and Elbow lane — always ran blood on Saturday nights. It was in Hughsie street, one lovely Summer evening in 1899, that I saw my first murderee — a nearly decapitated colored lady who had been caught by her beau in treason to her vows. And it was in the jungle of warehouses and railroad tracks on Locust Point that I covered my first fire.

De Bekker and I and the reporter for the *Sunpaper* (I forget his name) attended all these public events together, and since de Bekker was the eldest of the trio, and had a beard to prove it, he set the tone and tempo of our endeavors. If, on an expedition to the iron wilds of Locust Point, he decided suddenly that it was time for a hiatus and a beer, we downed tools at once and made for the nearest saloon, which was never more than a block away. Unhappily, the beers of those days, especially along the waterfront, ran only a dozen or so to the keg, and it was thus sometimes difficult for us youngsters, after two or three of them, to throw ourselves into gear again. At such times de Bekker's professional virtuosity and gift for leadership were demonstrated most beautifully.

" Why in hell," he would say, " should we walk our legs off trying to find out the name of a Polack stevedore kicked overboard by a mule? The cops are too busy dragging for the body to ask it, and when they turn it in at last, maybe tomorrow or the day after, it will be so improbable that no union printer in Baltimore will be able to set it up. Even so, they will only guess at it, as they guess at three-fourths of all the names on their books. Moreover, who gives a damn *what* it was? The fact that another poor man has given his life to engorge the Interests is not news: it happens every ten minutes. The important thing here, the one thing that brings us vultures of the press down into this god-forsaken wilderness is that the manner of his death was unusual — that men are not kicked overboard by mules every day. I move you, my esteemed contemporaries, that the name of the deceased be Ignaz Karpinski, that the name of his widow be Marie, that his age was thirty-six, that he lived at 1777 Fort avenue, and that he leaves eleven minor children."

It seemed so reasonable to the *Sun* reporter and me that we could think of no objection, and so the sad facts were reported in all three Baltimore morning papers the next day, along with various lively details that occurred to de Bekker after he had got down another beer. This labor-saving device was in use the whole time I covered South Baltimore for the *Herald*, and I never heard any complaint against it. Every one of the three city editors, comparing his paper to the other two, was surprised and pleased to discover that his reporter always got names and addresses right, and all three of us were sometimes commended for our unusual accuracy. De Bekker, I should add, was a fellow of conscience, and never stooped to what he called faking. That is to say, he never manufactured a story out of the whole cloth. If, under his inspiration, we reported that a mad dog had run amok down the Point and bitten twenty children, there was always an actual dog somewhere in the background, and our count of the victims was at least as authentic as any the cops would make. And if, when an immigrant ship tied up at the North German Lloyd pier, we made it known that fifteen sets of twins had been born during the voyage from Bremen, there were always some genuine twins aboard to support us.

Thus, in my tenderest years, I became familiar with the great art of synthesizing news, and gradually took in the massive fact that journalism is not an exact science. Later, as I advanced up the ladder of the press, I encountered synthesists less conscientious than de Bekker,[1] and indeed became one myself. It was well for me that I showed some talent, else my career might have come to disaster a year or so later, when I was promoted to the City Hall. There I found myself set against two enemy reporters of polished technic and great industry — Frank Kent of the *Sunpaper* and Walter Alexander of the *American*. Kent was a youngster only a little older than I was, but he was a smart fellow, and Alec was already covering his third or fourth city administration, and knew every rat-hole in the City Hall. He remained there for years afterward, and became, in the end, a bottomless abyss of municipal case and precedent. Mayors, comptrollers, health commissioners, city councilmen and other such transient jobholders consulted him as dili-

[1] He left Baltimore in 1901 to join the staff of the Brooklyn *Standard-Union,* and afterward worked for the New York *Tribune* and *Evening Post.* In 1908 he published a dictionary of music, and in 1921 a work on words and phrases in collaboration with Dr. Frank H. Vizetelly, editor of the Standard Dictionary. He died in 1931.

gently as they consulted the daily racing dope.
Even in 1900 he knew more than any of them, and
was thus a formidable competitor.

Once I had got my legs, Kent and I tried to rope
him into a camorra such as de Bekker operated in
South Baltimore, but he knew very well that he
would contribute a great deal more to its assets
than we would, so he played coy, and there was seldom a day that he didn't beat us. One week he let
us have it daily with both barrels, and we got into
trouble with our city editors. There was, of course,
only one remedy, and we were forced into it in
haste. Thereafter, we met every afternoon in
Reilly's ale-house opposite the City Hall, and concocted a fake to bounce him. That fake appeared
the next morning in both the *Sun* and the *Herald*,
with refinements of detail that coincided perfectly,
so all the city editors of the town, including Alec's,
accepted it as gospel. For a week or two Alec tried
to blitz and baffle us with real news beats, but when
we proceeded from one fake a day to two, and then
to three, four, and even more, he came in asking for
terms, and thereafter the three of us lived in broth-
erly concord, with Alec turning up most of the
news and Kent and I embellishing it. Our flames of
fancy having been fanned, we couldn't shut them
off at once, but whenever we thought of a prime
fake we let Alec have it also. If it was so improbable that his somewhat literal mind gagged at it
we refrained from printing it ourselves, but in such

cases we always saved it from going to waste by giving it to the City Hall man of the *Deutsche Correspondent*, a Mannheimer who was ready to believe anything, provided only it was incredible. Once we planted on him an outbreak of yellow fever in the City Jail, but inasmuch as his account of it was printed in German, and buried in columns of gaudy stuff about German weddings, funerals, bowling contests, and other such orgies, our city editors never discovered it.

Kent and I remained in the City Hall about a year, and until the end of that time our relations with Alec were kindly and even loving; in fact, we continued on good terms with him until his lamented death many years afterward. Unhappily, our successors never got next to him as we had, and in consequence he beat them almost every day, and often in a dramatic and paralyzing manner. In the end it was impossible for any rival reporter to stand up to him, and the rich *Sun* had to shanghai him from the poor *American* to avoid disgrace and ruin. More than once Baltimoreans of public spirit, even in the City Hall, proposed that he be elected Mayor himself, and in perpetuity, but like nearly every other good newspaper man, he looked on political office as ignominious, and preferred to remain a reporter. When he died at last the City Hall flag was at half-mast for a week.

The failure of the post-Kent-Mencken flight of City Hall reporters to bring him to a stand as the

Old Masters had done was probably due not only to the natural recession of talent among them, but also to a curious episode that had made a dreadful pother on the *Herald* and was still remembered uneasily by all the journalists of Baltimore. The central figure of that episode was a reporter whose name I shall suppress, for he was unhappily an addict to the hand-set whiskey of the Baltimore printers, and spent a large part of his time sleeping it off in police-stations. Let there be a murder, a fire or even an earthquake, and he would snore through it in one of the roomy barroom chairs that were then provided for the use of professional witnesses, straw bondsmen, and cops on reserve. Max Ways was a man of enlarged views, and had no objection to alcoholism as such, but a narcolept was of little more use to him than a dead man, and one rainy Sunday in the early Winter of 1898–99, being somewhat exacerbated by drink himself, he had the culprit before him, and gave him such a bawling out that even the office boys were aghast.

Moreover, that bawling out was reinforced by an ultimatum. If, by 6 p.m. of that same day, the culprit did not appear in the office with a story worth at least two sticks [2] he was to consider himself fired for the nth and last time, with no hope of appeal, pardon, commutation or reprieve, whether in this world or the next. The poor fish, alarmed,

2 A stick is about two inches of type.

shuffled off to police headquarters and begged the cops to help him, but they reported that the bleak, filthy weather had adjourned all human endeavor in the town, and that they had nothing in hand save two lost colored children and a runaway horse. He then proceeded to such other public offices as were open, but always he met with the same response. Somewhere or other he picked up the death of a saloonkeeper, but the saloonkeeper was obscure, and thus worth, at most, only a few lines. It began to look hopeless, and he slogged on despairingly, soaked by the rain and scarcely knowing where he was going.

This woeful tramp took him at last to the shopping district, and he started to plod it just as dusk was coming down. Simultaneously, the arc-lights which, in that era, hung outside every store of any pretensions began to splutter on, and in his gloomy contemplation of them he was suddenly seized with an idea — the first, in all likelihood, that had occurred to him for long months, and maybe even years. Those arc-lights were above the range of pedestrians on the sidewalks, but it would be easy to reach any of them with an umbrella. Suppose a passer-by carrying a steel-rodded umbrella should lift it high enough to clear another passer-by's umbrella, and its ferrule should touch the steel socket that held the lower carbon of one of the lights, and suppose there should be some leakage of electricity, and it should shoot down the umbrella rod, and into the umbrella's owner's arm, and then, facilitated by his wet clothes, down his legs and into the sidewalk — what would be the effect upon the man? The speculation was an interesting one, and the poor fish paused awhile to revolve it in his deteriorated mind.

The next morning the *Herald* printed a story saying that a man named William T. Benson, aged forty-one, a visitor from Washington, had made the experiment accidentally in West Baltimore street, and had been knocked, figuratively speaking, into a cocked hat. There was a neat description of the way the current had thrown him half way across the street, and a statement from him detailing his sensations *en route*. He had not, he said, lost consciousness, but gigantic pinwheels in all the colors of the rainbow whirled before his eyes, and in the palm of his right hand was a scarlet burn such as one might pick up by grasping a red-hot poker. Moreover, his celluloid collar had been set to smoking, and might have burst into flames and burned his neck if a stranger had not rushed up and quenched it with his handkerchief. The young doctors at the University Hospital, so it appeared, regarded Mr. Benson's escape alive as almost miraculous, and laid it to the fact that he had rubber heels on his shoes. Fortunately, their science was equal to the emergency, and they predicted that their patient would be as good as new, save for his burned hand, by morning. But they trembled to think of the possible fate of the next victim.

This story, which ran well beyond two sticks and rated a display head, saved the narcolept's job — but only temporarily. By ten o'clock the next morning more than 200 Baltimore merchants had called up the electric company and ordered the lights in front of their stores taken away at once. By noon the number was close to a thousand, and by 3 p.m. the lawyers of the electric company were closeted with Nachman, the business manager of the *Herald*, and his veins were running ice-water at their notice of a libel suit for $500,000. They were ready to prove in court, they said, that it was as impossible to get a shock from one of their lights as from a child's rattle. The whole apparatus was fool, drunk, boy, idiot, suicide, and even giraffe proof. It had been tested by every expert in the nation, and pronounced perfect.

What became of the poor fish no one ever learned, for he got wind of the uproar before coming to the office the next day, and in fact never came at all, but vanished into space. The check-up that went on, with half the staff thrown into it, produced only misery of a very high voltage. The cops knew nothing of any such accident, the doctors at the University Hospital had no record of it, and the only William T. Benson who could be found in Washington had not been in Baltimore for nine years. Nor was there any lifting of the gloom when the *Herald's* own lawyer was consulted. This gentleman (he afterward reached the eminence of a Federal circuit judge) was one of those old-fashioned attorneys who saw every case as lost, and liked to wring their clients' hearts. If the *Herald* went into court, he said, he would have to stand mute, for there was no conceivable defense, and if it offered a compromise the electric company would be insane to take anything less than $499,999.99. The most that could be hoped for was that a couple of implacable utilities-haters would sneak past the company's fixers and get on the jury, and there scale down the damages to something less brutal — say $250,000 or $300,-000.

During the month following the *Herald* printed twenty or thirty news stories acknowledging and denouncing the fake, and at least a dozen editorials apologizing for it, but many of the merchants had become immovably convinced that what could be imagined might some day actually happen, so the revenues of the electric company continued depleted, and the bellowing of its lawyers broke all records. When the case was finally set down for an early trial every *Herald* man felt relieved, for it was clearly best to get the agony over, go through a receivership, and start anew. On the day before the day of fate there was really a kind of gaiety in the office. Once more it was raining dismally, but everyone was almost cheerful. That afternoon a man carrying a steel-rodded umbrella lifted it to clear another pedestrian's umbrella in West Baltimore street, and the ferrule touched the lower carbon-socket of one of the few surviving arc-lights. When the cops got him to hospital he was dead.

I tell the tale as it was told to me: it all happened before I joined the staff. My own talent for faking fell into abeyance after I left the City Hall, and especially after I became city editor. In that office, in fact, I spent a large part of my energy trying to stamp it out in other men. But after I was promoted to managing editor, it enjoyed a curious recrudescence, and my masterpiece of all time, with the sole exception of my bogus history of the bathtub, printed in the New York *Evening Mail* on December 28, 1917, was a synthetic war dispatch printed in the *Herald* on May 30, 1905. The war that it had to do with was the gory bout between Japan and Russia, and its special theme was the Battle of Tsushimi or Korea Straits, fought on May 27 and 28. Every managing editor on earth knew for weeks in advance that a great naval battle was impending, and nearly all of them had a pretty accurate notion of where it would be fought. Moreover, they all began to get bulletins, on May 27, indicating that it was on, and these bulletins were followed by others on the day following. They came from Shanghai, Hongkong, Foochow and all the other ports of the China coast. They were set in large type and printed under what were

then called stud-horse heads, but they really offered nothing better than rumors of rumors.
Everyone knew that a battle was being fought, and
everyone assumed that the Japanese would win,
but no one had anything further to say on the subject. The Japs kept mum, and so did the Russians.

Like any other managing editor of normal appe-
tites I was thrown into a sweat by this uncertainty.
With the able aid of George Worsham, who was
then news editor of the *Herald,* I had assembled a
great array of cuts and follow stuff to adorn the
story when it came, and though the *Herald* had
changed to an evening paper by that time, he and
I remained at our posts until late in the evenings
of May 27 and 28, hoping against hope that the
story would begin to flow at any minute, and give
us a chance to bring out a hot extra. But nothing
came in, and neither did anything come in on May
29 — that is, nothing save more of the brief and
tantalizing bulletins from the China coast. On the
evening of this third day of waiting and lathering
I retired to my cubby-hole of an office — and wrote
the story in detail. The date-line I put on it was
the plausible one of Seoul, and this is how it began:

From Chinese boatmen landing upon the Korean coast
comes the first connected story of the great naval battle
in the Straits of Korea on Saturday and Sunday.

After that I laid it on, as they used to say in
those days, with a shovel. Worsham read copy on

me, and contributed many illuminating details. Both of us, by hard poring over maps, had accumulated a knowledge of the terrain that was almost fit to be put beside that of a China coast pilot, and both of us had by heart the names of all the craft in both fleets, along with the names of their commanders. Worsham and I worked on the story until midnight, and the next morning we had it set in time for our noon edition. It began on Page 1 under a head like a fire-alarm, jumped double-leaded to Page 2, and there filled two and three-quarters columns. It described in throbbing phrases the arrival of the Russians, the onslaught of the Japs, the smoke and roar of the encounter, and then the gradual rolling up of the Jap victory. No one really knew, as yet, which side had won, but we took that chance. And to give verisimilitude to our otherwise bald and unconvincing narrative, we mentioned every ship by name, and described its fate, sending most of the Russians to the bottom and leaving the field to Admiral Count Heihachiro Togo. With it we printed our largest, latest and most fierce portrait of the admiral, a smaller one of his unhappy antagonist, Admiral Zinivy Petrovitch Rozhdestvensky, and a whole series of pictures of the contending ships, with all the Russian marked either " damaged " or "sunk."

Thus the *Evening Herald* scored a beat on the world, and, what is more, a beat that lasted for nearly two weeks, for it took that long for any authentic details of the battle to reach civilization. By that time, alas, our feat was forgotten — but not by its perpetrators. Worsham and I searched the cables from Tokyo, when they began to come in at last, with sharp eyes, for we lived in fear that we might have pulled some very sour ones. But there were no such sour ones. We had guessed precisely right in every particular of the slightest importance, and on many fine points we had even beaten the Japs themselves. Years later, reading an astonishing vivid first-hand account of the battle by an actual participant, Aleksei Silych Novikov,[3] I was gratified to note that we were still right.

[3] Translated as Tsushima; New York, 1937.

XIV

Fire Alarm

At midnight or thereabout on Saturday, February 6, 1904, I did my share as city editor to put the *Sunday Herald* to bed, and then proceeded to Junker's saloon to join in the exercises of the Stevedores' Club. Its members, having already got down a good many schooners, were in a frolicsome mood, and I was so pleasantly edified that I stayed until 3:30. Then I caught a night-hawk trolley-car, and by four o'clock was snoring on my celibate couch in Hollins street, with every hope and prospect of continuing there until noon of the next day. But at 11 a.m. there was a telephone call from the *Herald* office, saying that a big fire had broken out in Hopkins Place, the heart of downtown Baltimore, and fifteen minutes later a reporter dashed up to the house behind a sweating hack horse, and rushed in with the news that the fire looked to be a humdinger, and promised swell pickings for a

dull Winter Sunday. So I hoisted my still malty
bones from my couch and got into my clothes, and
ten minutes later I was on my way to the office with
the reporter. That was at about 11:30 a.m. of
Sunday, February 7. It was not until 4 a.m. of
Wednesday, February 10, that my pants and shoes,
or even my collar, came off again. And it was not
until 11:30 a.m. of Sunday, February 14 — precisely a week to the hour since I set off — that I got
home for a bath and a change of linen.

For what I had walked into was the great Baltimore fire of 1904, which burned a square mile out
of the heart of the town and went howling and
spluttering on for ten days. I give the exact schedule of my movements simply because it delights
me, in my autumnal years, to dwell upon it, for it
reminds me how full of steam and malicious animal
magnetism I was when I was young. During the
week following the outbreak of the fire the *Herald*
was printed in three different cities, and I was present at all its accouchements, herding dispersed and
bewildered reporters at long distance and cavorting gloriously in strange composing-rooms. My
opening burst of work without a stop ran to sixty-
four and a half hours, and then I got only six hours
of nightmare sleep, and resumed on a working
schedule of from twelve to fourteen hours a day,
with no days off and no time for meals until work
was over. It was brain-fagging and back-break-
ing, but it was grand beyond compare — an adven-

ture of the first chop, a razzle-dazzle superb and elegant, a circus in forty rings. When I came out of it at last I was a settled and indeed almost a middle-aged man, spavined by responsibility and aching in every sinew, but I went into it a boy, and it was the hot gas of youth that kept me going. The uproar over, and the *Herald* on an even keel again, I picked up one day a volume of stories by a new writer named Joseph Conrad, and therein found a tale of a young sailor that struck home to me as the history of Judas must strike home to many a bloated bishop, though the sailor naturally made his odyssey in a ship, not on a newspaper, and its scene was not a provincial town in America, but the South Seas. Today, so long afterward, I too " remember my youth and the feeling that will never come back any more — the feeling that I could last forever, outlast the sea, the earth, and all men . . . Youth! All youth! The silly, charming, beautiful youth! "

Herald reporters, like all other reporters of the last generation, were usually late in coming to work on Sundays, but *that* Sunday they had begun to drift in even before I got to the office, and by one o'clock we were in full blast. The fire was then raging through a whole block, and from our fifth-floor city-room windows it made a gaudy show, full of catnip for a young city editor. But the Baltimore firemen had a hundred streams on it, and their chief, an old man named Horton, reported that they would knock it off presently. They might have done so, in fact, if the wind had not changed suddenly at three o'clock, and begun to roar from the West. In ten minutes the fire had routed Horton and his men and leaped to a second block, and in half an hour to a third and a fourth, and by dark the whole of downtown Baltimore was under a hail of sparks and flying brands, and a dozen outlying fires had started to eastward. We had a story, I am here to tell you! There have been bigger ones, of course, and plenty of them, but when and where, between the Chicago fire of 1871 and the San Francisco earthquake of 1906, was there ever one that was fatter, juicier, more exhilarating to the journalists on the actual ground? Every newspaper in Baltimore save one was burned out, and every considerable hotel save three, and every office building without exception. The fire raged for a full week, helped by that bitter Winter wind, and when it fizzled out at last the burned area looked like Pompeii, and up from its ashes rose the pathetic skeletons of no less than twenty overtaken and cremated fire-engines — some of them from Washington, Philadelphia, Pittsburgh and New York. Old Horton, the Baltimore fire chief, was in hospital, and so were several hundred of his men.

My labors as city editor during that electric week were onerous and various, but for once they did not include urging lethargic reporters to step into it. The whole staff went to work with the enthusiasm of crusaders shinning up the walls of Antioch, and all sorts of volunteers swarmed in, including three or four forgotten veterans who had been fired years before, and were thought to have long since reached the dissecting-room. Also, there were as many young aspirants from the waiting-list, each hoping for his chance at last, and one of these, John Lee Blecker by name, I remember brilliantly, for when I told him to his delight that he had a job and invited him to prove it he leaped out with exultant gloats — and did not show up again for five days. But getting lost in so vast a story did not wreck his career, for he lived to become, in fact, an excellent reporter, and not a few old-timers were lost, too. One of the best of them, sometime that afternoon, was caught in a blast when the firemen began dynamiting buildings, and got so coagulated that it was three days before he was fit for anything save writing editorials. The rest not only attacked the fire in a fine frenzy, but also returned promptly and safely, and by four o'clock thirty typewriters were going in the city-room, and my desk was beginning to pile high with red-hot copy.

Lynn Meekins, the managing editor, decided against wasting time and energy on extras: we got out one, but the story was too big for such banalities: it seemed like a toy balloon in a hurricane. " Let us close the first city edition," he said,

" at nine o'clock. Make it as complete as you can. If you need twenty pages, take them. If you need fifty, take them." So we began heaving copy to the composing-room, and by seven o'clock there were columns and columns of type on the stones, and picture after picture was coming up from the engraving department. Alas, not much of that quivering stuff ever got into the *Herald*, for a little before nine o'clock, just as the front page was being made up, a couple of excited cops rushed in, howling that the buildings across the street were to be blown up in ten minutes, and ordering us to clear out at once. By this time there was a fire on the roof of the *Herald* Building itself, and another was starting in the press-room, which had plate-glass windows reaching above the street level, all of them long ago smashed by flying brands. We tried to parley with the cops, but they were too eager to be on their way to listen to us, and when a terrific blast went off up the street Meekins ordered that the building be abandoned.

There was a hotel three or four blocks away, out of the apparent path of the fire, and there we went in a dismal procession — editors, reporters, printers and pressmen. Our lovely first edition was adjourned for the moment, but every man-jack in the outfit believed that we'd be back anon, once the proposed dynamiting had been done — every man-jack, that is, save two. One was Joe Bamberger, the foreman of the composing-room, and the other was Joe Callahan, my assistant as city editor. The first Joe was carrying page-proofs of all the pages already made up, and galley-proofs of all the remaining type-matter, and all the copy not yet set. In his left overcoat pocket was the front-page logotype of the paper, and in his left pocket were ten or twelve halftones. The other Joe had on him what copy had remained in the city-room, a wad of Associated Press flimsy about the Russian-Japanese war, a copy-hook, a pot of paste, two boxes of copy-readers' pencils — and the assignment-book!

But Meekins and I refused to believe that we were shipwrecked, and in a little while he sent me back to the *Herald* Building to have a look, leaving Joe No. 2 to round up such reporters as were missing. I got there safely enough, but did not stay long. The proposed dynamiting, for some reason unknown, had apparently been abandoned, but the fire on our roof was blazing violently, and the press-room was vomiting smoke. As I stood gaping at this dispiriting spectacle a couple of large plate-glass windows cracked in the composing-room under the roof, and a flying brand — some of them seemed to be six feet long! — fetched a window on the editorial floor just below it. Nearly opposite, in Fayette street, a sixteen-story office building had caught fire, and I paused a moment more to watch it. The flames leaped through it as if it had been made of matchwood and drenched with gasoline, and in half a minute they were roaring in the air at least 500 feet. It was, I suppose, the most melodramatic detail of the whole fire, but I was too busy to enjoy it, and as I made off hastily I fully expected the whole structure to come crashing down behind me. But when I returned a week later I found that the steel frame and brick skin had both held out, though all the interior was gone, and during the following Summer the burned parts were replaced, and the building remains in service to this day, as solid as the Himalayas.

At the hotel Meekins was trying to telephone to Washington, but long-distance calls still took time in 1904, and it was fifteen minutes before he raised Scott C. Bone, managing editor of the Washington *Post*. Bone was having a busy and crowded night himself, for the story was worth pages to the *Post*, but he promised to do what he could for us, and presently we were hoofing for Camden Station, a good mile away — Meekins and I, Joe Bamberger with his salvage, a copy-reader with the salvage of the other Joe, half a dozen other desk men, fifteen or twenty printers, and small squads of pressmen and circulation men. We were off to Washington to print the paper there — that is, if the gods were kind. They frowned at the start, for the only Baltimore & Ohio train for an hour was an accommodation, but we poured into it, and by midnight we were in the *Post* office, and the hospitable Bone and his men were clearing a place for

us in their frenzied composing-room, and ordering
the press-room to be ready for us.[1]

Just how we managed to get out the *Herald* that
night I can't tell you, for I remember only trifling
details. One was that I was the principal financier
of the expedition, for when we pooled our money
at Camden Station it turned out that I had $40 in
my pocket, whereas Meekins had only $5, and the
rest of the editorial boys not more than $20 among
them. Another is that the moon broke out of the
Winter sky just as we reached the old B. & O. Station in Washington, and shined down sentimen-
tally on the dome of the Capitol. The Capitol was
nothing new to Baltimore journalists, but we had
with us a new copy-reader who had lately come in
from Pittsburgh, and as he saw the matronly dome
for the first time, bathed in spooky moonlight, he
was so overcome by patriotic and aesthetic senti-
ments that he took off his hat and exclaimed " My
God, how beautiful!" And a third is that we all
paused a second to look at the red glow over Baltimore, thirty-five miles away as the crow flies. The
fire had really got going by now, and for four
nights afterward the people of Washington could
see its glare from their streets.

Bone was a highly competent managing editor,
and contrived somehow to squeeze us into the tu-

[1] Bone was an Indianan, and had a long and honorable
career in journalism, stretching from 1881 to 1918. In 1919 he
became publicity chief of the Republican National Committee,
and in 1921 he was appointed Governor of Alaska. He died in
1936.

multous *Post* office. All of his linotypes were already working to capacity, so our operators were useless, but they lent a hand with the make-up, and our pressmen went to the cellar to reinforce their *Post* colleagues. It was a sheer impossibility to set up all the copy we had with us, or even the half of it, or a third of it, but we nevertheless got eight or ten columns into type, and the *Post* lent us enough of its own matter to piece out a four-page paper. In return we lent the hospitable *Post* our halftones, and they adorned its first city edition next morning. Unhappily, the night was half gone before Bone could spare us any press time, but when we got it at last the presses did prodigies, and at precisely 6.30 the next morning we reached Camden Station, Baltimore, on a milk-train, with 30,-000 four-page *Heralds* in the baggage-car. By 8 o'clock they were all sold. Our circulation hustlers had no difficulty in getting rid of them. We had scarcely arrived before the news of our coming began to circulate around the periphery of the fire, and in a few minutes newsboys swarmed in, some of them regulars but the majority volunteers. Very few boys in Baltimore had been to bed that night: the show was altogether too gaudy. And now there was a chance to make some easy money out of it.

Some time ago I unearthed one of these orphan *Heralds* from the catacombs of the Pratt Library in Baltimore, and gave it a looking-over. It turned out to be far from bad, all things considered. The story of the fire was certainly not complete, but it was at least coherent, and three of our halftones adorned Page 1. The eight-column streamer-head that ran across its top was as follows:

HEART OF BALTIMORE WRECKED BY
GREATEST FIRE IN CITY'S HISTORY

Well, brethren, what was wrong about that? I submit that many worse heads have been written by pampered copy-readers sitting at luxurious desks, with vassals and serfs at their side. It was simple; it was direct; there was no fustian in it; and yet it told the story perfectly. I wrote it on a make-up table in the *Post* composing-room, with Meekins standing beside me writing a box for the lower right-hand corner of the first page, thanking the *Post* for its " proverbial courtesy to its contemporaries " and promising formally that the *Herald* would be " published daily by the best means it can command under the circumstances."

Those means turned out, that next day, to be a great deal short of ideal. Leaving Joe Callahan, who had kept the staff going all night, to move to another and safer hotel, for the one where we had found refuge was now in the path of the fire, Meekins and I returned to Washington during the morning to make arrangements for bringing out a larger paper. We were not ashamed of our four pages, for even the *Sunpaper*, printed by the Washington *Evening Star*, had done no better, but what were four pages in the face of so vast a story? The boys had produced enough copy to fill at least ten on the first day of the fire, and today they might turn out enough to fill twenty. It would wring our gizzards intolerably to see so much good stuff going to waste. Moreover, there was art to consider, for our two photographers had piled up dozens of gorgeous pictures, and if there was no engraving plant left in Baltimore there were certainly plenty in Washington.

But Bone, when we routed him out, could not promise us any more accommodation than he had so kindly given us the first night. There was, it appeared, a long-standing agreement between the *Post* and the Baltimore *Evening News*, whereby each engaged to take care of the other in times of calamity, and the *News* staff was already in Washington cashing in on it, and would keep the *Post* equipment busy whenever it was not needed by the *Post* itself. Newspapers in those days had no such plants as they now boast: if I remember rightly, the *Post* had not more than a dozen linotypes, and none of them could chew up copy like the modern monsters. The prospect seemed depressing, indeed, but Bone himself gave us a shot of hope by mentioning casually that the Baltimore *World* appeared to have escaped the fire. The *World*? It was a small, ill-fed sheet of the kind then still

flourishing in most big American cities, and its own
daily editions seldom ran beyond four pages, but it
was an *afternoon* paper, and we might hire its
equipment for the night. What if it had only four
linotypes? We might help them out with hand-set
matter. And what if its Goss press could print but
5,000 six- or eight-page papers an hour? We
might run it steadily from 6 p.m. to the middle of
the next morning, bringing out edition after edition.

We got back to Baltimore as fast as the B. & O.
could carry us, and found the *World* really un-
scathed, and, what is more, its management willing
to help us, and as soon as its own last edition was off
that afternoon Callahan and the gentlemen of the
Herald staff came swarming down on its little office
in Calvert street. The ensuing night gave me the
grand migraine of my life, with throbs like the
blows of an ax and continuous pinwheels. Every
conceivable accident rained down on us. One of the
linotypes got out of order at once, and when, after
maddening delays, Joe Bamberger rounded up a
machinist, it took him two hours to repair it, and
even then he refused to promise that it would work.
Meekins thereupon turned to his desperate plan to
go back to Gutenberg and set matter by hand —
only to find that the *World* had insufficient type in
its cases to fill more than a few columns. Worse,
most of this type appeared to be in the wrong
boxes, and such of it as was standing on the stones

had been picked for sorts by careless printers, and
was pretty well pied.[2]

Meekins sent me out to find more, but all the
larger printers of Baltimore had been burned out,
and the only supply of any size that I could discover was in the office of the *Catholic Mirror*, a
weekly. Arrangements with it were made quickly,
and Joe Bamberger and his gallant lads of the
union rushed the place and proceeded to do or die,
but setting type by hand turned out to be a slow
and vexatious business, especially to linotype operators who had almost forgotten the case. Nor did
it soothe us to discover that the *Mirror's* stock of
type (most of it old and worn) was in three or four
different faces, with each face in two or three sizes,
and that there was not enough of any given face
and size to set more than a few columns. But it was

[2] Perhaps I should explain some printers' terms here. The
stones are flat tables (once of actual stone, but now usually of
steel) on which printers do much of their work. Type is kept
in wooden cases divided into boxes, one for a character. As it
is set up by the compositor it is placed in galleys, which are
brass frames, and then the galleys are taken to the stone and
there made up. Sometimes, after the printing has been done,
the type is returned to a stone, and left there until a convenient
time to return it to the cases. To pick sorts is to go to such
standing type and pick out characters that are exhausted in the
cases. Pied type is type in such confusion that it cannot be returned to the cases by the usual method of following the words,
but must be identified letter by letter. To forget the case, mentioned below, is to lose the art of picking up types from the
boxes without looking at them. The boxes are not arranged al-
phabetically, and a printer learns the case as one learns the
typewriter keyboard. A face of type is a series of sizes of one
design. The face in which this line is set is called Scotch Modern and the size is eight point. The text above is in eleven and
one-half point Scotch Modern.

now too late to balk, so Joe's goons went to work, and by dark we had ten or twelve columns of copy in type, some of it in eight-point, some in ten-point and some in twelve-point. That night I rode with Joe's chief of staff, Josh Lynch, on a commandeered express-wagon as these galleys of motley were hauled from the *Mirror* office to the *World* office. I recall of the journey only that it led down a steep hill, and that the hill was covered with ice. Josh howled whenever the horse slipped, but somehow or other we got all the galleys to the *World* office without disaster, and the next morning, after six or eight breakdowns in the pressroom, we came out with a paper that at least had some news in it, though it looked as if it had been printed by country printers locked up in a distillery.

When the first copy came off the *World's* rickety Goss press Meekins professed to be delighted with it. In the face of almost hopeless difficulties, he said, we had shown the resourcefulness of Robinson Crusoe, and for ages to come this piebald issue of the *Herald* would be preserved in museums under glass, and shown to young printers and reporters with appropriate remarks. The more, however, he looked at it the less his enthusiasm soared, and toward the middle of the morning he decided suddenly that another one like it would disgrace us forever, and announced at once that we'd return to Washington. But we knew before we started that the generous Bone could do no more for us than he

had already done, and, with the *Star* monopolized
by the Baltimore *Sun*, there was not much chance
of finding other accommodation in Washington
that would be better than the *World's* in Baltimore.
The pressure for space was now doubled, for not
only was hot editorial copy piling up endlessly,
but also advertising copy. Hundreds of Baltimore
business firms were either burned out already or
standing in the direct path of the fire, and all of
them were opening temporary offices uptown, and
trying to notify their customers where they could
be found. Even in the ghastly parody printed in
the *World* office we had made room for nearly three
columns of such notices, and before ten o'clock
Tuesday morning we had copy for ten more.

But where to turn? Wilmington in Delaware?
It was nearly seventy miles away, and had only
small papers. We wanted accommodation for
printing ten, twelve, sixteen, twenty pages, for the
Herald had suffered a crippling loss, and needed
that volunteer advertising desperately. Philadelphia? It seemed fantastic, for Philadelphia was
nearly a *hundred* miles away. To be sure, it had
plenty of big newspaper plants, but could we bring
our papers back to Baltimore in time to distribute
them? The circulation men, consulted, were opti-
mistic. " Give us 50,000 papers at 5 a.m.," they
said, " and we'll sell them." So Meekins, at noon or
thereabout, set off for Philadelphia, and before
dark he was heard from. He had made an arrange-

ment with Barclay H. Warburton, owner of the Philadelphia *Evening Telegraph.* The *Telegraph* plant would be ours from 6 p.m., beginning tomorrow, and it was big enough to print any conceivable paper. Meekins was asking the Associated Press to transfer our report from Baltimore to Philadelphia, and the International Typographical Union to let our printers work there. I was to get out one more edition in Washington, and then come to Philadelphia, leaving Callahan in charge of our temporary office in Baltimore. But first I was to see Oscar G. Murray, president of the B. & O. Railroad, and induce him to give us a special train from Philadelphia to Baltimore, to run every night until further notice.

The B. & O.'s headquarters building in Baltimore had been burned out like the *Herald* office, but I soon found Murray at Camden Station, functioning grandly at a table in a storage warehouse. A bachelor of luxurious and even levantine tastes, he was in those days one of the salient characters of Baltimore, and his lavender-and-white striped automobile was later to become a major sight of the town. When he gave a party for his lady friends at the Stafford Hotel, where he lived and had his being, it had to be covered as cautiously as the judicial orgies described in Chapter XII.* He looked, that dreadful afternoon, as if he had just come from his barber, tailor and haberdasher. He

---

* I.e., Chapter XII in the complete edition of *Newspaper Days,* which does not appear in the present volume—Ed.

was shaved so closely that his round face glowed like a rose, and an actual rose was in the buttonhole of his elegant but not too gaudy checked coat. In three minutes I had stated my problem and come to terms with him. At two o'clock, precisely, every morning a train consisting of a locomotive, a baggage-car and a coach would be waiting at Chestnut Street Station in Philadelphia, with orders to shove off for Baltimore the instant our *Heralds* were loaded. It would come through to Camden Station, Baltimore, without stop, and we could have our circulation hustlers waiting for it there.

That was all. When I asked what this train would cost, the magnificent Murray waved me away. " Let us discuss that," he said, " when we are all back home." We did discuss it two months later — and the bill turned out to be nothing at all. " We had some fun together," Murray said, " and we don't want to spoil it now by talking about money." That fun consisted, at least in part, of some very exuberant railroading. If we happened to start from Philadelphia a bit late, which was not infrequent as we accumulated circulation, the special train made the trip to Baltimore at hair-raising speed, with the piles of *Heralds* in the baggage-car thrown helter-skelter on the curves, and the passengers in the coach scared half to death. All known records between Philadelphia and Baltimore were broken during the ensuing five weeks. Finally the racing went so far beyond the seemly that the proper authorities gave one of the engineers ten days lay-off without pay for wild and dangerous malpractice. He spent most of his vacation as the guest of our printers in Philadelphia, and they entertained him handsomely.

But there was still a paper to get out in Washington, and I went there late in the afternoon to tackle the dismal job. The best Bone could do for us, with the Baltimore *News* cluttering the *Post* office all day and the *Post* itself printing endless columns about the fire still raging, was four pages, and of their thirty-two columns nearly thirteen were occupied by the advertisements I have mentioned. I got the business over as soon as possible, and returned to Baltimore eager for a few winks of sleep, for I had not closed my eyes since Sunday morning, and it was now Wednesday. In the *Herald's* temporary office I found Isidor Goodman, the night editor. He reported that every bed in downtown Baltimore was occupied two or three deep, and that if we sought to go home there were no trolley-cars or night-hacks to haul us. In the office itself there was a table used as a desk, but Joe Callahan was snoring on it. A dozen other men were on the floor.

Finally, Isidor allowed that he was acquainted with a lady who kept a surreptitious house of assignation in nearby Paca street, and suggested that business was probably bad with her in view of the competing excitement of the fire, and that she might be able in consequence to give us a bed. But when we plodded to her establishment, which was in a very quiet neighborhood, Isidor, who was as nearly dead as I was, pulled the wrong door-bell, and a bass voice coming out of a nightshirt at a second-story window threatened us with the police if we didn't make off. We were too tired to resist this outrage, but shuffled down the street, silent and despairing. Presently we came to the Rennert Hotel, and went in hoping to find a couple of vacant spots, however hard, on a billiard-table, or the bar, or in chairs in the lobby. Inside, it seemed hopeless, for every chair in sight was occupied, and a dozen men were asleep on the floor. But there was a night-clerk on duty whom we knew, and after some mysterious hocus-pocus he whispered to us to follow him, and we trailed along up the stairs to the fourth floor. There he unlocked a door and pointed dramatically to a vacant bed, looking beautifully white, wide and deep. We did not wait to learn how it had come to be so miraculously vacant, but peeled off our coats and collars, kicked off our shoes, stepped out of our pants, and leaped in. Before the night-clerk left us we were as dead to this world and its sorrows as Gog and Magog. It was 4 a.m. and we slept until ten. When we got back to the *Herald's* quarters we let it be known that we had passed the night in the house of Isidor's friend in Paca street, along with two rich society women from Perth Amboy, N.J.

That night we got out our first paper in Philadelphia — a gorgeous thing of fourteen pages, with twenty columns of advertising. It would knock the eyes out of the *Sun* and *Evening News*, and we rejoiced and flapped our wings accordingly. In particular, we were delighted with the *Evening Telegraph's* neat and graceful head-type, and when we got back to Baltimore we imitated it. Barclay Warburton, the owner of the *Telegraph*, came down to the office to see us through — elegantly invested in a tail coat and a white tie. Despite this unprofessional garb, he turned out to be a smart fellow in the pressroom, and it was largely due to his aid that we made good time. I returned to Baltimore early in the morning on the first of Oscar Murray's special trains, and got a dreadful bumping on the curves and crossings. The circulation boys fell on our paper with exultant gurgles, and the next night we lifted the press-run by 10,000 copies.

We stayed in Philadelphia for five weeks, and gradually came to feel almost at home there — that is, if anybody not born in the town can ever feel at home in Philadelphia. The attitude of the local colleagues at first puzzled us, and then made us snicker in a superior way. Save for Warburton himself, not one of them ever offered us the slightest assistance, or, indeed, even spoke to us. We were printing a daily newspaper 100 miles from base — a feat that remains unparalleled in Amer-

ican journalism, so far as I know, to this day —
and it seemed only natural that some of the Philadelphia brethren should drop in on us, if only out
of curiosity. But the only one who ever appeared
was the managing editor of one of the morning
papers, and he came to propose graciously that we
save him a few dollars by lending him our halftones of the fire. Inasmuch as we were paying his
paper a substantial sum every day for setting ads
for us — the *Evening Telegraph* composing-room
could not handle all that crowded in — we replied
with a chilly nix, and he retired in a huff.

There was a press club in Philadelphia in those
days, and its quarters downtown offered a convenient roosting-place for the hour or two after the
night's work was done. In any other American
city we'd have been offered cards on it instantly
and automatically, but not in Philadelphia. At the
end of a week a telegraph operator working for us
got cards for us in some unknown manner, and a
few of us began using the place. During the time
we did so only one member ever so much as spoke to
us, and he was a drunken Englishman whose conversation consisted entirely of encomiums of Barclay Warburton. Whenever he saw us he would
approach amiably and begin chanting "Good ol'
Bahclay! Good ol' Bahclay! Bahclay's a good
sawt," with *sawt* rhyming with *caught*, and apparently meaning *sort*. We agreed heartily, but suffered under the iteration, and presently we forsook

the place for the saloon patronized by the *Herald* printers, where there was the refined entertainment described in Chapter X.

Meekins's arrangements for getting out the *Herald* so far from home were made with skill and worked perfectly. Callahan remained in Baltimore in charge of our field quarters outside the burned area, and on every train bound for Philadelphia during the afternoon he had an office-boy with such copy as had accumulated. At six o'clock, when the *Evening Telegraph* men cleared out of their office, we opened a couple of private wires, and they kept us supplied with later matter. Even after the fire burned out at last Baltimore was in an appalling state, and there were plenty of old Baltimoreans who wagged their heads despairingly and predicted that it would never be rebuilt. One such pessimist was the Mayor of the town: a little while later, yielding to his vapors, he committed suicide. But there were optimists enough to offset these glooms, and before we left Philadelphia the debris was being cleared away, many ancient and narrow streets were being widened, and scores of new buildings were started. All these debates and doings made for juicy news, and the men of the local staff, ably bossed by Callahan, poured it out daily. Meekins would come to Philadelphia two or three times a week to look over his faculty in exile, and I would drop down to Baltimore about as often to aid and encourage Joe. We had our

own printers in Philadelphia and our own pressmen. Our circulation department performed marvels, and the advertising department gobbled up
all the advertising in sight, which, as I have said,
was plenty. The *Herald* had been on short com-
mons for some time before the fire, but during the
two or three months afterward it rolled in money.

Once I had caught up on lost sleep I prepared
to do a narrative of the fire as I had seen it, with
whatever help I could get from the other *Herald*
men, but the project got itself postponed so often
that I finally abandoned it, and to this day no connected story has ever been printed. The truth is
that, while I was soon getting sleep enough, at least
for a youngster of twenty-four, I had been depleted by the first cruel week more than I thought,
and it was months before I returned to anything
properly describable as normalcy. So with the rest
of the staff, young and old. Surveying them when
the hubbub was over, I found confirmation for my
distrust, mentioned in Chapter X, of alcohol as a
fuel for literary endeavor. They divided themselves sharply into three classes. Those who had
kept off the stuff until work was done and it was
time to relax — there were, of course, no all-out teetotalers in the outfit — needed only brief holidays
to be substantially as good as new. Those who had
drunk during working hours, though in modera-
tion, showed a considerable fraying, and some of
them had spells of sickness. Those who had boozed

in the classical manner were useless before the end of the second week, and three of them were floored by serious illnesses, one of which ended, months later, in complete physical and mental collapse. I pass on this record for what it is worth.

FROM

HEATHEN DAYS

1890-1936

XV

Adventures of a
Y.M.C.A. Lad

[*1 8 9 4*]

WHEN I reach the shades at last it will no doubt astonish Satan to discover, on thumbing my *dossier*, that I was once a member of the Y.M.C.A. Yet a fact is a fact. What is more remarkable, I was not recruited by a missionary to the heathen, but joined at the suggestion of my father, who enjoyed and deserved the name of an infidel. I was then a little beyond fourteen years old, and a new neighborhood branch of the Y, housed in a nobby pressed-brick building, had just been opened in West Baltimore, only a few blocks from our home in Hollins street. The whole upper floor was given over to a gymnasium, and it was this bait, I gathered, that fetched my father, for I was already a bookworm and beginning to be a bit round-shouldered, and he often exhorted me to throw back my shoulders and stick out my chest.

Apparently he was convinced that exercise on the wooden horse and flying rings would cure my scholarly stoop, and make a kind of grenadier of me. If so, he was in error, for I remain more or less Bible-backed to this day, and am often mistaken for a Talmudist. All that the Y.M.C.A.'s horse and rings really accomplished was to fill me with an ineradicable distaste, not only for Christian endeavor in all its forms, but also for every variety of callisthenics, so that I still begrudge the trifling exertion needed to climb in and out of a bathtub, and hate all sports as rabidly as a person who likes sports hates common sense. If I had my way no man guilty of golf would be eligible to any office of trust or profit under the United States, and all female athletes would be shipped to the white-slave corrals of the Argentine.

Indeed, I disliked that gymnasium so earnestly that I never got beyond its baby-class, which was devoted to teaching freshmen how to hang their clothes in the lockers, get into their work-suits, and run round the track. I was in those days a fast runner and could do the 100 yards, with a fair wind, in something better than fourteen seconds, but how anyone could run on a quadrangular track with sides no more than fifty feet long was quite beyond me. The first time I tried it I slipped and slid at all four corners, and the second time I came down with a thump that somehow contrived to skin both my shins. The man in charge of the establishment — the boys all called him Professor — thereupon put me to the punching-bag, but at my fourth or fifth wallop it struck back, and I was floored again. After that I tried all the other insane apparatus in the place, including the horizontal bars, but I always got into trouble very quickly, and never made enough progress to hurt myself seriously, which might have been some comfort, at least on the psychological side. There were other boys who fell from the highest trapezes, and had to be sent home in hacks, and yet others who broke their arms or legs and were heroic figures about the building for months afterward, but the best I ever managed was a bloody nose, and that was caused, not by my own enterprise, but by another boy falling on me from somewhere near the roof. If he had landed six inches farther inshore he might have fractured my skull or broken my neck, but all he achieved was to scrape my nose. It hurt a-plenty, I can tell you, and it hurt still worse when the Professor doused it with arnica, and splashed a couple of drops into each of my eyes.

Looking back over the years, I see that that ghastly gymnasium, if I had continued to frequent it, might have given me an inferiority complex, and bred me up a foe of privilege. I was saved, fortunately, by a congenital complacency that has been a godsend to me, more than once, in other and

graver situations. Within a few weeks I was classi-
fying all the boys in the place in the inverse order
of their diligence and prowess, and that classifica-
tion, as I have intimated, I adhere to at the present
moment. The youngsters who could leap from bar
to bar without slipping and were facile on the tra-
peze I equated with simians of the genus *Hylobates*,
and convinced myself that I was surprised when
they showed a capacity for articulate speech. As
for the weight-lifters, chinners, somersaulters, leap-
ers and other such virtuosi of striated muscle, I dismissed them as *Anthropoidea* far inferior, in all
situations calling for taste or judgment, to school-
teachers or mules.

I should add that my low view of these prizemen
was unaccompanied by personal venom; on the contrary, I got on with them very well, and even had a
kind of liking for some of them — that is, in their
private capacities. Very few, I discovered, were
professing Christians, though the Y.M.C.A., in
those days even more than now, was a furnace of
Protestant divinity. They swore when they stubbed
their toes, and the older of them entertained us
youngsters in the locker-room with their adventures in amour. The chief free-and-easy trysting-
place in West Baltimore, at the time, was a Baptist
church specializing in what was called " young people's work." It put on gaudy entertainments, predominantly secular in character, on Sunday nights,
and scores of the poor working girls of the section

dropped in to help with the singing and lasso beaux.
I gathered from the locker-room talk that some of
those beaux demanded dreadful prices for their con-
sent to the lassoing. Whether this boasting was true
or not I did not know, for I never attended the Sab-
bath evening orgies myself, but at all events it
showed that those who did so were of an antinomian
tendency, and far from ideal Y.M.C.A. fodder.
When the secretaries came to the gymnasium to
drum up customers for prayer-meetings downstairs
the Lotharios always sounded razzberries and
cleared out.

On one point all hands were agreed, and that was
on the point that the Professor was what, in those
days, was called a pain in the neck. When he
mounted a bench and yelled " Fellows! " my own
blood always ran cold, and his subsequent remarks
gave me a touch of homicidal mania. Not until
many years afterward, when a certain eminent politician in Washington took to radio crooning, did
I ever hear a more offensive voice. There were tones
in it like the sound of molasses dripping from a barrel. It was not at all effeminate, but simply saccha-
rine. Had I been older in worldly wisdom it would
have suggested to me a suburban curate gargling
over the carcass of a usurer who had just left the
parish its richest and stupidest widow. As I was,
an innocent boy, I could only compare it to the official chirping of a Sunday-school superintendent.
What the Professor had to say was usually sensi-

ble enough, and I don't recall him ever mentioning either Heaven or Hell; it was simply his tone and manner that offended me. He is now dead, I take it, for many years, and I only hope that he has had good luck *post mortem*, but while he lived his harangues to his students gave me a great deal of unnecessary pain, and definitely slanted my mind against the Y.M.C.A. Even when, many years later, I discovered as a newspaper correspondent that the Berlin outpost thereof, under the name of the *christliche Verein junger Männer*, was so enlightened that it served beer in its lamissary, I declined to change my attitude.

But I was driven out of the Y.M.C.A. at last, not by the Professor nor even by his pupils in the odoriferous gymnasium — what a foul smell, indeed, a gymnasium has! how it suggests a mixture of Salvation Army, elephant house, and county jail! — but by a young member who, so far as I observed, never entered the Professor's domain at all. He was a pimply, officious fellow of seventeen or eighteen, and to me, of course, he seemed virtually a grown man. The scene of his operations was the reading-room, whither I often resorted in self-defense when the Professor let go with " Fellows! " and began one of his hortations. It was quiet there, and though most of the literature on tap was pietistic I enjoyed going through it, for my long interest in the sacred sciences had already begun. One evening, while engaged upon a pamphlet detailing devices for catching boys and girls who knocked down part of their Sunday-school money, I became aware of the pimply one, and presently saw him go to a bookcase and select a book. Dropping into a chair, he turned its pages feverishly, and presently he found what he seemed to be looking for, and cleared his throat to attract attention. The four or five of us at the long table all looked up.

"See here, fellows," he began — again that ghastly "fellows!" — "let me have your ears for just a moment. Here is a book " — holding it up — "that is worth all the other books ever written by mortal man. There is nothing like it on earth except the One Book that our Heavenly Father Himself gave us. It is pure gold, pure meat. There is not a wasted word in it. Every syllable is a perfect gem. For example, listen to this — "

What it was he read I don't recall precisely, but I remember that it was some thumping and appalling platitude or other — something on the order of " Honesty is the best policy," " A guilty conscience needs no accuser," or " It is never too late to mend." I guessed at first that he was trying to be ironical, but it quickly appeared that he was quite serious, and before his audience managed to escape he had read forty or fifty such specimens of otiose rubbish, and following nearly every one of them he indulged himself in a little homily, pointing up its loveliness and rubbing in its lesson. The poor ass, it appeared, was actually enchanted, and wanted

to spread his joy. It was easy to recognize in him
the anti-social animus of a born evangelist, but
there was also something else — a kind of voluptuous delight in the shabby and preposterous, a per-
verted aestheticism like that of a latter-day movie
or radio fan, a wild will to roll in and snuffle balder-
dash as a cat rolls in and snuffles catnip. I was, as I
have said, less than fifteen years old, but I had already got an overdose of such blah in the McGuffey
Readers and penmanship copybooks of the time, so
I withdrew as quickly as possible, unhappily aware
that even the Professor was easier to take than this
jitney Dwight L. Moody. I got home all tuckered
out, and told my father (who was sitting up reading for the tenth or twentieth time a newspaper account of the hanging of two labor leaders) that the
Y.M.C.A. fell a good deal short of what it was
cracked up to be.

He bade me go back the next evening and try
again, and I did so in filial duty. Indeed, I did so a
dozen or more nights running, omitting Sundays,
when the place was given over to spiritual exercises
exclusively. But each and every night that imbe-
cile was in the reading-room, and each and every
night he read from that revolting book to all within
ear-shot. I gathered gradually that it was having
a great run in devotional circles, and was, in fact,
a sort of moral best-seller. The author, it appeared,
was a Methodist bishop, and a great hand at incul-
cating righteousness. He not only knew by heart

all the immemorial platitudes, stretching back to the days of Gog and Magog; he had also invented many more or less new ones, and it was these novelties that especially aroused the enthusiasm of his disciple. I wish I could recall some of them, but my memory has always had a humane faculty for obliterating the intolerable, and so I can't. But you may take my word for it that nothing in the subsequent writings of Dr. Orison Swett Marden or Dr. Frank Crane was worse.

In a little while my deliverance was at hand, for though my father had shown only irritation when I described to him the pulpit manner of the Professor, he was immediately sympathetic when I told him about the bishop's book, and the papuliferous exegete's laboring of it. " You had better quit," he said, " before you hit him with a spittoon, or go crazy. There ought to be a law against such roosters." *Rooster* was then his counter-word, and might signify anything from the most high-toned and elegant Shriner, bank cashier or bartender to the most scurvy and abandoned Socialist. This time he used it in its most opprobrious sense, and so my career in the Y.M.C.A. came to an end. I carried away from it, not only an indelible distrust of every sort of athlete, but also a loathing of Methodist bishops, and it was many years afterward before I could bring myself to admit any such right rev. father in God to my friendship. I have since learned that some of them are very pleasant and amusing fellows, despite their professional enmity to the human race, but the one who wrote that book was certainly nothing of the sort. If, at his decease, he escaped Hell, then moral theology is as full of false alarms as secular law.

XVI

The Tone Art

[*1903*]

Wʜᴇɴ it was discovered by the music critic of the
Morning Herald, a little while after I went to work
as a cub reporter, that I could play the piano from
the printed music and knew how many sharps were
in the key of C major, he began borrowing me from
the city editor to cover his third-, fourth- and fifth-
string concerts, for he was not only a lazy dog but
also had a sensitive ear, and it pained him to have
to listen to the false notes so often struck at such
affairs. As for me, I did not mind them, for my own
playing, like Beethoven's, was pretty inaccurate,
and my general taste in music was still somewhat
low. I got no extra pay for this service, and indeed
no allowance of time: all my regular work had to
be done before I could go to a concert, and as a result I often arrived late, and heard only the termi-
nal or Cheyne-Stokes tumults of the performers.
But when a Summer opera company was in town, or

Sousa's band, or anything else of that loud and hearty order, I usually managed to get, as the phrase then went, a larger load of it, even at the expense of missing two-thirds of a colored murder, or the whole of a Democratic ward meeting. During my first Summer I thus heard the whole répertoire of bad opera from " Cavalleria Rusticana " to " The Chimes of Normandy," not once but three or four times, and in the intervals of this caterwauling I dropped in now and again on half a dozen Italian bands.

These bands were then at the height of their popularity in the United States, and every trolley park had one. They all put on substantially the same programme every night, beginning with one of the more deafening Rossini overtures and ending invariably with " The Star-Spangled Banner," played a couple of tones above the usual key of B flat to show off the trumpets, for the Spanish-American War was only a few years in the past, and patriotism was still bubbling in the national heart. There were two great set pieces that were never missed: indeed, the audiences of the day would have set down an Italian band leader as a fraud if he failed to play them. One was the sextette from " Lucia di Lammermoor," done with all the trumpets and trombones lined up on the apron of the platform, and the other was the anvil chorus from " Il Trovatore," with a row of real anvils in the same place, and a series of electric wires so arranged that big

blue sparks were struck off as the gentlemen of the
percussion section clouted the anvils with real ham-
mers. For this last effect, of course, the lights were
always turned out. It had been invented years before, so I learned long afterward, by the celebrated
Patrick Sarsfield Gilmore, the greatest of all American bandmasters, but by the turn of the century
he was dead and forgotten, and the wops who
worked his masterpiece all claimed credit for it.

They were, in fact, assiduous copy-cats, and
whenever one of them hit on anything really new
the rest imitated it at once. As a result it was hard
to tell one Italian band from another. They not
only played the same programme every night; they
also wore the same florid uniforms, and their leaders all exhibited the same frantic gestures and the
same barbaric hair-cuts. Any leader who, on coming to the coda of a Rossini overture, with its forty
or fifty measures of tonic and dominant chords,
did not throw his arms about like a maniac and contrive to make his back hair (it was always long and
coal black) flap up and down like a loose hatch in
a storm, would have seemed extremely strange. As
a matter of record, no such leader was known to
musical zoölogists — that is, not until I invented
one myself.

This was in 1903 or thereabout, after I had been
promoted to the office of dramatic editor. In that
rôle, as I have said, I was in charge of all advance
notices of musical and theatrical shows, and spent

a part of every day receiving press-agents. One day a member of the corps dropped in to introduce, according to the custom then prevailing, a band leader who had just come to town, and the leader informed me, as usual, that he had written a Baltimore *Morning Herald* march and proposed to dedicate it to me as a tribute to my national and even international celebrity as a friend of sound music. This, of course, was an old gag, and it made no impression on me. Every Italian leader had a portfolio of dog's-eared marches that he renamed after the principal papers of whatever city he happened to be playing in, and dedicated to such members of the staffs thereof as handled advance notices. I was thus not interested, for at least six other *Morning Herald* marches had been dedicated to me during my first few months in office. But there was something unusually attractive about this last imitator of imitators of imitators, and after the formal ritual was over I invited him to sit down, and asked him how the world was using him.

He was very young, and, as I could quickly see, not too sure of himself. He had come to the United States, he said, in the hope of getting a desk as a clarinetist in a first-rate symphony orchestra, but he found that it was the prevailing theory among the Germans who then conducted all American orchestras that the only good clarinetists were either Frenchmen or Belgians, and so he had been refused even an audition. He had thereupon joined an Italian band at $14.50 a week, and after a little while the *padrone* who owned it, and a dozen others exactly like it, had offered him the baton of one of them, at an advance, I gathered, to not more than $25. It was with this outfit that he had come to Baltimore, and as we got on easy terms he confessed to me that he greatly feared the competition of the six or eight other bands then playing in town, for his own was made up mainly of riffraff.

One of his tuba players, he said, could play only by ear, and was in fact not a musician at all but a barber, and that very morning at rehearsal it had been necessary to fire the second snare-drummer, a Black Hander from Palermo, for trying to disembowel a piccolo player with one of his drum-sticks. This snare-drummer was now threatening to throw a bomb at the opening concert. The only oboist in the band, who had to double in the English horn, was naturally insane, for mental aberration is almost normal among oboists, but he was worse than the common run, for his lunacy took the form of trying to blow the oboe and the English horn at once — a preposterous feat, of no practical use or sense. As for the six trumpet players — the very sinew and substance of a brass band — , three were red-ink drunkards, two were grappo addicts, and the sixth had to wear a false moustache to throw off the police, who suspected him of a trunk murder in Akron, O., and wanted to sweat him.

The woes of this earnest young Italian aroused

my sympathy, for I was young myself in those days
and had many tribulations of my own. Unhappily,
I could think of no way to help him against that
crew of scalawags, for my experience of musicians
had already gone far enough to convince me that
there was no cure for their eccentricities. Every
band leader in America had the same troubles, and
also every orchestra conductor, even the most eminent. There was boozing in the Boston Symphony,
and gang-wars were not unheard of at the rehear-
sals of the New York Philharmonic. He would have
to take his band as he found it, and content himself
with doing his level damndest: the Good Book itself
said that angels could do no more. But there was
still some chance of giving him help in the field of
public relations, and I let my mind play upon the
subject while he talked. Eventually I fished up an
idea.

Why, I asked him, go on leading an *Italian* band?
There were hundreds, and maybe even thousands of
them, in the country, and they were all precisely
alike, at least in the eyes of their public. Why not
start out from the reasonable assumption that that
public was more or less fed up with them, and proceed to give it something different? The professor
pricked up his ears, and so did the press-agent, and
my fancy began to flow freely. Why not have at the
fortissimo fans with a *Spanish* band? Why not,
indeed? The Spaniards, who had been fiends in human form only a few years ago, were now fast gath-

ering popularity in the United States — a phenomenon that follows all American wars. Nothing
had been too evil to say of them while they were
butchering Cubans and Filipinos, but the moment
Uncle Sam had to take over the job himself they
began, in retrospect, to seem innocent and even humane. Spanish singers were returning to the Metropolitan Opera House, and American women were
again wearing red and yellow, the Spanish colors.

The leader and his press-agent concurred after
only brief hesitation, and soon we were engaged in
preparing an announcement. The name of the
band, it appeared, was to be the Royal Palace Band
and Drum Corps of Madrid. Its leader was Lieut.
José de la Vega of the Spanish Army, a son to the
commander of the battleship *Vizcaya*, sunk by
Schley at Santiago. The lieutenant himself had
been present at that engagement as chief bugler of
the battleship *Infanta Maria Teresa*, and had been
blown overboard by one of Schley's shells, and then
rescued by Schley's gallant jackies, and brought to
Tampa and nursed back to normalcy by a beautiful
American nurse named Miss Mary Smith, and had
fallen in love with her and was about to marry her.
The press-agent, a competent craftsman, thought
of many interesting details, and even the leader, as
he heated up, made some useful contributions.
When the question of language was adverted to he
relieved the press-agent and me by saying that he
knew a few words of Spanish — *Cuanto? De quien*

es esta sombrero? Siento! La cerveza no es buena,
and so on — enough to fool Americans. So far as I
was aware, there was only one actual Spaniard in
Baltimore, and he was a man of eighty, floored by
rheumatism. There were, of course, plenty of Cubans and Porto Ricans, but none of them would
speak to a Spanish officer.

The scheme was launched the next week, and to
the tune of considerable friendly réclame in the local press. No one, to my knowledge, detected the
imposture, not even the critic of the Baltimore *Sunpapers*, who was not let in on the secret. The leader
and his men wore the same uniforms that they had
been wearing all the while, and played the orthodox
programme, with the addition of the *habanera* from
" Carmen " and " La Paloma." The only real concession to verisimilitude was offered by the press-
agent, who had a large Spanish flag made and hung
it behind the band. At the end of the first half of
the first concert the large audience leaped to its feet
and cheered, and when the last note of the evening
was played there was so vociferous a demand for en-
cores that Lieut. de la Vega did " La Paloma "
twice more, the second time *pianissimo* with the
lights dimmed. During the intermission I encountered one of the professors at the Peabody Con-
servatory of Music, and he told me that he was
greatly enjoying the evening. Italian bands, he
said, drove him wild, but the Spaniards at least
knew how to get decent sounds out of the wood-

wind. " If this fellow," he said, " would sneak in four or five Italian trumpet players he would have a really good band."

Unhappily, the innovation, though an artistic success, was killed in its infancy by the Italian *padrone* who owned the band. When he heard that it had gone Spanish he raised a considerable pother, mainly on prudential grounds. If the news ever got to Italy, he said, he would be disgraced forever, and the Black Hand would probably murder his old mother. Moreover, he was presently reinforced by the members of the band, and especially by the gorilla moiety thereof. They demanded an immediate raise of $2 a week as compensation for the infamy of being turned into Spaniards, and when it was refused they took to sabotage. On the opening night of the second week, when the time came to launch the first dose of " La Paloma," the whole band began to play " Funiculi-Funicula " instead, greatly to Lieut. de la Vega's astonishment and chagrin. There was, of course, nothing for him to do save go along, but during the intermission he gave the performers a piece of his mind, and they responded by threatening to plant a bomb under his podium. Before the end of that second week the band was demanding a raise of $4, and the *padrone* came to Baltimore to make peace. The upshot was that in return for a solemn promise to let his old mother in Naples live he burned the Spanish flag, fired the press-agent, and ordered Lieut. de la Vega

to resume the style and appelation of Antonio Brac-
ciolini, which he had been before. A little while later
the band gave place to another from the same stable, and in the course of time, I suppose, it succumbed to the holocaust which engulfed all the Italian bands in America. I never heard from Lieut. de
la Vega-Bracciolini again. But now and then I got
news of the press-agent. He was going about the
country telling newspaper colleagues that I was a
smartie who deserved a kick in the pants.

I got to know a good many other musicians in
those days, and found many of them pleasant fellows, though their ways of life were strange. I well
recall a talented lady pianist who came to Baltimore for six seasons running, and each time brought
a new husband, always of a new nationality. The
last that I saw was a Turk, and afterward, so I
have heard, she proceeded to a Venezuelan, a South
African Dutchman and a native of Monte Carlo,
but on that point I can't speak from personal
knowledge. I also remember a French tenor who
traveled with no less than three wives, but that was
before the passage of the Mann Act. Two of them
sang in the chorus of his company, and while they
were on the stage the third took care of their and
her own infants in the baggage-room. This company had come up from South America, and carried on its affairs according to provincial Italian
principles. Everything was sung in the fashion of
the sextette in " Lucia " — that is, with the singers

in a long row at the footlights. This was done even
in the final agonies of "Traviata," with *Violette*
dying of tuberculosis. As the curtain fell the lady
playing the rôle — she weighed at least 200 pounds
— was lined up with *Alfred, Annina, Germont* and
Dr. Grenvil, howling *Gran Dio! morir si giovane!*
(Great God! to die so young!) in a voice of brass.
One warm evening, approaching the opera-house
somewhat late, I could hear the screams of the po-
lygamous tenor two blocks away. He was throwing
a lot of violent and supernumerary high C's, many
of them *sforzando,* into *Deserto sulla terra.*

I soon found that, among the instrumental players, the register of the instrument apparently had
some effect upon the temperament of the artist.
The bull-fiddle players were solid men who played
the notes set before them, however difficult, in a
dogged and uncomplaining manner, and seldom
gave a conductor any trouble, whether by alcoholism or Bolshevism. The cellists were also pretty reliable fellows, but in the viola section one began to
encounter boozers, communists and even spiritual-
ists, and when one came to the fiddlers it was reasonable to expect anything, including even a lust
to maim and kill. So, also, in the brass and wood-
wind. No one ever heard of a bassoon or tuba player
saying or doing anything subversive, but the trum-
peters were vain and quarrelsome, the flautists and
clarinetists were often heavy drinkers, and the oboists, as I have noted, were predominantly *meshug-*

gah. Learning these instructive facts, I began to have some sympathy with orchestra conductors, a class of men I had hitherto dismissed as mere athletes, comparable to high-jumpers, circus acrobats and belly-dancers. I now realized that their lives were full of misery, and when, a few years later, I became well acquainted with a number of them, it seemed only natural to learn that they were steady readers of Schopenhauer and Nietzsche and heavy consumers of aspirin, mineral oil and bicarbonate of soda.

Indeed, my gradually growing familiarity with musicians taught me many interesting things about them, and also helped my comprehension of the general mystery of man. It did not surprise me to discover that a great many of them, in their professional capacity, hated music, for I was already aware that most bartenders of any sense were teetotalers and that some of the most eminent medical men at the Johns Hopkins Hospital took patent medicines when they were ill, but it *did* surprise me to find that this animosity to the tone art as a trade was often accompanied by a deep love of it as a recreation. I well recall my delight when I was invited by a Baltimore brewer to a party at his brewery in honor of a dozen members of the Boston Symphony Orchestra, and saw them strip off their coats and fall upon a stack of chamber music that kept them going until 4 a.m. These men, all of whom were first-rate performers, had put in the early part of the evening playing a heavy concert, with a new tone-poem by Richard Strauss, bristling with technical snares, as its principal ingredient. They agreed unanimously that Strauss was a scoundrel, that his music was an outrage upon humanity, and that anyone who paid good money to hear it was insane. Yet these same men, after nearly two hours of professional suffering, now spent four more hours playing for the pleasure of it, and one of the things they played with the greatest gusto was Strauss's serenade in E flat for wind instruments, opus 7. All they got for their labor, save for a keg of beer to each man and the applause of the brewer and of the customers he had invited to meet them, was a hot inner glow, obviously extremely grateful. As I sat listening to them I could not help pondering upon the occult satisfaction that arises from the free and perfect performance of a function, as when a cow gives milk or a dog chases a cat. If the stars were sentient they would no doubt get the same kick out of their enormous revolutions, otherwise so pointless. These reflections, in some way or other, induced me to resume music myself, abandoned since my boyhood, and I was presently playing trios and quartettes with an outfit that devoted four hours of every week to the job — that is, two hours to actual playing and the other two to the twin and inseparable art of beer-drinking.

The members of this little club were all very

much better performers than I was, and it puzzled me at the start to find them so tolerant of my inferiority. I discovered the secret when, after a little while, they took in a recruit even worse, for I was a good deal less pained by the dreadful sounds he made than cheered by his pious enthusiasm. In brief, he really loved music, and that was enough to excuse a great many false entrances and sour notes. I could stand him, at least up to a point, just as the rest could stand me, again up to a point. That club goes on to the present day, though I am the only survivor of the era of my own admission. It has included through the years some first-rate professionals and it has also included some amateurs hardly worth shooting, but they have got on together very amicably, and though they are now mainly elderly men, with kidneys like sieves, they still meet once a week, Winter or Summer, in wartime or peace-time, rain or shine. From end to end of World War I an Englishman sat between two Germans at every meeting, and in World War II a Czech has his place, and two Jews flank the Germans. What this signifies I refrain, on the advice of counsel, from venturing to suggest: in all probability it is downright unlawful. But there it is.

The club, in its day, has had some men of more or less note among its members, and there were times during its earlier stages when the question of honorifics presented a certain difficulty. Should a distinguished university, governmental or ecclesias-

tical dignitary be addressed by his simple surname
or given his title? In the case of those who sat regularly the problem was soon solved in the Rotarian
fashion by calling him Julius or Charlie, but when
he came only occasionally it was got round by giving him a satirical lift. Thus a plain Mister became
Doctor, a Doctor became Professor, and a Professor became *Geheimrat*. If there had ever been a colonel in the club we'd have made him a general, and
if there had ever been an archbishop we'd have addressed him as Your Eminence or perhaps even
Your Holiness. Once, when a baron sat in for a few
sessions, we called him Count, and another time we
promoted a judge to Mr. Chief Justice. The club
has always had a few non-performing members, but
they have been suffered only on condition that they
never make any suggestions about programmes or
offer any criticism of performances. The same rule
has applied to occasional guests: they are welcome
if they keep their mouths shut and do not sweat visibly when the flute is half a tone higher than the
first violin, but not otherwise. The club has never
gone on the air or had its disturbances recorded on
wax, but nevertheless it has done more than one
humble service to the tone art, and in the dark forward and abysm of the future those services may
be acknowledged and even rewarded. For one thing,
it has produced, from its composers' section, at
least one peerless patriotic hymn, to wit, " I Am a
100% American," by William W. Woollcott. This

magnificent composition has everything. It is both chaste and voluptuous. It radiates woof and it reeks with brrrrrrrr. I am frankly tender toward it, for when the inspiration for it seized the composer I had the honor of taking it down at the piano: he was, at the moment, suffering from a sprained arm, and moreover, he plays no instrument save the triangle, and that only in a dilettante fashion. A print of it exists and may be found in libraries, but so far it has not got its deserts from the public. Perhaps it will take a third World War or even a fourth to bring it out. National hymns, as everyone knows, sometimes linger a long while in the dog-house before they win universal acceptance and acclaim. Even " The Star-Spangled Banner " was formally adopted by Congress only a few years ago; indeed, it outran " God Bless America " by hardly more than a neck.

But the greatest of all of Willie Woollcott's inspirations was his plan to play the first eight Beethoven symphonies seriatim, with only brief halts for refreshments between them. He omitted the Ninth only because the club's singing section, at that time, lacked castrati, and in fact consisted of but two men, both of them low, growling basses. We had excellent arrangements of the first eight symphonies, and after debating the project for two or three years resolved at last to give Willie's bold project a whirl. This must have been in 1922 or thereabout, when the club had the largest membership in its history, including a great many bold and reckless men, some of them aviators or ex-marines. Willie not only supplied the idea; he also proposed to supply the scene — his house in a dense woods near Baltimore, with no neighbors within earshot — and the refreshments. It seemed a reasonable arrangement, and so we fell to — at 4 o'clock of a Summer afternoon.

The First Symphony was child's play to us, and we turned it off in record time, with a pause of only ten minutes afterward. By six o'clock we had also finished the Second, and then we stopped for cocktails and dinner. After dinner there was some relaxation, and we dallied a bit with some excellent malt liquor, so that it was eight o'clock before we tackled the Eroica. It began so badly that we played the first movement twice, but after that it picked up momentum, and by 9.30 we had finished it. Then we paused again, this time for sandwiches, a walk in the woods — it was a lovely moonlit night — and another resort to the malt, but at 11.30 or maybe a little later we were back in the trenches, and the Fourth was begun. For some reason or other it went even worse than the Eroica, though it actually makes much less demand on technic, and the clock must have been near to 1 a.m. when we decided finally that it had been done well enough. Our struggles with it had naturally tired us, so we decided to knock off for an hour and find out what the malt had to offer in the way of encouragement.

This hiatus, unhappily, was a fatal one, for when the time came to resume the hullabaloo it was discovered that two of the members had sneaked off for home, and that two more were so sound asleep that we could not arouse them without risk of hurting them. Thus the C minor was begun under unfavorable circumstances, and by the time it was over the band was reduced to what amounted to a mere fragment, and the four-hand piano was making so much noise that the other surviving instruments were barely audible. The Pastoral followed at once, but how it was done I can't say, for I fell asleep myself somewhere in the *scherzo*, and by the time Willie got me back on the piano bench the end had been reached and there was a debate going on about No. 7. It was now nearly 5 a.m., and the east was rosy with the dawn. One faction, it appeared, was in favor of giving up and going home; another insisted that a round of ham and eggs and a few beers would revive us enough to take us to the end. As to what actually happened there are two legends. The official story, inscribed by Willie upon the scrolls of the club, is that we tackled the Seventh, banged through it in circus time, and then dispatched the Eighth. A rump account says that we blew up in the middle of the Seventh, leaped to the Eighth, blew up again, and were chased out by our host, assisted by his hunting dogs. According to this rump account, but three performers were left at the end — the *primo* pianist, one fiddler and a man trying to play a basset-horn.

My own feeling is that in such bizarre matters precise facts are only intrusions. If we actually played the eight symphonies, then no other group of *Tonkünstler* has ever done it, on this or any other earth. And if we only tried, then no one else has ever tried.

XVII

Gore in
the Caribbees

[1917]

No reporter of my generation, whatever his genius, ever really rated spats and a walking-stick until he had covered both a lynching and a revolution. The first, by the ill-favor of the gods, I always missed, usually by an inch. How often, alas, alas, did I strain and puff my way to some Christian hamlet of the Chesapeake Bay littoral, by buggy, farm-wagon or pack-mule, only to discover that an anti-social sheriff had spirited the blackamoor away, leaving nothing but a seething vacuum behind. Once, as I was on my travels, the same thing happened in the charming town of Springfield, Mo., the Paris and Gomorrah of the Ozarks. I was at dinner at the time with the late Edson K. Bixby, editor of the Springfield *Leader*, along with Paul Patterson and Henry M. Hyde, my colleagues of the Baltimore *Sunpapers*. When the alarm reached us we abandoned our victuals instantly, and leaped and galloped downtown to the jail. By the time we got there, though it was in less than three minutes, the cops had loaded the candidate — he was a white man — into their hurry-wagon and made off for Kansas City, and the lynching mob had been reduced to a hundred or so half-grown youths, a couple of pedlars selling hot-dogs and American flags, and a squawking herd of fascinated but disappointed children.

I had rather better luck with revolutions, though I covered only one, and that one I walked into by a sort of accident. The year was 1917 and I was returning from a whiff of World War I in a Spanish ship that had sailed from La Coruña, Spain, ten days before and was hoping, eventually, to get to Havana. It was, at the moment, somewhat in the maze of the Bahamas, but a wireless reached it nevertheless, and that wireless was directed to me and came from the *Sunpaper* office in Baltimore. It said, in brief, that a revolution had broken out in Cuba, that both sides were doing such rough lying that no one north of the Straits of Florida could make out what it was about, and that a series of succinct and illuminating dispatches describing its issues and personalities would be appreciated. I wirelessed back that the wishes of my superiors were commands, and then sent another wireless to a friend in Havana, Captain Asmus Leonhard, marine superintendent of the Munson Line, saying that I itched to see him the instant my ship made port. Captain Leonhard was a Dane of enormous knowledge but parsimonious speech, and I had a high opinion of his sagacity. He knew everyone worth knowing in Latin America, and thousands who were not, and his estimates of them seldom took more than three words. " A burglar," he would say, characterizing a general played up by all the North American newspapers as the greatest trans-Rio Grande hero since Bolívar, or " a goddam fraud," alluding to a new president of Colombia, San Salvador or Santo Domingo, and that was all. His reply to my wireless was in his usual manner. It said: " Sure."

When the Spanish ship, after groping about for two or three days in Exuma Sound, the North-East Providence Channel, the Tongue of Ocean and various other strangely-named Bahaman waterways, finally made Havana and passed the Morro, a smart young mulatto in Captain Leonhard's launch put out from shore, took me aboard his craft, and whisked me through the customs. The captain himself was waiting in front of the Pasaje Hotel in the Prado, eating a plate of Spanish bean-soup and simultaneously smoking a Romeo y Julietta cigar. " The issues in the revolution," he said, tackling the business in hand at once, " are simple. Menocal, who calls himself a Conservative, is president, and

José Miguel Gomez, who used to be president and calls himself a Liberal, wants to make a come-back. That is the whole story. José Miguel says that when Menocal was reëlected last year the so-called Liberals were chased away from the so-called polls by the so-called army. On the other hand, Menocal says that José Miguel is a porch-climber and ought to be chased out of the island. Both are right."

It seemed clear enough, and I prepared to write a dispatch at once, but Captain Leonhard suggested that perhaps it might be a good idea for me to see Menocal first, and hear the official version in full. We were at the palace in three minutes, and found it swarming with dignitaries. Half of them were army officers in uniform, with swords, and the other half were functionaries of the secretariat. They pranced and roared all over the place, and at intervals of a few seconds more officers would dash up in motor-cars and muscle and whoop their way into the president's office. These last, explained Captain Leonhard, were couriers from the front, for José Miguel, having taken to the bush, was even now surrounded down in Santa Clara province, and there were high hopes that he would be nabbed anon. Despite all the hurly-burly it took only ten minutes for the captain to get me an audience with *el presidente*. I found His Excellency calm and amiable. He spoke English fluently, and was far from reticent. José Miguel, he said, was a fiend in human form who hoped by his treasons to provoke American intervention, and so upset the current freely-chosen and impeccably virtuous government. This foul plot would fail. The gallant Cuban army, which had never lost either a battle or a war, had the traitor cornered, and within a few days he would be chained up among the lizards in the fortress of La Cabaña, waiting for the firing-squad and trying in vain to make his peace with God.

So saying, *el presidente* bowed me out, at the same time offering to put a motor-car and a secretary at my disposal. It seemed a favorable time to write my dispatch, but Captain Leonhard stayed me. " First," he said, " you had better hear what the revolutionists have to say." " The revolutionists!" I exclaimed. " I thought they were out in Santa Clara, surrounded by the army." " Some are," said the captain, " but some ain't. Let us take a hack." So we took a hack and were presently worming our way down the narrow street called Obispo. The captain called a halt in front of a bank, and we got out. " I'll wait here in the bank," he said, " and you go upstairs to Room 309. Ask for Dr. ―― " and he whispered a name. " Who is this Dr. ――? " I whispered back. " He is the head of the revolutionary junta," replied the captain. " Mention my name, and he will tell you all about it."

I followed orders, and was soon closeted with the doctor — a very tall, very slim old man with a straggling beard and skin the color of cement.

While we gabbled various persons rushed in and out of his office, most of them carrying papers which they slapped upon his desk. In a corner a young Cuban girl of considerable sightliness banged away at a typewriter. The doctor, like *el presidente*, spoke excellent English, and appeared to be in ebullient spirits. He had trustworthy agents, he gave me to understand, in the palace, some of them in high office. He knew what was going on in the American embassy. He got carbons of all official telegrams from the front. The progress of events there, he said, was extremely favorable to the cause of reform. José Miguel, though somewhat bulky for field service, was a military genius comparable to Joffre or Hindenburg, or even to Hannibal or Alexander, and would soon be making monkeys of the generals of the army. As for Menocal, he was a fiend in human form who hoped to provoke American intervention, and thereby make his corrupt and abominable régime secure.

All this naturally struck me as somewhat unusual, though as a newspaper reporter I was supposed to be incapable of surprise. Here, in the very heart and gizzard of Havana, within sight and hearing of thousands, the revolutionists were maintaining what amounted to open headquarters, and their boss wizard was talking freely, and indeed in a loud voice, to a stranger whose only introduction had been, so to speak, to ask for Joe. I ventured to inquire of the doctor if there were not some danger that his gold-fish globe of a hideaway would be discovered. " Not much," he said. " The army is hunting for us, but the army is so stupid as to be virtually idiotic. The police know where we are, but they believe we are going to win, and want to keep their jobs afterward." From this confidence the doctor proceeded to boasting. " In ten days," he said, " we'll have Menocal jugged in La Cabaña. Shoot him? No; it would be too expensive. The New York banks that run him have plenty of money. If we let him live they will come across."

When I rejoined the captain downstairs I suggested again that it was high time for me to begin composing my dispatch, and this time he agreed. More, he hauled me down to the cable office, only a block or two away, and there left me. " If you get into trouble," he said, " call me up at the Pasaje. I'll be taking my nap, but the clerk will wake me if you need me." I found the cable office very comfortable and even luxurious. There were plenty of desks and typewriters, and when I announced myself I was invited to make myself free of them. Moreover, as I sat down and began to unlimber my prose a large brass spittoon was wheeled up beside me, apparently as a friendly concession to my nationality. At other desks a number of other gentlemen were in labor, and I recognized them at once as colleagues, for a newspaper reporter can always spot another, just as a Freemason can spot a Freemason, or a detective a detective. But I didn't know any of them, and fell to work without speaking to them. When my dispatch was finished I took it to the window, and was informed politely that it would have to be submitted to the censor, who occupied, it appeared, a room in the rear.

The censor turned out to be a young Cuban whose English was quite as good as Menocal's or the doctor's, but unhappily he had rules to follow, and I soon found that they were very onerous. While I palavered with him several of the colleagues came up with copy in their hands, and in two minutes an enormous debate was in progress. He was sworn, I soon gathered, to cut out everything even remotely resembling a fact. No names. No dates. Worse, no conjectures, prognostications, divinations. The colleagues, thus robbed of their habitual provender and full of outrage, put up a dreadful uproar, but the censor stood his ground, and presently I slipped away and called up Captain Leonhard. My respect for his influence was higher than ever now, and it had occurred to me that the revolutionists up the street might have a private cable, and that if they had he would undoubtedly be free of it. But when, in response to his order, I met him in front of the Pasaje, he said nothing about a cable, but heaved me instead into a hack. In ten minutes we were aboard an American ship just about to cast off from a wharf down in the region of the customs-house, and he was introducing me to one of the mates. " Tell him what to do," he said,

" and he will do it." I told the mate to file my dispatch the instant his ship docked at Key West, he nodded silently and put the copy into an inside pocket, and that was that. Then the siren sounded and the captain and I returned to the pier.

It all seemed so facile that I became somewhat uneasy. Could the mate be trusted? The captain assured me that he could. But what of the ship? Certainly it did not look fit for wrestling with the notorious swells of the Straits of Florida. Its lines suggested that it had started out in life as an excursion boat on the Hudson, and it was plainly in the last stages of decrepitude. I knew that the run to Key West was rather more than a hundred miles, and my guess, imparted to the captain, was that no such craft could make it in less than forty-eight hours. But the captain only laughed. " That old hulk," he said, " is the fastest ship in the Caribbean. If it doesn't hit a log or break in two it will make Key West in five and a half hours." He was right as usual, for that night, just as I was turning in at the Pasaje I received a cable from the *Sunpaper* saying that my treatise on the revolution had begun to run, and was very illuminating and high-toned stuff.

Thereafter, I unloaded all my dissertations in the same manner. Every afternoon I would divert attention by waiting on the censor and filing a dispatch so full of contraband that I knew he would never send it, and then I would go down to the wharf and look up the mate. On the fourth day he was *non est* and I was in a panic, for the captain had gone on a business trip into Pinar del Rio and no one else could help me. But just as the lines were being cast off I caught sight of a likely-looking Americano standing at the gangway and decided to throw myself upon his Christian charity. He responded readily, and my dispatch went through as usual. Thereafter, though the mate never showed up again — I heard later that he was sick in Key West — I always managed to find an accommodating passenger. Meanwhile, the censor's copy-hook accumulated a fine crop of my rejected cablegrams, and mixed with them were scores by the colleagues. Every time I went to the cable office I found the whole corps raising hell, and threatening all sorts of reprisals and revenges. But they seldom got anything through save the official communiqués that issued from the palace at hourly intervals.

These communiqués were prepared by a large staff of press-agents, and were not only couched in extremely florid words but ran to great lengths. I had just come from Berlin, where all that the German General Staff had to say every day, though war was raging on two fronts, was commonly put into no more than 300 words, so this Latin exuberance rather astonished me. But the stuff made gaudy reading, and I sent a lot of it to the *Sun-paper* by mail, for the entertainment and instruction of the gentlemen of the copy-desk. The Cuban mails, of course, were censored like the cable, but the same Americano who carried my afternoon dispatch to Key West was always willing to mail a few long envelopes at the same place. Meanwhile, I hung about the palace, and picked up enough off-record gossip to give my dispatches a pleasant air of verisimilitude, soothing to editors if not to readers. Also, I made daily visits to the headquarters of the revolutionists, and there got a lot of information, some of it sound, to the same end. In three days, such is the quick grasp of the reportorial mind, I knew all the ins and outs of the revolution, and in a week I was fit to write a history of Cuban politics from the days of Diego Velazquez. I was, of course, younger then than I am now, and reporters today are not what they used to be, but into that we need not go.

After a week it began to be plain, even on the evidence supplied by the revolutionists, that the uprising was making heavy weather of it, and when, a day or two later, the palace press-agents announced, in a communiqué running to 8,000 words, that José Miguel Gomez was about to be taken, I joined the colleagues in believing it. We all demanded, of course, to be let in on the final scene, and after a long series of conferences, with speeches by Menocal, half a dozen high army officers, all the press-agents and most of the correspondents, it was so ordered. According to both the palace and the revolutionists, the front was down at Placetas in Santa Clara, 180 miles away, but even in those days there were plenty of Fords in Havana, and it was arranged that a fleet of them should start out the next morning, loaded with correspondents, type-writers and bottled beer. Unhappily, the trip was never made, for at the precise moment the order for it was being issued a dashing colonel in Santa Clara was leading his men in a grand assault upon José Miguel, and after ten minutes of terrific fire and deafening yells the Cuban Hindenburg hoisted his shirt upon the tip of his sword and surrendered. He did not have to take his shirt off for the pur-pose: it was already hanging upon a guava bush, for he had been preparing for a siesta in his ham-mock. Why he did not know of the projected attack I could never find out, for he was held incommuni-cado in La Cabaña until I left Cuba, and neither the palace nor the revolutionists seemed willing to discuss the subject.

The palace press-agents, you may be sure, spit on their hands when they heard the news, and turned out a series of communiqués perhaps unsur-passed in the history of war. Their hot, lascivious rhetoric was still flowing three or four days later, long after poor José Miguel was safely jugged among the lizards and scorpions. I recall one canto of five or six thousand words that included a minute autopsy on the strategy and tactics of the final bat-tle, written by a gifted military pathologist on the staff of the victorious colonel. He described every move in the stealthy approach to José Miguel in the minutest detail, and pitched his analysis in highly graphic and even blood-curdling terms. More than once, it appeared, the whole operation was in dire peril, and a false step might have wrecked it, and thereby delivered Cuba to the wolves. Indeed, it might have been baffled at its very apex and apogee if only José Miguel had had his shirt on. As it was, he could not, according to Latin notions of decorum, lead his men, and in consequence they skedaddled, and he himself was forced to yield his sword to the agents of the New York banks.

The night of the victory was a great night in Havana, and especially at the palace President Menocal kept open house in the most literal sense: his office door was wide open and anyone was free to rush in and hug him. Thousands did so, including scores of officers arriving home from the front. Some of these officers were indubitably Caucasians, but a great many were of darker shades, including saddle-brown and coffin-black. As they leaped out of their Fords in front of the palace the bystanders fell upon them with patriotic gloats and gurgles, and kissed them on both cheeks. Then they struggled up the grand staircase to *el presidente's* reception-room, and were kissed again by the superior public there assembled. Finally, they leaped into the inner office, and fell to kissing His Excellency and to being kissed by him. It was an exhilarating show, but full of strangeness to a Nordic. I observed two things especially. The first was that, for all the uproar, no one was drunk. The other was that the cops beat up no one.

José Miguel was brought to Havana the next morning, chained up in a hearse, and the palace press-agents announced in a series of ten or fifteen communiqués that he would be tried during the afternoon, and shot at sunrise the day following. The colleagues, robbed of their chance to see his capture, now applied for permission to see him put to death, and somewhat to their surprise it was granted readily. He was to be turned off, it appeared, at 6 a.m. promptly, so they were asked to be at the gate of La Cabaña an hour earlier. Most of them were on hand, but the sentry on watch refused to let them in, and after half an hour's wrangle a young officer came out and said that the execution had been postponed until the next day. But the next day it was put off again, and again the next, and after three or four days no more colleagues showed up at the gate. It was then announced by the palace literati that President Menocal had commuted the sentence to solitary confinement for life in a dungeon on the Cayos de la Doce Leguas off the south coast, where the mosquitoes were as large as bullfrogs, along with confiscation of all the culprit's property, whether real, personal or mixed, and the perpetual loss of his civil rights, such as they were.

But even this turned out to be only tall talk, for President Menocal was a very humane man, and pretty soon he reduced José Miguel's sentence to fifty years, and then to fifteen, and then to six, and then to two. Soon after that he wiped out the jugging altogether, and substituted a fine — first of $1,000,000, then of $250,000, and then of $50,-000. The common belief was that José Miguel was enormously rich, but this was found to be an exaggeration. When I left Cuba he was still protesting that the last and lowest fine was far beyond his means, and in the end, I believe, he was let off with the confiscation of his yacht, a small craft then laid up with engine trouble. When he died in 1921 he had resumed his old place among the acknowledged heroes of his country. Twenty years later Menocal joined him in Valhalla.

XVIII

◆

Romantic
Intermezzo

———

[1 9 2 0]

TAKE wine, women and song, add plenty of A-No. 1
victuals, the belch and bellow of oratory, a balmy
but stimulating climate and a whiff of patriotism,
and it must be obvious that you have a dose with a
very powerful kick in it. This, precisely, was the
dose that made the Democratic national convention of 1920, holden in San Francisco, the most
charming in American annals. No one who was
present at its sessions will ever forget it. It made
history for its voluptuous loveliness, just as the
Baltimore convention of 1912 made history for its
infernal heat, and the New York convention of
1924 for its 103 ballots and its unparalleled din.
Whenever I meet an old-timer who took part in it
we fall into maudlin reminiscences of it, and tears

drop off the ends of our noses. It came within an inch of being perfect. It was San Francisco's brave answer to the Nazi-inspired earthquake of April 18, 1906.

The whole population shared in the credit for it, and even the powers and principalities of the air had a hand, for they provided the magnificent weather, but chief praise went justly to the Hon. James Rolph, Jr., then and for eleven years afterward mayor of the town. In 1920, indeed, he had already been mayor for nine years, and in 1931, after five terms of four years each in that office, he was promoted to the dignity of Governor of California. He was a man of bold imagination and spacious ideas. More than anyone else he was responsible for the superb hall in which the convention was held, and more than any other he deserved thanks for the humane and enlightened entertainment of the delegates and alternates. The heart of that entertainment was a carload of Bourbon whiskey, old, mellow and full of pungent but delicate tangs — in brief, the best that money could buy.

The persons who go to Democratic national conventions seldom see such wet goods; in truth, they had never seen any before, and they have never seen any since. The general rule is to feed them the worst obtainable, and at the highest prices they can be cajoled and swindled into paying. Inasmuch as large numbers of them are Southerners, and most of the rest have Southern sympathies, it is assumed that they will drink anything, however revolting, provided only it have enough kick. In preparation for their quadrennial gathering to nominate a candidate for the Presidency the wholesale booze-sellers of the country ship in the dregs of their cellars — rye whiskey in which rats have drowned, Bourbon contaminated with arsenic and ptomaines, corn fresh from the still, gin that is three-fourths turpentine, and rum rejected as too corrosive by the West Indian embalmers. This stuff the Democrats put away with loud hosannas — but only for a few days. After that their livers give out, they lose their tempers, and the country is entertained with a rough-house in the grand manner. There has been such a rough-house at every Democratic national convention since Jackson's day, save only the *Ja*-convention at Chicago in 1940 and the incomparable gathering at San Francisco in 1920. The scene at the latter was one of universal peace and lovey-dovey, and every Democrat went home on his own legs, with his soul exultant and both his ears intact and functioning.

The beauty of this miracle was greatly enhanced by the fact that it was unexpected. Prohibition had gone into force only five months before the convention was scheduled to meet, and the Democrats arrived in San Francisco full of miserable forebodings. Judging by what they had already experienced at home, they assumed that the convention booze would be even worse than usual; indeed, most

of them were so uneasy about it that they brought
along supplies of their own. During the five months
they had got used to hair oil, Jamaica ginger and
sweet spirits of nitre, but they feared that the San
Francisco booticians, abandoning all reason, would
proceed to paint remover and sheep dip. What a
surprise awaited them! What a deliverance was at
hand! The moment they got to their hotels they
were waited upon by small committees of refined
and well-dressed ladies, and asked to state their de-
sires. The majority, at the start, were so suspicious
that they kicked the ladies out; they feared entrap-
ment by what were then still called revenuers. But
the bolder fellows took a chance — and a few hours
later the glad word was everywhere. No matter
what a delegate ordered he got Bourbon — but it
was Bourbon of the very first chop, Bourbon aged
in contented barrels of the finest white oak, Bourbon of really ultra and super quality. It came in
quart bottles on the very heels of the committee
of ladies — and there was no bill attached. It was
offered to the visitors with the compliments of
Mayor James Rolph, Jr.

The effects of that Bourbon were so wondrous
that it is easy to exaggerate them in retrospect.
There were, of course, other links in the chain of
causation behind the phenomena I am about to describe. One, as I have hinted, was the weather — a
series of days so sunshiny and caressing, so cool
and exhilarating that living through them was like

rolling on meads of asphodel. Another was the hall
in which the convention was held — a new city au-
ditorium so spacious, so clean, so luxurious in its
comforts and so beautiful in its decorations that the
assembled politicoes felt like sailors turned loose in
the most gorgeous bordellos of Paris. I had just
come from the Republican national convention in
Chicago, and was thus keen to the contrast. The
hall in Chicago was an old armory that had been
used but lately for prize fights, dog shows and a
third-rate circus, and it still smelled of pugs, ken-
nels and elephants. Its walls and gallery railings
were covered to the last inch with shabby flags and
bunting that seemed to have come straight from a
bankrupt street carnival. Down in the catacombs
beneath it the victualling accommodations were of
a grab-it-and-run, eat-it-if-you-can character, and
the rooms marked " Gents " followed the primordial design of Sir John Harington as given in his
" Metamorphosis of Ajax," published in 1596. To
police this foul pen there was a mob of ward heelers
from the Chicago slums, wearing huge badges,
armed with clubs, and bent on packing both the
gallery and the floor with their simian friends.

The contrast presented by the San Francisco
hall was so vast as to be astounding. It was as clean
as an operating room, or even a brewery, and its
decorations were all of a chaste and restful character. The walls were hung, not with garish bunting,
but with fabrics in low tones of gray and green,

and in the whole place only one flag was visible. Downstairs, in the spacious basement, there were lunch-counters served by lovely young creatures in white uniforms, and offering the whole repertory of West Coast delicacies at cut-rate prices. The Johns were lined with mirrors, and each was staffed with shoe-shiners, suit-pressers and hat-cleaners, and outfitted with automatic weighing-machines, cigar-lighters, devices releasing a squirt of Jockey Club perfume for a cent, and recent files of all the principal newspapers of the United States. The police arrangements almost deserved the epithet of dainty. There were no ward heelers armed with clubs, and even the uniformed city police were confined to a few garrison posts, concealed behind marble pillars. All ordinary ushering and trouble-shooting was done by a force of cuties dressed like the waitresses in the basement, and each and every one of them was well worth a straining of the neck. They were armed with little white wands, and every wand was tied with a blue ribbon, signifying law and order. When one of these babies glided into a jam of delegates with her wand upraised they melted as if she had been a man-eating tiger, but with this difference: that instead of making off with screams of terror they yielded as if to soft music, their eyes rolling ecstatically and their hearts going pitter-pat.

But under it all, of course, lay the soothing pharmacological effect of Jim Rolph's incomparable

Bourbon. Delegates who, at all previous Democratic conventions, had come down with stone in the
liver on the second day were here in the full tide of
health and optimism on the fifth. There was not a
single case of mania à potu from end to end of the
gathering, though the place swarmed with men who
were subject to it. Not a delegate took home gastri-
tis. The Bourbon was so pure that it not only did
not etch and burn them out like the horrible hooches
they were used to; it had a positively therapeutic
effect, and cured them of whatever they were suffering from when they got to town. Day by day
they swam in delight. The sessions of the convention, rid for once of the usual quarreling and caterwauling, went on like a conference of ambassadors,
and in the evenings the delegates gave themselves
over to amicable conversation and the orderly
drinking of healths. The climax came on June 30,
the day set apart for putting candidates for the
Presidency in nomination. It was, in its way, the
loveliest day of the whole fortnight, with a cloud-
less sky, the softest whisper of a breeze from the
Pacific, and a sun that warmed without heating.
As the delegates sat in their places listening to the
speeches and the music they could look out of the
open doors of the hall to the Golden Gate, and
there see a fleet of warships that had been sent in
by the Hon. Josephus Daniels, then Secretary of
the Navy, to entertain them with salutes and ma-
noeuvres.

There was an excellent band in the hall, and its leader had been instructed to dress in every speaker with appropriate music. If a gentleman from Kentucky arose, then the band played " My Old Kentucky Home "; if he was followed by one from Indiana, then it played " On the Banks of the Wabash." Only once during the memorable day did the leader make a slip, and that was when he greeted a Georgia delegate with " Marching Through Georgia," but even then he quickly recovered himself and slid into " At a Georgia Campmeeting." An entirely new problem confronted him as the morning wore on, for it was at San Francisco in 1920 that the first lady delegates appeared at a Democratic national convention. His test came when the earliest bird among these stateswomen got the chairman's eye. What she arose to say I do not recall, but I remember that she was a Mrs. FitzGerald of Massachusetts, a very handsome woman. As she appeared on the platform, the leader let go with " Oh, You Beautiful Doll! " The delegates and alternates, struck by the artful patness of the selection, leaped to their legs and cheered, and La FitzGerald's remarks, whatever they were, were received with almost delirious enthusiasm. The next female up was Mrs. Izetta Jewel Brown of West Virginia, a former actress who knew precisely how to walk across a stage and what clothes were for. When the delegates and alternates saw her they were stricken dumb with admiration, but when the band leader gave her "Oh, What a Pal Was Mary," they cut loose with yells that must have been heard half way to San José.

It was not these ladies, however, who made top score on that memorable day, but the Hon. Al Smith of New York. Al, in those days, was by no means the national celebrity that he was to become later. He had already, to be sure, served a year of his first term as Governor of New York, but not many people west of Erie, Pa., had ever heard of him, and to most of the delegates at San Francisco he was no more than a vague name. Thus there was little sign of interest when the Hon. W. Bourke Cockran arose to put him in nomination — the first of his three attempts upon the White House. Cockran made a good speech, but it fell flat, nor did the band leader help things when he played "Tammany" at its close, for Tammany Hall suggested only Romish villainies to the delegates from the Bible country. But when, as if seeing his error, the leader quickly swung into "The Sidewalks of New York" a murmur of appreciation ran through the hall, and by the time the band got to the second stanza someone in a gallery began to sing. The effect of that singing, as the old-time reporters used to say, was electrical. In ten seconds a hundred other voices had joined in, and in a minute the whole audience was bellowing the familiar words. The band played six or eight stanzas, and then switched to "Little Annie Rooney," and then to

" The Bowery," and then to " A Bicycle Built For Two," and then to " Maggie Murphy's Home," and so on down the long line of ancient waltz-songs. Here the leader showed brilliantly his subtle mastery of his art. Not once did he change to four-four time: it would have broken the spell. But three-four time, the sempiternal measure of amour, caught them all where they were tenderest, and for a solid hour the delegates and alternates sang and danced.

The scene was unprecedented in national conventions and has never been repeated since, though many another band leader has tried to put it on: what he lacked was always the aid of Jim Rolph's Bourbon. The first delegate who grabbed a lady politico and began to prance up the aisle was full of it, and so, for all I know, was the lady politico. They were joined quickly by others, and in ten minutes Al was forgotten, the convention was in recess, and a ball was in progress. Not many of the delegates, of course, were equal to actual waltzing, but in next to no time a ground rule was evolved which admitted any kind of cavorting that would fit into the music, so the shindig gradually gathered force and momentum, and by the end of the first half hour the only persons on the floor who were not dancing were a few antisocial Hardshell Baptists from Mississippi, and a one-legged war veteran from Ohio. For a while the chairman, old Joe Robinson, made formal attempts to restore order, but

after that he let it run, and run it did until the last
hoofer was exhausted. Then a young man named
Franklin D. Roosevelt got up to second Al's nomination. He made a long and earnest speech on the
heroic achievements of the Navy in the late war,
and killed Al's boom then and there.

That great and singular day was a Wednesday,
and the bosses of the convention made plans the
next morning to bring its proceedings to a close on
Saturday. But the delegates and alternates simply
refused to agree. The romantic tunes of " East
Side, West Side " and " A Bicycle Built For Two "
were still sounding in their ears, and their veins
still bulged and glowed with Jim Rolph's Bourbon.
The supply of it seemed to be unlimited. Day by
day, almost hour by hour, the ladies' committee
produced more. Thus Thursday passed in happy
abandon, and then Friday. On Saturday someone
proposed boldly that the convention adjourn over
the week-end, and the motion was carried by a vote
of 998 to 26. That afternoon the delegates and alternates, each packing a liberal supply of the Bourbon, entered into taxicabs and set out to see what
was over the horizon. San Francisco was perfect,
but they sweated for new worlds, new marvels, new
adventures. On the Monday following some of them
were roped by the police in places more than a hundred miles away, and started back to their duties
in charge of trained nurses. One taxicab actually
reached Carson City, Nev., and another was re-

ported, probably apocryphally, in San Diego. I myself, though I am an abstemious man, awoke on Sunday morning on the beach at Half Moon Bay, which is as far from San Francisco as Peekskill is from New York. But that was caused, not by Jim Rolph's Bourbon, but by George Sterling's grappo, a kind of brandy distilled from California grape skins, with the addition of strychnine.

After the delegates went home at last the Methodists of San Francisco got wind of the Bourbon and started a noisy public inquiry into its provenance. Jim Rolph, who was a very dignified man, let them roar on without deigning to notice them, even when they alleged that it had been charged to the town smallpox hospital, and offered to prove that there had not been a case of smallpox there since 1897. In due time he came up for reëlection, and they renewed their lying and unChristian attack. As a result he was reëlected almost unanimously, and remained in office, as I have noted, until 1931. In that year, as I have also noted, he was promoted by the appreciative people of all California to the highest place within their gift, and there he remained, to the satisfaction of the whole human race, until his lamented death in 1934.

XIX

The Noble Experiment

[*1924*]

PROHIBITION went into effect on January 16, 1920, and blew up at last on December 5, 1933 — an elapsed time of twelve years, ten months and nineteen days. It seemed almost a geological epoch while it was going on, and the human suffering that it entailed must have been a fair match for that of the Black Death or the Thirty Years' War, but I should say at once that my own share of the blood, sweat and tears was extremely meagre. I was, so far as I have been able to discover, the first man south of the Mason and Dixon line to brew a drinkable home-brew, and as a result my native Baltimore smelled powerfully of malt and hops during the whole horror, for I did not keep my art to myself, but imparted it to anyone who could be trusted

— which meant anyone save a few abandoned Methodists, Baptists and Presbyterians, most of them already far gone in glycosuria, cholelithiasis or gastrohydrorrhea, and all of them soon so low in mind and body that they could be ignored.

My seminary was run on a sort of chain-letter plan. That is to say, I took ten pupils, and then each of the ten took ten, and so on *ad infinitum*. There were dull dogs in Baltimore who went through the course forty or fifty times, under as many different holders of my degrees, and even then never got beyond a nauseous *Malzsuppe*, fit only for policemen and Sunday-school superintendents. But there were others of a much more shining talent, and I put in a great deal of my time in 1921 and 1922 visiting their laboratories, to pass judgment on their brews. They received me with all the deference due to a master, and I was greatly bucked up by their attentions. In fact, those attentions probably saved me from melancholia, for during the whole of the twelve years, ten months and nineteen days I was a magazine editor, and a magazine editor is a man who lives on a sort of spiritual Bataan, with bombs of odium taking him incessantly from the front and torpedoes of obloquy harrying him astern.

But I would not have you think that I was anything like dependent, in that abominable time, upon home-brew, or that I got down any really formidable amount of it. To be sure, I had to apply my critical powers to many thousands of specimens, but I always took them in small doses, and was careful to blow away a good deal of the substance with the foam. This home-brew, when drinkable at all, was a striking proof of the indomitable spirit of man, but in the average case it was not much more. Whenever the mood to drink purely voluptuously was on me I preferred, of course, the product of professional brewmasters, and, having been born lucky, I usually found it. Its provenance, in those days, was kept a kind of military secret, but now that the nightmare is over and jails no longer yawn I do not hesitate to say that, in so far as my own supply went, most of it came from the two lowermost tiers of Pennsylvania counties. Dotted over that smiling pastoral landscape there were groups of small breweries that managed successfully, by means that we need not go into, to stall off the Prohibition agents, and I had the privilege and honor of getting down many a carboy of their excellent product both in Baltimore, where I lived, and in New York, where I had my office.

When I say New York I mean the city in its largest sense — the whole metropolitan region. As a matter of fact, the malt liquor on tap on the actual island of Manhattan was usually bad, and often downright poisonous. When I yearned for a quaff of the real stuff I went to Union Hill, N. J., and if not to Union Hill, then to Hoboken. Both of these great outposts radiated a bouquet of malt and hops almost as pungent as Baltimore's, and in Union Hill there was a beer-house that sticks in my memory as the most comfortable I have ever encountered on this earth. Its beers were perfect, its victuals were cheap and nourishing, its chairs were designed by osteological engineers specializing in the structure of the human pelvis, and its waiters, Axel, Otto, Julius and Raymond, were experts at their science.[1] This incomparable dump was discovered by the late Philip Goodman, then transiently a theatrical manager on Broadway and all his life a fervent beer-drinker, and he and I visited it every time I was in New York, which was pretty often. We would ease into our canons' stalls in the early evening and continue in residence until Axel, Otto, Julius and Raymond began to snore in their corner and the colored maintenance engineer, Willie, turned his fire-hose into the washroom. Then back by taxi to Weehawken, from Weehawken to Forty-second street by the six-minute ferry, and from Forty-second street by taxi again to the quick, lordly sleep of quiet minds and pure hearts.

The fact that the brews on tap in that Elysium came from lower Pennsylvania naturally suggested

---

[1] Raymond, like Axel, was from upper Schleswig-Holstein, and hence technically a Dane. I naturally assumed that his baptismal name was an Americanized form of the old Teutonic name of Reimund, signifying a sagacious councilor. But one night he told me that his father, a *Stadtpfeiffer*, had named him after the " Raymond " overture by Ambrose Thomas, a work he greatly admired.

an expedition to the place of their origin, and Goodman and I laid many plans for making the trip in his car. But every time we started out we dropped in on Axel, Otto, Julius and Raymond for stirrup cups, and that was as far as we ever got. Alone, however, I once visited Harrisburg on newspaper business, and there had the felicity of drinking close to the *Urquell*. That was in the primitive days when New York still bristled with peepholes and it was impossible to get into a strange place without a letter from a judge, but in Harrisburg there were no formalities. I simply approached a traffic cop and asked him where reliable stuff was to be had. " Do you see that kaif there? " he replied, pointing to the corner. " Well, just go in and lay down your money. If you don't like it, come back and I'll give you another one." I liked it well enough, and so did not trouble him further.

I should add, however, that I once came so near going dry in Pennsylvania, and in the very midst of a huge fleet of illicit breweries, that the memory of it still makes me shiver. This was at Bethlehem in the Lehigh Valley, in 1924. I had gone to the place with my publisher, Alfred Knopf, to hear the celebrated Bach Choir, and we were astounded after the first day's sessions to discover that not a drop of malt liquor was to be had in the local pubs. This seemed strange and unfriendly, for it is well known to every musicologist that the divine music of old Johann Sebastian cannot be digested without the aid of its natural solvent. But so far as we could make out there was absolutely none on tap in the Lehigh Valley, though we searched high and low, and threw ourselves upon the mercy of cops, taxi-drivers, hotel clerks, the Elks, the rev. clergy, and half the tenors and basses of the choir. All reported that Prohibition agents had been sighted in the mountains a few days before, and that as a result hundreds of kegs had been buried and every bar-tender was on the alert. How we got through the second day's sessions I don't know; the music was magnificent, but our tonsils became so parched that we could barely join in the final Amen. Half an hour before our train was scheduled to leave for New York we decided to go down to the Lehigh sta-tion and telegraph to a bootician in the big city, desiring him to start westward at once and meet us at Paterson, N. J. On the way to the station we dis-cussed this madcap scheme dismally, and the taxi-driver overheard us. He was a compassionate man, and his heart bled for us.

"Gents," he said, "I hate to horn in on what ain't none of my business, but if you feel that bad about it I think I know where some stuff is to be had. The point is, can you get it?"

We at once offered him money to introduce us, but he waved us off.

"It wouldn't do you no good," he said. "These Pennsylvania Dutch never trust a hackman."

"But where is the place?" we breathed.

"I'm taking you to it," he replied, and in a moment we were there.

It was a huge, blank building that looked like a forsaken warehouse, but over a door that appeared to be tightly locked there was the telltale sign, "Sea Food" — the universal euphemism for beerhouse in Maryland and Pennsylvania throughout the thirteen awful years. We rapped on the door and presently it opened about half an inch, revealing an eye and part of a mouth. The ensuing dialogue was *sotto voce* but *staccato* and *appassionata*. The eye saw that we were famished, but the mouth hesitated.

"How do I know," it asked, "that you ain't two of them agents?"

The insinuation made us boil, but we had to be polite.

"*Agents!*" hissed Knopf. "What an idea! Can't you *see* us? Take a good look at us."

The eye looked, but the mouth made no reply.

"Can't you tell musicians when you see them?" I broke in. "Where did you ever see a Prohibition agent who looked so innocent, so moony, so dumb? We are actually fanatics. We came here to hear Bach. Is this the way Bethlehem treats its guests? We came a thousand miles, and now — "

"*Three* thousand miles," corrected Knopf.

"*Five* thousand," I added, making it round numbers.

Suddenly I bethought me that the piano score

of the B minor mass had been under my arm all the
while. What better introduction? What more per-
suasive proof of our *bona fides?* I held up the score
and pointed to the title on the cover. The eye read:

J. S. Bach
Mass in B Minor

The eye flicked for an instant or two, and then
the mouth spoke. " Come in, gents," it said. As the
door opened our natural momentum carried us into
the bar in one leap, and there we were presently
immersed in two immense *Humpen.* The quality
we did not pause to observe; what we mainly recalled later was the astounding modesty of the bill,
which was sixty-five cents for five *Humpen* —
Knopf had two and I had three — and two sandwiches. We made our train just as it was pulling
out.

It was a narrow escape from death in the desert,
and we do not forget all these years afterward that
we owed it to Johann Sebastian Bach, that highly
talented and entirely respectable man, and especially to his mass in B minor. In the great city of
Cleveland, Ohio, a few months later, I had much
worse luck. I went there, in my capacity of newspaper reporter, to help cover the Republican national convention which nominated Calvin Cool-
idge, and I assumed like everyone else that the
Prohibition agents would lay off while the job was

put through, if only as a mark of respect to their commander-in-chief. This assumption turned out to be erroneous. The agents actually clamped down on Cleveland with the utmost ferocity, and produced a drought that was virtually complete. Even the local cops and newspaper reporters were dry, and many of the latter spent a large part of their time touring the quarters of the out-of-town correspondents, begging for succor. But the supplies brought in by the correspondents were gone in a few days, and by the time the convention actually opened a glass of malt liquor was as hard to come by in Cleveland as an honest politician.

The news of this horror quickly got about, and one morning I received a dispatch in cipher from a Christian friend in Detroit, saying that he was loading a motor-launch with ten cases of bottled beer and ale, and sending it down the Detroit river and across Lake Erie in charge of two of his goons. They were instructed, he said, to notify me the instant they arrived off the Cleveland breakwater. Their notice reached me the next afternoon, but by that time the boys were nominating Cal, so I could not keep the rendezvous myself, but had to send an agent. This agent was Paul de Kruif, then a young man of thirty-four, studying the literary art under my counsel. Paul was a fellow of high principles and worthy of every confidence; moreover, he was dying of thirst himself. I started him out in a rowboat, and he was gone three hours.

When he got back he was pale and trembling, and I could see at a glance that some calamity had befallen. When he got his breath he gasped out the story.

The two goons, it appeared, had broken into their cargo on the way down from Detroit, for the weather was extremely hot. By the time they anchored off the Cleveland breakwater they had got down three cases, and while they were waiting for de Kruif they knocked off two more. This left but five — and they figured that it was just enough to get them back to Detroit, for the way was uphill all the way, as a glance at a map will show. De Kruif, who was a huge and sturdy Dutchman with a neck like John L. Sullivan, protested violently and even undertook to throw them overboard and pirate the launch and cargo, but they pulled firearms on him, and the best he could do was to get six bottles. These he drank on his return in the rowboat, for the heat, as I have said, was extreme. As a result, I got nothing whatsoever; indeed, not a drop of malt touched my throat until the next night at 11.57, when the express for Washington and points East crossed the frontier of the Maryland Free State.

This was my worst adventure during Prohibition, and in many ways it remains the worst adventure of my whole life, though I have been shot at four times and my travels have taken me to Albania, Trans-Jordan and Arkansas. In Maryland there was always plenty, and when I was in New York Goodman and I made many voyages to Union Hill. One hot night in 1927, while we were lolling in the perfect beerhouse that I have mentioned, a small but excellent band was in attendance, and we learned on inquiry that it belonged to a trans-Atlantic liner of foreign registry, then berthed at one of the North river docks. Through Axel and Raymond we got acquainted with the leader, and he told us that if we cared to accompany him and his men back to the ship they would set up some real Pilsner. We naturally accepted, and at five o'clock the next morning we were still down in the stewards' dining-room on H-deck, pouring in *Seidel* after *Seidel* and victualing royally on black bread and *Leberwurst*. The stewards were scrupulous fellows and would not bootleg, but Goodman had some talent for mathematics, and it was not hard for him to figure out a tip that would cover what we had drunk of their rations, with a reasonable *Zuschlag* added.

Thereafter, we visited that lovely ship every time it was in port, which was about once every five weeks, and in a little while we began to add other ships of the same and allied lines, until in the end we had a whole fleet of them, and had access to Pilsner about three weeks out of four, and not only to Pilsner but also to Münchner, Dortmunder, Würzburger and Kulmbacher. It was a long hoof down the dark pier to the cargo port we had to use, and a long climb from the water-line down to H-deck, but we got used to the exertion and even came to welcome it, for we were both under medical advice to take more exercise. When we went aboard, usually at 10 or 11 p.m., there was no one on the dock save a customs watchman sitting on a stool at the street entrance, chewing tobacco, and when we debarked at 4 or 5 a.m. the same watchman was still there, usually sound asleep.

Gradually, such being the enticements of sin, we fell into the habit of sneaking a couple of jugs past the watchman — most often, of Germany brandy, or *Branntwein*. It was abominable stuff, but nevertheless it was the real McCoy, and Goodman and I found it very useful — he for drugging his actors and I for dishing out to the poets who infested my magazine office. One night there was some sort of celebration aboard ship — as I recall it, the birthday of Martin Luther — and the stewards put on a special spread. The *pièce de résistance* was a *Wurst* of some strange but very toothsome kind, and Goodman and I got down large rashers of it, and praised it in high, astounding terms. The stewards were so pleased by our appreciation that they gave us two whole ones as we left, and so we marched up the pier to the street, each with a bottle of *Branntwein* in one coat pocket and a large, globulous sausage in the other. To our surprise we found the customs watchman awake. More, he halted us.

" What have you got there in your pockets? " he demanded.

We turned them out, and he passed over the two bottles without a word, but the sausages set him off to an amazing snorting and baying.

"God damn me," he roared, "if I ever seen the like. Ain't you got *no* sense *whatever?* Here I try to be nice to you, and let you get something 100% safe into your system, and what do you hand me? What you hand me is that you try to do some *smuggling* on me. Yes, *smuggling*. I know the law and so do you. If I wanted to turn you in I could send you to Atlanta for the rest of your life. God damn if I ain't *ashamed* of you."

With that he grabbed the two sausages and hugged them to him. Goodman and I, conscious of guilt, stood silent, with flushed faces and downcast eyes. What was there to say? Nothing that we could think of. We had been taken red-handed in a deliberate violation of the just laws of this great Republic. We had tried with malice prepense to rob the Treasury of the duty on two valuable sausages — say, 67½ cents at 25% *ad valorem* on a valuation of $2.50 for the pair. The amount, to be sure, was small, but the principle was precious beyond price. In brief, we were common felons, dirt criminals, enemies to society, and as reprehensible, almost, as so many burglars, hijackers or Prohibition agents.

The watchman howled on for two or three minutes, seeking, apparently, to impress upon us the heinousness of our offense. We needed no such exposition. Our consciences were devouring us with red-hot fangs. There was no need for us to say a word, for we radiated repentance and regret. But finally, as the watchman dismissed us with a parting blast, Goodman ventured upon a question.

" Do you," he asked, " want the bottles too? "

" Hell, no," replied the watchman. " What *I* am trying to bust up is *smuggling*."

XX

Vanishing
Act

[1934]

Taking one day with another I have but little han-
kering to see ruins, but when, in the early part of
1934, I found myself aboard a ship approaching
the French port of Tunis, in the Mediterranean,
and a Catholic bishop who was a fellow-passenger
proposed that we go ashore the next day and have
a look at the remains of Carthage I agreed at once,
for the Carthaginians have always fascinated me,
if only because they made so thorough a job of dis-
appearing from the earth. His Excellency, it appeared, was but little interested in them himself,
for they were heathens as I was, and hence outside
his ordinary jurisdiction; what made him want to
see their capital was simply the fact that the Roman city built upon its site had been the stamping-
ground of the celebrated Tertullian, who wrote his
" Apologeticus " there, and a frequent resort of
the even more renowned and much less dubious St.

Augustine. The actual see of Augustine, however, was not Carthage but Hippo, and the bishop and I put in a couple of hours trying to find out where Hippo was, for if it was nearby we might very well make a side trip to it. Unhappily, none of the guide-books in the ship's library threw any light on the question, and we had about given it up as unanswerable when we happened upon a dog's-eared German encyclopedia and learned from it that there were actually two Hippos, both of them to the west of Carthage. The first, it appeared, was still carried on the books of the Vatican as Hippo Diarrhytus and the second as Hippo Regius, but now they were only the theoretical cathedral towns of titular dioceses, without anything in them even remotely resembling cathedrals. If they actually had bishops then those bishops had probably never seen them, nor made any serious inquiries into their spiritual condition, but were engaged instead upon paper work at Rome. Which Hippo was Augustine's? The encyclopedia was not altogether clear on the point, but we concluded after some speculation (as it turned out, rightly) that it must be Hippo Regius, and dug up an atlas to find out where it lay. There was no such town in the atlas, and it was not until we landed at Tunis the next day that we learned that Hippo Regius had changed its name to Bône, and was so far from Tunis that getting there and back would take us three or four days. So we gave up the idea of vis-

iting the see of Augustine, and contented ourselves
with taking a look at Carthage.

What is left of it, we found, lies about ten miles
northeast of the city of Tunis, on the brow of a
little hill now called Byrsa, jutting out into the
Gulf of Tunis, with the blue of the Mediterranean
fading off into the distance beyond. The slope of
the hill is steep in front, and the pea-green inshore
waters of the gulf come quite close to the site, but
on the landward side the descent is gradual, and
vague farms that seem almost level show themselves now and again through the dust of the Tunisian plain. There is an automobile road up from
Tunis, and also a trolley line that stops at the foot
of the hill. Down on the beach a few fishermen haul
in their nets, and in the other direction balls of
denser dust show where some laborious husband-
man is plowing with donkey or camel. The landscape looks almost as peaceful as that of Iowa.
There is no quick movement in it, not even from
birds, and the ear catches no sound. Yet it has seen
some of the wildest fighting ever recorded, and the
climaxes of that fighting were almost always mas-
sacres. The earliest navigators of the Mediterranean, coming probably from Crete, fought for a
toe-hold on the shore against the primeval anthro-
pophagi, and then against one another for the trade
that, even in those remote days, flowed up to the
gulf from the black abysm of Africa. By the Ninth
Century B.C. the Phoenicians, who were the Eng-

lish of the ancient world, had driven out all the rest and built a handsome *cart hadash,* or new town, on the bluff, and by the Third Century it was greater than Tyre, their capital, and its sailors and traders roved all the waters from Syria to the Pillars of Hercules, and even beyond. There is, indeed, every reason to believe that they circumnavigated Africa at least 1,800 years before Vasco da Gama. The chief port of this Western trade was always Carthage. From it radiated routes that reached to the farthest frontiers of the known world The Carthaginians controlled the sea-borne carrying trade of that world, and were its greatest jobbers and bankers, and whenever they found a good harbor they set up a colony, and reached out from it for the business of the back country. One of those colonies, Tarshish in Spain, was so prosperous that it became, in Biblical times, a sort of common symbol of opulence. Also, it became a refuge for the broken and outlawed men of the whole Mediterranean littoral, and it was there that Jonah tried to hide himself when he got into trouble with Jahveh, as your pastor will tell you. But today Tarshish is only a measly fishing village at the mouth of the Guadalquiver, bearing about the same relation to Cadiz that Sagaponack, L. I., does to New York. As for Carthage itself, it is not even a village, but only a spot.

Certainly there must be few parallels in history to the completeness of its destruction. The Romans,

like all the other Japs and Nazis of antiquity, threw
their hearts into the job when they undertook to
pull an enemy town to pieces, but there is no record that they ever went so far anywhere else as at
Carthage. Consider, for example, the kindred case
of Jerusalem, destroyed in the year 70 A.D. That
was an earnest and comprehensive piece of work,
as such things go, and the Jews still wail it as their
worst disaster since the Babylonian Captivity; but
let us not forget that the wall before which they
do their wailing survived the Roman mortars and
torpedo-bombs almost undamaged, and remains in
excellent repair to this day. Nor is it the only
healthy relic of the days before Jerusalem was
hypothetically wiped out, to rise no more; the
town, in fact, is full of odds and ends that are
ascribed, at least by the guides, to the ages of Sol-
omon, Moses, Abraham and even Adam. But at
Carthage the Romans really spit on their hands,
and in consequence the remains of the city, once so
rich and so puissant, are no greater in bulk and
hardly greater in significance than the remains of
a barn struck by lightning. The French fathers
settled in the place have raked up everything they
could find and stored it in what they call a museum, but you could get the whole contents of that
museum into a couple of boxcars, and most of them
are mere scraps and potsherds, unidentified and
unidentifiable. For when the Romans demolished
Carthage they not only tore down and removed all

its buildings, and plowed up its streets, and filled its wells, and emptied its graves; they also devoured and annihilated all its records, so that what is known about it today, save for the major outlines of its history, is next to nothing. Of its people we have only a few names — Hannibal, Hamilcar and so on, nearly all of them of military men. The one Carthaginian author who is remembered is Sanchuniathon, and he is remembered only because a fifth-rate Greek once mentioned him, and probably also invented him.

The bishop and I were through with the relics in half an hour, and when we had finished we were no wiser than we had been before. What use did the Carthaginians make of the little stone boxes that were stretched out in a meagre row? The prevailing theory is that they were coffins for the ashes of children sacrificed to the national god, who is assumed to have been the Phoenician Moloch, but that is only a guess, and for all anyone knows to the contrary the name of the god may have been Goldberg or McGinnis, and the creatures sacrificed to him may have been, not children at all, but dogs, cats or goats. If he had a temple that temple is now less than dust, and if it had priests then all the gold, silver, myrrh and frankincense accumulated by those priests is now the same. Even the new town that the Romans built on the site long after the old one was destroyed is far along the road to annihilation and forgetfulness. Its best preserved relic is the shell of a theatre — now greatly resembling a stone quarry in the last stages of bankruptcy and decay. While His Excellency and I contemplated what is left of it, some boys who were passengers in our ship recreated themselves by leaping up and down its moldering tiers. Presently one of these boys missed his step and skinned his shins, and under cover of his caterwauling we withdrew. There was an Englishman nearby engaged upon a lecture to such visitors as cared to hear him. We listened for a while and found his patter far superior to that of the average guide, but what he had to say was, after all, precisely nothing, and that was what we already knew.

So we moved away to a quiet place overlooking the dusty Tunisian plain, and fell into silent pondering, each on his own. I can't tell you what form the bishop's meditations took, for high ecclesiastics are not given to confidences in that field, but my own, I recall, dwelt altogether on the complete obliteration, not only of Carthage the town, but also of its people. They were, I have no doubt, divided into groups and moieties as we are today, and showed all the sharp differences of fortune, virtue, capacity and opinion that have marked human societies at all times and everywhere. There must have been Carthaginians who were admired and envied by the rest, and other Carthaginians who were envied and disliked. Whenever a new source of cocoanuts, ivory or ebony was discovered along the Af-

rican coast, or a new tin mine in Cornwall, or a new
fishing bank in the waters to the North, there must
have been a heavy inflow of fresh money, and a
large part of that fresh money, you may be sure,
was collared by individual Carthaginians of superior smartness, and laid out in ostentations of
the sort that win public respect and lay the founda-
tions of doggy families. It is not hard to imagine
what followed, for the same thing is going on today, not only in all the great nations of Christendom, but also in the black kingdoms of the African
jungle and the barbarisms of Inner Asia. Once Father had the money the rest followed almost automatically. If there were any daughters in the family the general estimation of their pulchritude went
up by 200 or 300%, and all save the one who fell
in love with a lieutenant in the army made elegant
and even gaudy marriages — maybe with the sons
of old families that traced their ancestry back to
the motherland of Phoenicia and claimed descent
from a Duke of Byblus or Zarephath; maybe even
with some actual member of the Phoenician nobility, sent out to the colonies to recoup the failing
fortunes of his house. As for the sons of the new
plutocrat, they went through the Harvard of the
time (first missing Groton, but making Lawrence-
ville), put in five or six years playing polo and
keeping dancing women, and then married soberly
and settled down to sitting on boards of directors,
serving as vestrymen of the temple of Moloch (or

Goldberg, or McGinnis), and waiting patiently for the exitus of their now venerable pa.

By the time he shuffled off at last, leaving doctors' bills to the amount of at least a ton of gold, they were fathers themselves, with wives growing bulky and pious, daughters who never had enough clothes, and sons who broke the legs of the family elephants playing polo and had to be ransomed ever and anon from the clutches of designing wenches from Crete, Sicily and Spain. The grandchildren continued the sempiternal and inevitable round, familiar in Sumer and still familiar in this great free republic. Some of them, born idiots, became philosophers and refused to bathe. Others went in for gambling and were soon in hock to their brothers and cousins. Others succumbed to the evangelists of new religions who were constantly coming in from the eastward, and went about arguing that Moloch (or Goldberg, or McGinnis) was really not a god at all, but only the emanation of a god, and that his parent divinity was someone of the same name, or some other name, in Mesopotamia, the Hittite country, or elsewhere. Yet others laid out their heritage backing schemers who claimed to have discovered tin mines in Carthage itself, not twenty miles from the City Hall; or assembled vast collections of unintelligible papyri from the upper Nile, and employed Greeks with long whiskers to catalogue them; or bought large ranches in the hinterland and undertook to raise

elephants, camels or giraffes; or organized gangs
of gladiators and took them along the North African coast, challenging all comers; or drove chariots
down the main street to the peril of the cops, street-
sweeps, blind men and school children, and landed
finally in the sanitarium on the mountain over behind what is now Tunis. The fourth generation
produced a high percentage of whores and drunkards, and began to slip back to the primordial nonentity. Some of the cadets of the younger lines en-
listed in the army, or in the Phoenician Foreign
Legion, and were killed fighting Assyrians, Per-
sians, Greeks or Romans. Others became policemen,
bookkeepers, sailors, collectors for the orphans,
schochets or *mohels* (for the Carthaginians were
Semitic), school teachers, fortune tellers, barbers,
priests, stone masons or horse doctors, or even garbage haulers, fish pedlars or jail wardens. But not
infrequently there was at least one line that kept
its money and held up its collective head, and after
a century or two it came to be accepted as ancient
and eminent, and began to look down its nose at
the rest of the people. The gradual accumulation
of such lines produced an aristocracy — an inevitable phenomenon in human society, then as now.
That aristocracy had arisen from the trading class,
but in the end it was clearly and admittedly superior to the trading class. Its members were regarded
with deference by the commonalty, and had a long
list of special opportunities and privileges. One of

its constituent families, in the later days of Carthage, was that of Hannibal and Hamilcar.

But that it actually ruled the country is not very probable, for aristocracies, taking one century with another, are hardly more than false-faces. They sit in the parlor, so to speak, but down in the boiler-room quite different gangs are at work. Those gangs, whatever the form of government, are composed of professional governors, which is to say, of politicians, orators, intriguers, demagogues. They commonly occupy, in the hierarchy of caste, a place below the salt, and it is unusual for them to transmit their talents and power to their descendants, but while they last all real power is in their hands, whether the country they infest be a monarchy, an oligarchy or a free republic. As I have said, we know next to nothing of the internal history of Carthage, but the little we know indicates that it went through the same upheavals that periodically wrack all the great states of today. Every now and then the parliament, or grand council, or steering committee or whatever the governing body was called suffered a wholesale purging, and as the old gang took to the hills a new gang came in. We know nothing of the issues involved, or of the personalities participating, but it is not unreasonable to assume that what happened then was substantially what happens now. Let us not be deceived by recalling that in Carthage, so far as the meagre record shows, the proletariat had no voice in the government, and that demagogy in our sense was thus impossible. Let us recall, rather, that demagogues do not operate on the proletariat only, but also on aristocracies, plutocracies and even kings and emperors. Nay, I have seen them, with my own eyes, operating upon bishops, university presidents and newspaper editors. They are the most adept practical psychologists of the race, and when they rise to their full gifts it is impossible to prevail against them by any means whatsoever, save only by the sorry means of setting another and worse gang of demagogues upon them.

Thus Carthage lived and had its being for 668 glorious years, constantly reaching out for new trade, setting up new bridgeheads on ever remoter and remoter coasts, and piling up wealth as no other nation had ever piled it up before. Its liners and tramp freighters went everywhere, and its ships of war controlled all the seas. Now and then, to be sure, some other nation objected to this relentless penetration, and especially to the monopoly that usually followed it, and there were bloody wars, but the Carthaginians took such unpleasantnesses in their stride, for they were well aware that blood was the price of admiralty. One of their wars lasted a hundred years, but they drew profits out of it all the while it was going on, and came out of it richer than ever. Every savage tribe from the Congo to the Baltic got a taste of their steel, and they did not hesitate to

tackle the greatest empires. Even mighty Rome, at
the apex of its power, found them formidable an-
tagonists, and on several occasions they came within
an ace of sacking the Imperial City itself. Altogether, it took the Romans 119 years to knock them
off, and when it was accomplished at last it was
made possible only by the fact that the blackamoors of Africa, tired at last of Carthaginian rule,
joined Rome against them. As I looked out over
the scene of what must have been the decisive battle of the war, I could not help wondering what
these blackamoors had got out of the victory. Perhaps the Romans let them carry off a few women,
and maybe a share of the lesser bric-a-brac. Otherwise, they got nothing, for the Romans grabbed
everything really valuable for themselves, and a little while later they were running the blackamoors
precisely as prisoners are run in an efficient house
of correction, which is to say, precisely as the Carthaginians had been running them before the war.

The descendants of those poor people were before me as I pondered — laboriously plodding the
Tunisian plain behind their archaic plows and spavined donkeys and camels, each surrounded by his
ball of dust. It seemed a bleak and miserable life
that they were leading, but I couldn't help adding
to myself that they had at least survived. Of their
old masters, the Carthaginians, there was nothing
left save a Valhalla of blurred and incredible
ghosts. I tried, though cold sober, to conjure up

some of them as I contemplated their jumping-off place, but it was a vain undertaking, for even conjuring needs materials, and I had next to none. Who was the chief poet of Carthage in, say, the year 500 B.C., and what sort of poetry did he write? I asked myself the question, but that is as far as I got, for I was not too sure that Carthage had any poets, and if they existed no specimens of their work have come down to us. Well, then, what of the executive secretary of the Carthage Chamber of Commerce in the year 400? Here I got a little further, for a people as excessively commercial as the Carthaginians must have had a chamber of commerce, and it is impossible to imagine one without an executive secretary. I therefore imagined him, but having gone so far I was stalled again, for I could not figure out what he must have looked like, or what sort of office he did his work in, or how much of his time he devoted to port statistics and how much to writing speeches for the shipping magnates, grain exporters and bringers in of ivory, apes and peacocks who were his employers.

It was easier, somehow, to contrive plausible phantoms of lesser folk — for example, the stevedores down at the docks, the rowers of galleys, the cops patrolling their beats, the wine-sellers behind their bars, the hawkers of charms and images, the farmers in from the country with their loads of turnips and cabbages, the soldiers sparking the housemaids, the barbers with their sharp razors and clattering tongues. But even the barbers, when I got to them, hauled me up, for I was not sure that the Carthaginians shaved. Did the other Semites of that era? The portraits of Moses, Abraham and company in the art galleries of the world seem to indicate that they didn't, and I recalled that even the orthodox Jews of New York, up to the time they moved to the Bronx, still wore their beards. In the end the old gentry of Carthage gave me less trouble than any of the other folks, for the gentry are much the same everywhere. As the motorman of the Tunis trolley began to bang his gong and the bishop and I climbed aboard his car I was thinking of the ancient families that saw at one stroke the ruin of their nation and the annihilation of their own lines. Some of them, by 146 B.C., had been set tled in Carthage for five or six hundred years, and their position in its society must have been quite the equal of that of the Percys in England. Whenever there was a public procession they marched at its head. No one ever dared to flout them, not even the politicoes in whose puppet-show they served as glittering dummies. They were the living symbols of half a millennium of Carthaginian power and glory, pomp and circumstance, and each of them was a living repository of honor, dignity, *noblesse oblige*. Not a few of them, I daresay, were so finely bred that they had lost the calves of their legs and were more or less hollow in the head, but they would not lie and they could not be bought. So they stood as the third Punic War came to its catastrophic end, and the ruffianly Romans closed in. By the time the burning and slaying, the raping and looting were over they had all vanished — and this is the first friendly mention that they have had in print, I suppose, for 2,088 years.

The bishop and I were silent as we were hauled back to Tunis, each sunk in his own thoughts. When the trolley-car finally stopped at the Tunis four corners we debarked from it and looked for a hack to haul us down to the wharf where a launch from our ship was waiting. At that moment a brisk and handsome young man, obviously an American, emerged from the assembled crowd, approached me politely, and asked me if I were not Mr. Mencken from Baltimore. When I replied that I was he introduced himself as a Baltimorean who had come out to the North African coast some years before, and was at present living in Tunis. I naturally asked him what he was doing there, and his reply was so astounding that I could only stare at him like an idiot. He was, he said, the manager of a baseball league stretching all along the coast, from Casablanca in the west to Cairo in the east, with a couple of outlying clubs in Syria and the Holy Land and another at Gibraltar. But where, I faltered, did he get his pitchers and catchers, his batters and fielders? What did the Moroccans, Berbers, Copts, Syrians, Arabs, Jews and the rest know about the national game of the United States?

His reply was that they knew a lot, for he had taught them. They were young fellows with plenty of enthusiasm in them, and hence quick to learn. Baseball, he said, was now the favorite sport along the whole south shore of the Mediterranean, and when two good teams met for an important game a large crowd turned out and there was a great deal of loud rooting. There was to be one the next day, and if I were free he would be delighted to have me see it as his guest. He had lived in Tunis so long, he said, that he was now almost a native, but his thoughts still turned to old Baltimore, and whenever he heard that a Baltimorean was in town he looked him up.

There was no time to cross-examine this amazing stranger, for the bishop and I had to get back to our ship, but he was a very well-appearing fellow, so I swallowed his tale without too much resistance. When I got back to Baltimore I found that it had been true in every detail. There was, in fact, a thick envelope of clippings about him in the morgue of the Baltimore *Sunpapers*. I went through those clippings with great interest, and was not surprised to discover that not one of them mentioned the fact that the home grounds of his Tunis club were on the site of what had once been Carthage.

Permissions